Emma Rayner

In Castle and Colony

Emma Rayner

In Castle and Colony

ISBN/EAN: 9783744708838

Printed in Europe, USA, Canada, Australia, Japan

Cover: Foto ©ninafisch / pixelio.de

More available books at **www.hansebooks.com**

CASTLE AND COLONY

IN
CASTLE & COLONY

BY

EMMA RAYNER

AUTHOR OF "FREE TO SERVE"

HERBERT S. STONE AND COMPANY
CHICAGO AND NEW YORK
MDCCCXCIX

In Castle and Colony

CHAPTER I

She was a very tiny maiden to take part in so great a ceremony, and the white linen robes that covered her from head to foot swept the ground and impeded the childish movements. Startled blue eyes looked out from amidst the whiteness, and up into the face of the gentleman who led her, guiding her footsteps carefully. The little Swedish maiden was so small, and her five years of experience so short, that as she followed in the long funeral procession there was a needs be for the care her companion bestowed upon her. The care was ever present. The face above her was grave, but the dark brown eyes shone down into hers encouragingly, and the hand that guided her was warm and soft.

"Courage, little Agneta! 'Twill soon be over."

The lips did not appear to move, the whole figure was decorously still, yet the child's companion contrived that the words should reach her ears, and the little girl walked on obediently, never once turning her head to the long line of mourners that followed.

She *did* want to glance round once, to assure herself of the presence of the tall lady who walked immediately behind her. It would have comforted her to look into that face, though at the moment it was very white and stately. Not even for the little Agneta would there have been a relaxing of the muscles about the mouth, or a movement of the eyelids that drooped over the sad eyes. But it was the face of the mother, and to look back at it would have been reassuring to the childish heart.

The procession was imposing, as befitted the position of him whom they were bearing to the grave. When it started from the door of the lonely dwelling on the hill above the lake, the old Swedish house, half castle, half mansion, was left without a master. Slowly the funeral cortége wound its way down, through the pine wood, and out to the road to the village. The dead whom they were to bury out of sight that day was a young man, but many had gathered from far to show him respect.

"It is for his father's sake," the tall lady who walked behind the child said when the funeral procession was set in order.

It was not two years since the father himself was carried along the same road.

The eyes of the little Agneta wandered from the long winding road to the figures that moved before, and back to her in unmelodious and doleful strains was borne the sound of solemn requiem, sung by the singing boys and men belonging to the church in the village. No breath of wind from among the pine trees above came to soften the sound, but mingled with it could be heard now and then the footfalls of the horse that had place behind the singers. The animal was richly covered with caparisons embroidered with gold, and on it rode a horseman armed as a cuirassier, his armor gilt, his sword naked, with its point turned towards his own breast. The little Agneta shuddered at that naked sword. She wondered why the man did not put it in its scabbard, and then she tripped over the long linen robe of mourning, and would have fallen if her companion had not held her up.

When she looked again another horse, that had place behind the grand horseman, was being led by two men in mourning around the bend in the road, full in view of her wondering eyes. She knew it well. It belonged to brother Adolf, and he would never ride it again. It was covered to the ground with a black cloth with a white cross in the middle, and closely following it came a gentleman bearing a standard having upon it the arms of her brother.

"They are all walking before Adolf," mused the little girl, and fixed her eyes on the bier covered with black cloth and borne by six men in mourning. She gave little heed to the banners that were carried on either side of it. To her they were only strange accessories. She was too young to know them as so many tokens of family honor and position, and to recognize on each the arms of some ancestor stately and proud.

They had all passed beyond the bend in the road

now, and another horse, covered to the ground, and following the bier, was being led out of sight. There was nothing more for Agneta to look upon except the figures of those who followed on foot, men of noble bearing many of them, friends of the child's father—gray-bearded and solemn. They had come to do honor to the son for the sake of the father. And there were younger men there who had called the dead man their friend. These were of another type, of lighter vein, and less noble bearing.

There were no women for the little Agneta to watch, for these all walked behind. The tiny, child mourner, led by the tall, dark-eyed cavalier, appeared at the head of this division of the procession, and close behind her came the stately lady who wore her linen robes in queenly style, and needed no care from the gentleman appointed as her escort. Other women followed, also clad in the spotless linen robes of mourning, and behind these more immediate relatives came a goodly line of women friends, testifying their sympathy and respect by their presence at the funeral rites. The procession was further augmented by many coaches, some grand and gay, as befitted the wealthy, some old and dilapidated like the fortunes of their owners.

And thus the body of Adolf Botorpa was laid to rest, and the Swedish mansion on the hill finally lost its master, and stood desolate on that autumn day of the year 1641, none being left to return to it as rightful inmates save the little Agneta and the queenly woman, who, when the ceremony was over, folded the child in her arms as she whispered: "What next, little one?"

But that was later, after the return to the house, and when the mistress was for the moment free from her duties as hostess. For the moment, but only that. The long banqueting was yet to come, and not one detail of it all would the stately lady omit. That night the old house showed lights in every story, and in the banqueting hall upon the third floor, where supper was laid, the feast was protracted and ceremonious. The dignity of the dead must be maintained, and she into whose hands the duty fell was little likely to shirk the task, even when it stretched out to a week beyond the actual funeral. Her husband's son should be buried as became his position, and then—. At that point the thoughts of the mother always turned to the dark-eyed cavalier who led the little Agneta in the procession, and her own eyes gathered a more troubled gloom.

To the little girl herself the week was long and lonely. The household was given over to solemn feasting. From old Brita in the kitchen to the stately mother, all were engrossed in the special duties of the hour. The sweet red lips many a time quivered, and the empty arms reached out pitifully, and then were drawn back with a brave determination to wait. The little maid was lonely, and oppressed with the solemnity of all this pomp and ceremony, but the banquets in memory of brother

Adolf must be given, and the friends who had come to show their respect for him must be suitably entertained, and even the little Agneta could understand that her own claim must wait. The blood of the Botorpas ran in her veins, and she not only waited, but waited without complaint. And there came at last a night when the mother arms folded again about her, and the proud head, crowned with hair as fair and soft as that of the child herself, was lowered till it rested on the golden curls.

"Is brother Adolf buried as befits his rank?" asked the small maiden, unconsciously quoting words heard often in the days that were past.

"Yes, child; we have done our duty by him." The answer came with a long sigh. In her heart the mother added bitterly: "Would that he had done as much by us!"

Just how far he had fallen short of it she had yet to learn, and again her thoughts went to the tall, handsome man who had led little Agneta. When she thought of her husband's only son, the half-brother of Agneta, she must necessarily think also of the friend who had enjoyed all his confidence. They had been always together of late. And it was of late that the character of Adolf had changed so much for the worse; of late—since the death of his father. And yet her husband had trusted Monsieur Pors fully, as fully as he had trusted Adolf. And he was not usually deceived.

Madam Botorpa rose, and put the child from her. Aye, surely her husband had trusted him, and she had trusted him also, else would he never have been given the right to stand by the tiny maiden and print upon her lips the more than brotherly kiss, else would he never have presumed to claim the privilege of walking by her side and caring for her on the day of the funeral. He had claimed, rather than asked it.

"He was my friend, and she—belongs to me," he said, with an appealing gesture but a confident mien.

She would have given all she possessed to be able to tell him that he overestimated that right, but she could not. Memory reminded her grimly of a day when, with much ceremony, the hand of the little maiden was placed in that of the young man, and the father laid his hand upon both, and the pastor blessed the betrothal. A shiver ran through her as she remembered the kiss he pressed on the baby lips, and the satisfied smile that rested on his face as he said: "Mine now, little one! Betrothed to-day—bride at some future time!"

The father had believed in him so implicitly. For herself—she had believed in him too, but that winning smile and musical voice had even then sometimes wrought on her an opposite effect from that produced on others. More than once a doubt had come, though it never stayed. Now—she doubted no more, but she trembled, and that for the future of her child.

CHAPTER II

The old stone house was very still. The funeral ceremonies were ended, and the living were at liberty to go their way and leave the dead in peace. Below the hill the lake shimmered in the autumn sunlight, and between the house and the water the winds played soft melodies among the pines. The melodies were all outside of the house. There was no suggestion of them in the face of the lady who sat in an upper room of the mansion, with eyes fixed on the lake, and thoughts as far as possible removed from it.

It was a large room, impressive with the dignity of age. The figures on the tapestry that covered its walls had lost their prominence by reason of the dulling of the colors. Time had softened all things, extending its ministrations even to the bare floor, dark with years. The table carpet had once been brilliant with crimson and gold, but now its hues flaunted no longer. The harmony of age prevailed there also, and the ancient stools and long, high seats reflected the firelight with a grave decorum that was in full keeping with their years. Even the fire displayed no rollicking tendencies, but was content to burn soberly and moderately, as became it in such surroundings. No shining brass andirons held up the short cleft sticks. They stood stiffly against the back of the chimney, scant in quantity, since their mission was rather to combat the chill of the damp than to provide actual warmth.

On one object in that room time had not yet tried its skill. There was no toning down of the colors in the childish face that gravely fronted the fire. The lips were red with warm blood, and the gold and blue of hair and eyes were brilliant enough to make a dash of brightness among the prevailing neutral tints.

The mother eyes were not the only ones that rested on that bit of brightness. From the half-open door another looked approvingly on the child. The intruder was tall and well formed, singularly graceful in movement and distinguished in bearing. Time had done little in the way of toning down there, though he had had twenty-five years in which to try his skill. The man who stood in the opening of the door was strong of body and of will, more particularly of will. Evidently he was not in haste, for he stood motionless, watching the two within. That his scrutiny pleased him was manifested by the slight relaxing of the lips that neared but did not reach a smile. It was at the moment when he saw another pair of eyes turned toward his that he advanced.

"Do I come at an unwelcome hour?" he asked, gravely approaching the lady.

"Nay, I would have all business matters settled as soon as may be."

Madam Botorpa let her fingers rest for a moment

in his, and then quietly drew away the hand he would have retained.

"Are you wise?" he asked gently. "Your sorrow is yet new, and business is a burden that the fair should carry only when the shoulders are strong."

She motioned him to be seated, and he drew a stool close to hers, and with grave courtesy waited for her to speak. He had not to wait long.

"My son Adolf was taken away too suddenly to explain to me the position in which he left his little sister," she said slowly. "He tried to tell me, but was able only to intimate that you could give me all the information I needed."

"He spoke truly, madam."

The voice was low, the eyes inscrutable.

"I know that he was extravagant, that he got into difficulties," she continued. "I think that he came to you for relief."

"He did."

Nothing could be more gentle than tone and words.

"Did he involve the estate? To what length did his follies go?"

There was a ring in her voice that did not escape the ear of the listener.

"Madam, we speak of the dead," he said softly.

"And of the living," she replied, looking towards the child.

"Verily," he responded, with a smile brilliant as it was transitory. "You ask me—what?"

"Did Adolf remember his sister's rights?" asked

Madam Botorpa plainly. "When my husband died the estate was impoverished. There was little actual money. He gave all that remained to his son, with the understanding that he would seek to improve the fortunes of the place, and hold his sister's interests sacred. Has he done so?"

"The interests of the little Agneta have not suffered—*shall* not suffer," said her listener fervently.

"*Shall* not? In whose hands then do they lie?"

"In mine."

"In yours?"

"I have that honor, madam."

"What do you mean? What am I to understand?"

She rose, and stood before him. With quick courtesy he also abandoned his seat.

"Madam," he said gently, "I would rather you should understand nothing. It were better so, believe me. But if you *must* eat of the tree of knowledge, I am fain to explain that my dead friend was somewhat reckless—that finding his difficulties increase, he, to save himself from disgrace, made over to me his paternal estate, which, after a descent, and when he himself had no issue, was, as you know, alienable."

"He gave you all?"

"Nay, he *gave* me naught. For all that I hold he had ample return. The estate was already deeply involved. The loss, I assure you, was not on his side."

"And his sister has nothing?"

"I pray you, kind lady, do you count me nothing?"
The tone was light, the gesture deprecating.
She took note of neither.

"You have legal proof of this?" she said, but while she asked the question she knew that answer was unnecessary. Adolf's uneasiness during his short illness, his manifest remorse, his reckless career before that time—all were proofs that Monsieur Pors did not lie. Madam found no room for doubt that the old mansion, which for so long had owned the Botorpas as master, had passed into other hands.

"Certainly. They are at your service. Nay, madam, let not this distress you," continued the young man. "I swear it shall make no difference either to my little betrothed or to her mother. I beg of you to forget that you have thus rashly courted sorrow by a too curious scrutiny of existing circumstances. Think you that I would have exerted myself to aid Adolf in the way I did had not the interests of my little lady been very near my heart? Along with my friend's estate, I gladly accept his responsibilities. Now, as ever, this is the home of my betrothed, and her welfare shall be the first consideration."

She turned from him with a motion of impatience. He answered the movement.

"You doubt my will to serve her?" he asked.

"Methinks that we deal in conflicting terms," she said. "Service and robbery were not wont to be interchangeable words."

Her eyes flashed straight into his as she spoke. There was no corresponding gleam there. The lips that answered even smiled.

"Gentle lady, you have me at a disadvantage," he said. "The tongue of man would utter such words at its peril. But you—say on, yet stand not thus, I pray."

She seated herself mechanically. He stood before her, tall, patient, courteous, waiting for her to speak. No ripple of annoyance passed over his face. It expressed nothing but deferential attention.

"Madam, wherein lies my sin?" he asked, when her words were long delayed. "Was it in aiding my friend that I erred? Would you have exonerated me had I allowed another to meet Adolf's need? Then would you have had a stranger to deal with to-day."

"Wherein have you erred?" she repeated, in a voice that was calm only by force of a strong will. "Sir, were it not wiser to ask that question of your own heart? Did it never speak to you words that 'man may utter at his peril'? Does it seem to you a light thing to lead a weaker than yourself to ruin? 'Tis a gift, surely, that of being able to throw a glamour over evil, till even he who is not a fool may well mistake darkness for light. A coarser nature would have made sin repulsive where you gave it attraction. Such a one Adolf would never have followed. Then would there have been no necessity for this interview, with you or any other."

"Nay, you do me too great an honor," he said,

and his bow was grave, though in his tone was a half hidden ring of mockery. "In the eyes of such fair mentors as yourself a man's deeds may well gather blackness. Would that masculine nature were as near sainthood as that of man's gentle reprovers. I claim not innocence, madam, yet can I not flatter myself that my friend's career was ever materially changed through act of mine. He is dead. It becomes me not even to hint at his faults. Yet methinks there was less weakness than your gentle heart finds as excuse. A man's will is his own, and none intermeddleth therewith except with his consent. My friend was unwise, I admit, yet must I humbly claim that he alone was responsible for his mistakes."

He turned slightly, and noticed that the little Agneta had approached, and with parted lips and eyes that expressed the strongest disapproval, was regarding him closely. He bent towards her with a smile suggestive of relief.

"Come hither, little maiden, and plead my cause," he said. "Nay, sweet one, set not your face against me, even as does the mother," he added, playfully. "Those pretty lips were meant to smile—yes, and to kiss also. Is it not so?"

He put out his hand and drew her to him, looking down laughingly into the soft blue eyes. Something in his own caused them to change, hesitatingly and reluctantly, though surely, from grave disapproval, through the stages of doubt, unwilling surrender, and growing attraction, to open friendliness. The tiny maiden could not resist the laughing glamour of his eyes, and the caressing smile on his lips. The hand that clasped her was delicate as a woman's, though bronzed by out-door sports beyond all charge of effeminacy, but the muscles of the arm were closely knit. Hand and arm held her in an embrace strong enough to mean possession. To the child the close clasp was altogether a caress, to the mother it had a double character. The arm that held could keep, aye, and *would* keep, did it so desire.

"You must not vex my mother," said the little maiden seriously, though her eyes smiled back into his. "You must do what she says. You must be good."

"Why, sweet one, it is that she will not allow. When I would be good to her she says me nay."

His glance went from child to mother, resting with the same easy grace on each. The eyes of the little Agneta followed his questioningly till they reached her mother's face. It was grave and sad, but it held itself well under control. The child was too young to note the slight quiver of the lips, or the flash in the steady blue eyes. She did not know that the hand which lay motionless on her mother's lap was with difficulty restrained from plucking her fiercely out of the arm that held her. The hand lay rigidly still, apparently as well under command as the voice that answered the spoken words.

"Good, say you?" replied the lady, and the touch of scorn was well regulated. " 'Tis a strange perversion of terms, surely, to call that good which is the seal of the wrong done to this child and to me."

He smiled upon her still.

"Nay, you are determined to do me injustice," he said softly. "What could my gentle friend ask further? I have begged of her to let the past be as if it were not. Madam, your hand alone shall administer the affairs of this household, as of yore. What matters it whom the servants call master?"

"Aye, what matters it," she replied, "that this child remain as a beggar where she should rule as mistress? It is all one whether I hold the home of her ancestors for her as her right, or accept residence in it as a dole from the hand that—"

She hesitated, and left the sentence unfinished.

"Madam, say on," her companion urged. "The hand that—?"

"That was not ashamed to possess itself of the spoil and now proffers a portion of it to the despoiled, and dubs itself virtuous in the act," she said scornfully.

"You deal in ugly names, fair lady," he replied, and except that his words came more slowly, there was no change in his manner. "To me it savors not of wisdom to meet a just—I had well nigh said a generous—offer with such lack of grace."

"Generous!" she said, and sat looking at him. He returned the gaze steadily. As she looked into the depths of those brown eyes her own slowly lost their fire and their last gleam of hope. Those others darkened and strengthened with the passing moments. The words on her tongue were silenced. She felt the impotence of speech. Whatever else those eyes said to her, they told her plainly of the strength of her opponent and the weakness of her own cause. They made protest look like foolishness. Why babble like a child railing in helpless wrath? The strength in those eyes was conclusive. She accepted it with all that it entailed. She had feared the worst. It had but come.

Her eyes abandoned their scrutiny. There was no more to find out. She rose, with a dignity of movement from which all trace of passion had vanished.

"You have no more to tell me, I think," she said. "We understand each other."

"Madam, I hope not," he replied, and now there was surely some eagerness in his voice. "I would fain believe that all that which you think you understand of me is not my due, and that the denial of my wish, that I read in your face, is a misunderstanding on my part."

"I do not think we either of us misunderstand," she said, and her manner gave him no alternative but to bring the interview to an end. He bent down over the little Agneta, and pressed a kiss on the rosy lips. Did he know just how hard it was for the woman who stood so calmly by him to endure the sight of that kiss?

"Little one," he said lightly, "dost ever look at a

certain silver plate, where thy name and mine are joined? Ask the mother to show it thee sometimes, child. 'Twas not meant to be put away and forgotten. It means a very real union one day, little sweetheart."

She looked at him questioningly.

"Where is it?" she asked.

"In safe keeping, as is the little girl to whose future that to which it refers was meant to give direction," said her mother calmly. "Bid Monsieur Pors adieu, Agneta. He is waiting to go."

The child held out her hand. He took it, and held it; then stooped and kissed it.

"Some day you will give it to me to keep," he said, and with a low bow to the lady turned and left mother and child alone.

When darkness had fallen over hill and lake, and the wind among the pines had changed its song to a dirge, and was moaning over the gladness of summer departed, with here and there an interlude of half suppressed shrieks in anticipation of winter's wild frolics, the light from the uncurtained windows of the upper room sent out long beams across the blank spaces. The hearth had been replenished with lengths of cleft pine trunks, and was the heart from which a warm glow sallied out and filled the room, causing the candles to pale on their stands. Not so the plate of silver that lay in the hand of the lady kneeling in the fire-shine. It showed no pallor of humility in presence of that full light. The rather, it gave back the glow proudly, as became noble metal, chosen for its purity to commemorate the betrothal of Agneta Botorpa, of ancient lineage, to Gustavus Pors, of no less worthy family. The sheet of engraved silver was the seal of the compact. That was why the lady's face darkened above it.

Gustavus Pors came of a sufficiently honorable race. Had the present representative of the family been of the calibre of his ancestors, that bit of shining metal would not have sent back the glint of the flame into such disquieted eyes. As regarded the exterior man, no better specimen of the race had been found in all the years of the past. The strength and grace of generations had descended upon the young man. In all but one respect he was a Pors to the heart's core. In that particular alone he had missed his heritage. The lives of the men of his people had ever, until now, been without reproach.

Not that Gustavus Pors met with the reproach of men. Surely not. To the majority of those who knew him, and knew him well, he was the worthy descendant of worthy forefathers. His thriving estates bore witness that he was no reckless squanderer. A few only of those who had a closer acquaintance with him smiled, and hinted that the feet of the young man did not tread precisely the path beaten smooth by the footsteps of his ancestors. Madam Botorpa was one of the few—but *she* did not smile. To marry the little Agneta to a man less pure and loyal and true than her father, was to her to fail in her trust.

The father himself had betrothed her, in gladness of heart and full faith in the man who would one day claim the fulfillment of the promise.

Always provided fancy did not change in the meantime. Thirteen years is a long interval over which to look, and prophesy of a young man's mood. More than once, during the last months, Madam Botorpa had flattered herself that the purpose which had been strong when the compact was made, had already become to Gustavus Pors a thing of questionable good, and that he would yet be not unwilling to be freed from his promise. His attitude to-day had undeceived her. It was in keeping with the testimony of that gleaming silver, rather than with her desire.

The presence of that betrothal gift irritated her. She would have liked to toss it into the fire, and heap fresh sticks about it till it curled and twisted and gave to the flames its record, becoming once more a piece of harmless metal. She rose to her feet, the little silver plate in her hand. The slender arm swung out, but the fingers did not relax their grip. They held the glistening silver full over the fire, and the blaze came up and scorched the delicate fingers. Even then they did not loosen their grasp. They hovered over the flames for a minute before the arm was slowly drawn back. They dropped the obnoxious sheet of metal then, and it went clanging on to the hearth, well out of the reach of danger. After all it was but the record of a fact that would remain though the silver plate ran in a molten stream among the ashes at her feet. There was a more potent element than that of fire, and with it Gustavus Pors had yet to contend. Time was a power on which the fickle fancy of youth did not count. Thirteen years would hardly pass and leave the young man of the same mind as to-day. To set his fancy on a winsome child, and to feel the same attraction toward the maiden grown, were different things. When circumstances had matured the man, and time had led the little maid to the verge of womanhood, the union which Madam Botorpa would fain prevent might seem as undesirable to one as to the other.

It *might*, if time could have fair play. But time would be deprived of half its power if to the attraction already exerted by the child were added the chivalrous impulse called into being by her dependence upon the man. Monsieur Pors had possessed himself of the surest means of keeping alive the affection in his own heart, as well as of awakening it in the heart of the little Agneta.

Madam Botorpa turned from the fire, replacing the betrothal present upon the table. Through the weakness of the child's brother the young man had forestalled her. She would have set time to work against him—he had already enlisted it on his side. He would surround the little Agneta with care and love. What could she give in return but gratitude and girlish affection?

Madam Botorpa's thoughts went far afield, seeking for a safe issue from the position in which she found herself. That position was the more straitened that the funeral ceremonies had been beyond criticism. She had done her duty by her husband's son. Not the strictest exponent of Swedish custom could have accused her of the omission of a single detail that should have been included. Neither expense nor trouble had been considered. The dead had been laid aside with all due honor, and the living were the poorer in proportion. To find a way for the living to walk safely, the thoughts of the only waking occupant of the house on the hill went back and forth, while the firelight shone out into the night, and the wind played strange variations of its dirge among the pines.

The best room the village inn afforded was that night occupied by a young man, who was apparently engrossed in a survey of the sprigs of juniper beneath his feet. In reality he was unaware of their presence. He was letting his thoughts go over almost the same ground traveled by those of the lady in the upper room of the castle. The odor of the juniper pervaded the room, and the broken twigs scattered upon the floor imparted to it the regulation rustic air, but instead of the fresh greenery from the forest the young man saw a silver plate bearing his own name and that of a little child.

"It was an odd fancy," he muttered, "and yet—I have a notion I shall never repent it. The little witch exerts a charm even now that I cannot quite throw off. At eighteen, if present promise be fulfilled, she will be a bride worth waiting for. And then—well, who knows? Pleasure will have had its swing. I may be ready to extend open arms to virtue, to prove myself such a one as will not disappoint the stately mother herself. Verily she does me injustice. Adolf was a fool—would have been no less in any event. As well lose the castle to me as to another. I have at least the wherewithal to uphold it, and the will to do justice to the little maid. But 'tis well I have a hold upon her, other than that formal betrothal. Madam cannot easily set *that* aside, I trow, but the home of the family— she will think twice before she deprive the little Agneta of that."

He smiled, and the dark eyes gave forth a momentary gleam. Then the smile died away, and a look half tender took its place.

"Little maiden, you have a trick of leaving a soft place in my heart," he said. " 'Tis the touch of baby fingers perhaps. And yet my old friend's hand could effect the same end. The best thing in human nature would always come to the fore when he was by. Well, I'll not prove him in the wrong, even yet. He trusted his daughter to me. In spite of madam herself the little witch shall thank him."

He laughed, stretched himself lazily, and got up and went out into the darkness.

CHAPTER III

"Here Lars, man, stir them long legs of yours a little faster, will you? Know you not that madam is in haste?"

The woman opened the mouth of the great oven as she spoke, and shut it again with a heavy bang. There was no light in the broad kitchen save that on the hearth, nor was any needed. That was big enough and bright enough to light a wider space than even the roomy kitchen of the stone house on the hill. Old Brita had not spared fuel this early morning. It was one of the things that were plentiful, and to-day she used it royally. Why not? Madam did not often go on a journey, and when she did she was not going like a beggar. Bread of Brita's own baking, and a few dainties for "the bairn," must needs go with her. Who could tell, quoth Brita, whether in the hamlets passed by the way, food of any kind would be found at the lady's coming? Madam would lie at strange inns, and be dependent on strange provender. With the wings of wild fowl well nigh flapping in your face when you set foot outside the door, why should madam go hungry, or eat that which was fit only for the mouth of the slatternly housewife whose heart was well satisfied if only her jaws had enough to work on?

So the birds had yielded up their lives, and Brita had dressed and prepared and cooked, heating the big oven more than once, and drawing from it stores savory enough to make the mouth of the watchful Lars water.

"In haste, is she?" growled Lars, taking long, slow strides across the kitchen. "In haste she must be, of a truth, else would not a man be routed out of his bed before the stars have half burned out their lamps."

"Stars!" retorted Brita, scornfully. "Would you wait for them, at this time of the year? They put not out their lamps till the sun bids them, and the sun is up late enough now, I trow. None but the sluggard would wait on its beams. 'Tis well for you that others were out of their beds before your lazy pate was lifted, else might you have gone hungry to-day. You will need a bite or two on the way, as well as madam, and you'll want something better than your finger nails to exercise your teeth on. That mouth of yours can open to eat as well as to grumble, I'll warrant."

"Aye, aye, good Brita, that can it," said the worthy Lars, with a return of good humor at the prospect before him. "And right good promise that oven holds out to a man. Driving is hungry work, I tell you."

"You'll be like to get neither to the driving nor the eating, if you stand staring at my fire," said Brita.

Thus admonished, Lars disappeared through the

heavy outer door of the kitchen, and Brita bustled about making much ado over the final preparations. Lars himself was to drive madam's coach. The great sturdy fellow was even now giving the six horses a special measure of grain, in anticipation of the hard work before them, for a journey over Swedish roads at a time when summer had finally abandoned the land, and the skies took occasion to weep over its departure, was an undertaking requiring strength of limb and stoutness of heart on the part of driver and beasts. The latter munched their early meal contentedly, troubling their brains not at all over the wherefore of their unexpected good fortune. And in the kitchen Brita nodded her satisfaction after her last peep into the oven, and began to set on the table a breakfast worthy of hungry men about to go on a journey.

" 'Tis my belief the place will see her no more," muttered the old woman, as she passed from oven to table. "She keeps a still tongue in her head, but there's them that say the bairn will ne'er be mistress of her father's house, more's the pity. We shall miss her sorely, pretty dear, and madam too. She's been a good mistress, and a kind, though a bit proud. I've served the old family long. 'Twill go against the grain to see any but a Botorpa on these lands."

In a room on the third floor the last of the Botorpas in a direct line lay sleeping tranquilly. By her side Madam Botorpa stood irresolute, her fingers softly touching the tumbled curls. She hesitated to wake the sleeper. The day would be long, and the journey irksome to one so young. The mother repented of her purpose, and turned away, leaving the little girl to her slumbers. There was time enough yet. She shaded the candle and went to the window. The land of the Botorpas lay about her everywhere, though it showed now only as limitless blackness beneath the stars. The little sleeping girl and the Botorpa lands belonged of right to one another. They ought never to be separated. And they need not be separated, though another than a Botorpa to-day called those lands his own. He called the representative of the family his own also. And he was as jealous about the possession of the one as the other.

In the month that had passed since the funeral, he had given madam full proof of his right to the lands. She did not try to dispute it. She did not doubt that he had paid for them their full value. But his right to the child was another matter.

"Better the loss of lands than the loss of happiness," she said, standing there by the window between the darkness without and the dim light of the screened candle at the further end of the room. "He can give her everything but one—a heart as pure as her own."

Old Brita was not far wrong. Madam was bidding farewell to the home to which her husband had brought her ten years before. It was a double renunciation. She was giving it up for herself and the child.

CHAPTER IV

The day was just breaking when the big family coach, resplendent yet without and within in faded purple velvet, was brought with much manipulation of reins and flourish of whip well up to the door of the mansion. It looked very big and lonely when the one sad-faced lady and the little child climbed into it, and the door was shut. With the eight people it was meant to accommodate inside, it might present a cheery appearance, but with only the present occupants, and in the chill morning air, it seemed dark and gloomy.

Sturdy Lars was on the driver's seat, comfortably conscious of a certain hamper packed away beneath it. When the lady and child had entered, he rose, and flourished his whip over the coach. It was the signal for the wagoners who were waiting at a distance to range themselves behind the carriage. They were all either madam's own servants, or tenants on the Botorpa estate, and their wagons, six in number, were well filled with goodly chests and rougher boxes, that held the personal effects of the two travelers, and the provisions Brita had deemed necessary for mistress and servants during the journey.

Many of those chests had been packed by madam's own hands. Old silver that had come with her from her father's house, personal gifts from her husband, jewels belonging to herself, and those set aside by the father for his little daughter, and therefore not included in his gift to his son—these were carefully stowed away in the strong chests. Nothing that could by any interpretation be considered the property of Monsieur Pors found place there. Of this madam was scrupulously particular. Everything that he had claimed, or could ever claim, was left behind. He would find it all when he came to take possession—all but the child. And that was the claim in which he was most interested.

When the horses had drawn the coach from the door, and the travelers were clear of the house, so that a good view of it could be obtained, madam motioned the little Agneta to the window.

"Look out now, child," she said. "Look well at the house. You are going a long way away from it."

And the little girl looked, and wondered why she was told to do so, and put her head inside again, and found the old coach more entertaining, because she had not seen it so often.

She was interested in the wagons that followed. Her small fingers had helped to wrap up the old silver ewers and basins, and the great tankards, and she had seen them consigned to the chests. She put her head outside again to assure herself that those chests were in motion, and as she did so she saw old Brita standing without the house, and waving her hand. The old woman's other hand was rubbing something from her cheek, Agneta did not know what. But a serving man who stood by recognized the object as a round briny drop, and wondered what ailed the woman that she pulled such a long face over the mistress's journey, though, to be sure, troubles had come thick on the house of late, and it was enough to make a body feel low. None could tell what might happen before madam returned, nor, for the matter of that, whither madam was bound. She was not one to tell her business to every serving man and maid.

On the evening of the second day of her journey, Madam Botorpa stayed her foot as she was entering the wayside inn at which they had arrived.

"Lars," she said, "your horses' heads will tomorrow be turned towards home. The coach goes with me no further. The wagons also will return."

"You are going back?" cried the sturdy Lars, in such surprise that he could in no wise keep his feelings within his own breast. "Well, I'd rather drive back than go forward, I'll swear. The roads get worse with every mile."

"The question is not whither *I* am going, but whither the coach is to go," said madam quietly. "I have no further use for it. And since your desires point the same way as your duties, it is well," she added with a smile.

That smile proved too much for Lars.

"Madam, I'll drive you whither you want to go," he said, "though I get not back to the castle by doomsday."

There was another smile for him now. Madam held out her hand. Lars, scarcely knowing what he did, took it in his own clumsy one, holding it as if he feared it would break.

"Nay, you will serve me best by returning," she said. "My journey is not ended, yet I no longer wish to use the coach. A less heavy vehicle will suit better the state of the roads."

He turned away bewildered. And that night, by madam's order, he engaged wagons to take her and her possessions a day's journey, the direction of which she would herself decide. With his own hands Lars, next morning, transferred boxes and chests to the four-wheeled vehicles which one by one came straggling to the inn at early day-dawn. They were very small, so that only one large chest and two little ones could by any possibility be placed on each. A yoke of oxen, or two cows, supplied the motive power as often as did a single horse. To harness a pair of horses to a wagon seemed to be a proceeding unheard of by these slowly arriving wagoners.

Lars shook his head gravely as he turned a critical eye on the harness. Old rope was the mainstay of the same, the knots tied in sundry places remaining as mementoes of former mishaps. Like useful rope answered the driver for reins, and if the whole arrangement held together at the start he was well content. Breakages by the way could be repaired with a new knot, or an extra piece of hempen cord, after the style of previous journeys. The bits in the horses' mouths, fashioned from rams' horns, were not more primitive than the equipment in general, and the manners of the drivers accorded well with the whole. Nobody was in a hurry, or in any degree anxious to add to his savings by helping the lady forward on her journey. The wagons drove up leisurely, and as the shaky vehicles drew near, more than one wagoner turned out to be a woman.

The yard of the inn presented a semi-animated appearance when the sun's outriders, sent to warn the land of the approach of his chariot, swept down into it. Oxen stood half asleep before partially loaded wagons. Madam Botorpa's own vehicles, easily to be distinguished from those of the newcomers, were being slowly emptied. Lanterns moved lazily about, except where Lars himself swung one on high to inspect a freshly arrived wagon, or thrust it beneath a horse's neck to make sure that the animal had not been brought hither without even the usual allowance of knotted rope. On one side of the yard the big coach rested in its splendor, and close beneath its shadow an undersized pony, harnessed to a particularly dilapidated wagon, hung its head almost to the ground in a last effort to finish the night's slumber before day was fairly in possession of the field. From her room above madam looked down upon the scene, but she did not descend until her own servants were ready for departure. Then she sent for Lars.

"Are all things in forwardness for my journey?" she asked.

"As forward as they are like to be, with such as yon to carry you and your goods," replied the man bluntly. "Better change your mind, madam, while yet you may do so to some purpose. It's my belief it will be changed for you fast enough before the day is done, if so be that you trust yourself to such a crew."

"What, are not the men honest?" asked the lady.

"Honest as may be, I doubt not," said Lars, "but that is more than can be said of the thongs and cords that should make horse and wagon work together as one, and 'tis to the honesty of these you'll have to trust when you are being dragged out of a hole in the road."

"Yet they are the best you can procure. Is it not so?" demanded his mistress.

"The best and the worst. There are no others to be had for fair words or for foul," said Lars.

"Then I will abide by the arrangement," she said. "And you—I would have you set off at once. Good luck to you, and a swift journey to Brita's fireside!"

Madam Botorpa ate her breakfast while her servants were putting in the horses for the return to the castle, and the little Agneta ran backwards and forwards to the window, dividing her attention between the indoor attractions and those without.

"They are going now," she cried. "There is the coach, and Lars is looking back. There is nobody to ride inside to-day."

They had no more than fairly started when madam herself came out, and gave the order to put her train also in motion. She and the child rode in the most trusty looking of the wagons, and the others followed in irregular line. The drivers had only covenanted to go one day's journey from home. If madam wished to travel further, she must find fresh vehicles to convey her and her goods. For them, they went not more than a day's distance from their own dwellings.

"It is well. I hold you responsible only for that upon which you agreed," said madam, and though the arrangement would entail much trouble at the next stopping place, it seemed not to please her ill.

She mounted the wagon, and the little Agneta seated herself gleefully by her mother's side. The journey had not grown wearisome to her yet.

"This is better than the coach," she declared. "I can see without putting my head out."

But before the day was over she had cause to regret the shelter of the sombre, stately coach. A few breakages in the harness, that had to be repaired before a fresh start could be made, and several delays through the wagons sticking in broken parts of the road, were the only episodes of the morning.

The road itself was the worst they had yet traversed. They had turned off that day from the more frequently traveled highways, and were going through a district upon which recent rains had set a seal of mud effectual enough to close it against all intruders not of an especially persistent character. But the present intruder was persistent, and though her progress was slow, it was still progress—until noon was past. Then, when the solitary farmhouse at which they had rested was left in the distance, the skies joined forces with the road, and the travelers had to encounter water above and below.

"Better go back to where you stopped at noon," counseled the wagoner, "and break your journey there, if so be they will take you in."

But Madam Botorpa wrapped herself and the child in thick traveling cloaks, and bade the driver proceed.

"Rain is to be expected before our journey is over," she said. "If we turn aside at the first shower, we may be long on the way."

"This is no shower, as you'll find out before long," growled the man, but he urged his horse forward, and nothing was heard for a time but the creaking of harness, and the rattle of wheels, and the beating of the rain at each access of energy in the storm. The dark trees of a pine forest changed position group by group, ranging themselves behind instead of in front of the travelers, and for every one that was passed there seemed a corresponding one yet ahead. The rain became more persistent. For more than twenty-four hours the skies had been threatening. Now the clouds settled down to a steady outpour, that was not long in having its effect on the already softened roads. Stoppages were more lengthy than advances, and muttered growls proceeded from all along the line.

It was no use going back. The pine forest lay between the travelers and the house they had left at noon, and no other habitation was within reach. They were skirting the low shores of a lake, the rough, wet road stretching before them without a single encouraging sign. The hind wheels of the wagon were for the twentieth time stuck fast in a mud hole, out of which the horse had for the last few minutes been vainly endeavoring to pull them.

"How far are we from the nearest village?" asked Madam Botorpa, as the wagoner desisted from his efforts and stood looking helplessly at the horse.

"Nearer a mile and a half than a mile," replied the man sullenly, without looking at the lady.

Her fears had fallen short of the fact. She had believed herself much nearer the village. A Swedish mile and a half, or more than ten English miles of this bog to be traversed before shelter and refreshment could be had! And somewhere behind the clouds the sun was even now sweeping the horizon. Darkness would not be much longer delayed. She gave no sign of her anxiety, however.

"There would be more chance of starting an empty wagon," she said, and rose to exchange the wet vehicle for the muddy road.

But the hands of the little Agneta held her fast. For the first time during the journey the courage of the small maiden had failed her. She lifted a pitiful face down which tears and rain were making watercourses, and clung sobbing to her mother.

"What, crying?" said the lady gently. "Nay, nay, little daughter, take courage. The rain will soon be over, and so will these tears."

"When are we going back home?" whispered the child between her sobs.

Ah, when? The low spoken words fell like a blow, and for a moment the face of the lady paled. Then she lifted the little girl in her arms, and stepped down into the road.

"Where is thy courage, little one?" she said cheerily, picking out the least miry spot on which to deposit her burden. "See, we shall soon be started again. Even now the wheel stirs. By and by there will be the village, and then supper and rest."

"I would rather go home," moaned the child. It was a very pitiful moan, with no suspicion of temper in it, but only a sorrowful longing for past joys.

As she seated herself again Madam Botorpa looked back. The more heavily laden wagons were far behind, some of them not even in sight. When they would make their way to the village, and whether she should ever see all her strong chests again, she did not know. A low sigh escaped her lips. She too was longing for home.

The little Agneta had long slept beneath her mother's cloak, when the horse, as fully tired out as the temper of the driver, struggled to the door of the small building that served as inn. Madam Botorpa hammered long at the door before a head was thrust from a second story window, and a sleepy voice asked:

"Who stands there, disturbing honest people in their beds?"

"A traveler who needs rest sorely," was the answer.

"And why did you not ask it at a decent hour, before the household slept?" demanded the voice, in unconciliatory tone.

"Because the storm delayed us," returned Madam Botorpa. "Hasten, my friend, and undo the door. A lady and child stand without, and the little one is sore weary and wet."

The wagoner seconded the appeal by a resounding thump on the woodwork, at the same time crying in tones not to be disregarded:

"Look you, landlord! If your feet hasten not down to let in those who wait without, 'tis your door that will suffer. I want shelter for myself and my beast. May he who withholds it stand himself in like plight, and that before long!"

The head was withdrawn from the window, and slow, heavy footsteps were presently heard descending the stairs. The door being at length unfastened, the landlord swung a lantern full in the faces of his guests. The half opened eyes of the child blinked at the sudden light.

"Come in," said the man. "We can give you shelter till morn."

More than that he declared himself unable to furnish, and Madam Botorpa did but stay to place the child under shelter before she plunged again into darkness in pursuit of the wagon, in which Brita's store of provisions was disappearing. The driver was in too much of a hurry to get himself and his horse under the roof of the stable to give heed to her request that the hamper might be brought to the house.

"There it is. Take it if you want it," he said, bringing his horse to a stand.

It was easier to carry out her own behests than to secure obedience. Madam lifted the hamper and stumbled back through the darkness to the inn door.

That night the lady and child slept upon straw, and would have gone hungry but for Brita's forethought.

The morning saw no break in the clouds. To proceed was out of the question. The wagons had all come up in the course of the night. Madam paid the drivers and saw the empty conveyances depart. The next consideration was where to procure more. But that was not a question for to-day. The rain held its own, and Madam Botorpa waited, and looked out upon the stream of water that showed where the road should be, and in her heart thanked old Brita that the child was not hungry.

The house afforded nothing in the shape of food, and scarcely more in the way of accommodation. The landlord and his wife were a fair match for their habitation. One solace only Madam Botorpa drew from her surroundings. That which availed to shut her in might very well avail to shut others out, and a landlord who took no interest in his guests would have the less to say of them if questioned.

And the weather *did* clear in the end, though it took its time about it. A day came when the skies were bright, and the roads had settled down into a thick mud, instead of the water into which they had of late seemed to be resolved. Then the lady sallied out and scoured the country round, and as a result obtained one vehicle for her own use, and a corresponding one to convey a portion of her goods to the next stopping place, which might, or might not, prove a more manageable region. As a matter of fact it was a degree better than the one she had left, and here she stayed while her chests were being slowly dragged over the heavy mud, and brought within her reach again. That, as only four wagoners were at work on the transfer, was not accomplished in a day.

It was a question—judging entirely by the weather—whether the season remained late autumn or had become early winter, when, sixteen days later than the morning on which Lars turned his horses' heads homewards, madam stood again by the side of the sleeping Agneta, this time not hesitating to wake her. The days were shorter and the traveling slower now, and it was wise not to wait for the sun's appearance before making a start.

"Come, little one, open those sleepy eyes."

The mother's hand touched the closed lids. They opened slowly, then quivered and dropped again. They were heavy with sleep.

"Wake, lazy one! 'Tis full time we were astir."

The reluctant lids lifted afresh.

"Are we going in the wagon again to-day?" asked the child sleepily.

"Yes, and already I hear the sound of wheels. If we would not go hungry, we must hasten, for breakfast has yet to be eaten."

The voice was cheerful, and the tired ring in it not sufficiently apparent to manifest itself to the undiscerning ears of a child.

"I am so tired of the wagons," said the little girl reflectively. "I wish we had kept the coach. No— I wish we had gone back in it. Is Lars at home now?"

"Surely he is. Lars is not such a great traveler as my little daughter."

"Are we going to travel always?" asked the child plaintively. "Shan't we go home too?"

"How long we have to travel depends on how far we go in a day, and how far we go in a day depends on how early we start, and how early we start depends on how quickly we are ready," said madam, upon which the little Agneta gave her attention to the business in hand, and forbore further question.

The last of Brita's provisions were consumed that morning.

"We must depend now on what we can procure by the way," said Madam Botorpa. "The district we seek should lie not many days' journey from here, though I know not well whether we are taking the most direct course thereto."

The chill of frost was in the air when the lady and

child came out into the pale light. A star or two yet held out against the day-dawn, slow to acknowledge a superior. Madam had been fortunate in the matter of wagons. Her property was all to go with her to-day. She looked critically round on the drivers. He who was waiting for her by the door, having only a few light packages in his wagon, was of stout build and surly mien. Madam Botorpa passed him over, and signed to one further back.

"My friend, transfer your load to this waiting wagon," she said. "Your horse pleases me well. I will ride behind it to-day."

The face of the horse's owner brightened. Not so that of the wagoner who stood near the inn door.

"Your goods are already in my wagon," he said angrily. " 'Tis folly to change them. I was hired to drive a lady and child, and not to drag heavy chests over such roads as these."

"Not hired by me, my friend," said the lady quietly. "With the rest, you were engaged to go a day's journey at my expense. The service I desire of you is the transportation of the chests in yonder wagon. Its owner will help you on with your load."

The man turned away with a growl, and Madam Botorpa's new charioteer took his place. He was a man of short stature and intelligent face. Man and horse had an air of willingness that was the most refreshing thing to be seen that chilly morning. Madam Botorpa placed herself behind the horse, and then turned to the driver.

"Know you the whereabouts of the farm lands of

Axel Bonde?" she asked. "They should lie somewhere within the knowledge of the men of this region, I think, though it may well be that in my journeying I have gone somewhat out of the way."

"The farm lands of Axel Bonde?" answered the man. "Nay, if 'tis Axel you seek, you have not gone a great way astray."

A low sigh of relief escaped the lady's lips.

"Does the farm lie far from here?" she asked.

"It lies not near," replied the man, "and the house is yet further removed. 'Tis a weary distance by the highway, and would scarce be reached on the second day from now. Nay, at this time of the year it might easily take the better part of three days to go thither. But there is a way by which men reach the farm, by cross roads, and though it is rough enough, it might perchance be traveled."

The lady hesitated.

"You are sure it is the place I seek?" she asked. "This Axel? Tell me—of what age is he?"

"He yet falls short of three-score and ten, and is as hale as one who has seen fifteen years less of life," was the answer. "If the Axel you seek be a man long of limb and straight of backbone, I can put you in the way of meeting with him."

"It is the same," said madam. "I am near my journey's end."

"Will you seek him by the highway, or the cross road?" asked the driver, standing yet by his horse.

"Can the cross road be traversed in a day?" she questioned.

"If the day be long enough, madam. It has been done many a time," said the driver, "but in the present state of the roads I promise you neither a quick nor an easy journey. I am willing to try it."

"I also am willing," said Madam Botorpa, and the man climbed to his seat and turned to those who were to follow.

"We go by the cross road to the farm lands of Axel Bonde," he shouted.

"More fool you!" came the response, and Madam Botorpa recognized in the loudest of the voices the tones of her would-be charioteer.

CHAPTER V

The road upon which Madam Botorpa had started in no respect belied its reputation. It was rough at the beginning, rougher further on, and, if it had an end—which seemed problematical—might by analogy be expected to be roughest there. As the travelers proceeded it became nothing more than a rude track, along which the wagons jolted and creaked dismally.

The weather grew colder as the day advanced. A shrill wind whistled past the travelers, in more haste than they, judging by the comparative speed. Only one house was passed, and at that madam descended, and asked for food for herself and the child. A piece of bread was reluctantly furnished, and from this the little Agneta, hungry with her long ride in the sharp air, made her dinner. Madam returned to the wagon and told the driver to push on. The farm of Axel Bonde must be reached before the travelers slept.

"Better wrap up all you can," said the man, as they took their seats. "We shall meet the wind now. It is going to be rough before we get to the end. It will make the end a little later in coming, too."

He was not wrong. The wind increased in strength, and a driving sleet, that froze upon the front of the wagon, came with stinging force into the faces of the occupants.

The tempers of the drivers behind grew perceptibly akin to the weather. Breakages were repaired less readily, and wagons that stuck in a hole were slower in coming out of it. The horses, too, were growing tired. It was a steady, hard pull at every step, and the sleet tried the courage of the animals. Madam Botorpa thought it best not to get too far ahead of her train.

Darkness fell early. It was while it was yet possible to consider it day rather than night, that madam's disputant of the morning made his voice heard.

"How much longer is this going on?" he called gruffly. "This is no road to travel on after sunset. The day is spent, and a hard enough day it's been. I, for one, have not a mind to break my neck stumbling along in the dark."

"It is about as easy to go forward as to go back," said madam's driver. "Better push on, friend. 'Twill bring the end nearer."

"The wrong end for me," was the answer, and there was a savage ring in the voice. "Let who will go forward. For me, since I must needs risk the going one way or the other in the darkness, I will let my nose follow my inclinations. It will the sooner feel the warmth of my own hearth."

"Yet if you return thither without finishing your journey, such home-coming may well be comfort at the expense of profit. I pay not a wagoner who only performs half his task."

The wind carried the sound of the lady's voice to the ears of the grumbler behind. There was a quiet determination in it that had a cooling effect on the man's temper, or on his ardor to return. He hesitated.

"I made no agreement to work night as well as day," he said.

"At this season your journey could hardly be completed by daylight. Nor did you expect it," said madam firmly.

"It is like enough to *be* daylight before it is over," growled the man.

But he put his horse in motion again, and the fight with weather and road continued for a season. The weather was becoming more decidedly aggressive. In long, heavy gusts the wind swooped down, imparting a spiteful energy to the sleet that, changing its character somewhat, had now assumed the form of hard, frozen particles, which had a cutting power trying enough to the faces that met them. It grew very dark, so that the roadway could be discerned only by the aid of lanterns. The little Agneta slept, and woke shivering when the wagon wheel went suddenly down into a dangerous rut, and crept closer to her mother to sleep uneasily again.

Madam Botorpa's driver retained his composure during all the mishaps, but he became more and more silent. The courage of his horse was not yet exhausted, though the same could not be said of some that followed.

A loud oath from behind presently broke in on the steady howl of the storm. A horse went down violently, and the procession came to a stand.

"What is the matter?" asked madam, her voice a little less steady than usual.

"Matter enough!" was the savage answer, and again Madam Botorpa recognized the voice of the man who had that morning elected himself as her charioteer. "You'll have a horse to pay for as well as a day's journey. That's about all."

"Go back and see," said madam to her own driver, and man and lantern turned back, leaving the lady and child alone in the darkness. Before the point of light which showed the position of the lantern had reached the first of the belated vehicles, there was a sound of struggling and plunging, and then a heavy thud, followed by another and another. The little Agneta awoke, and sat up bewildered, her eyes vainly trying to pierce the darkness.

"Where are we?" she asked, with a little gasp of fear.

"Alone on the road. The man has gone back with the lantern. A horse has fallen."

Even the ears of the child could not fail to discern the lack of hopefulness in the voice that hitherto had never failed to comfort. Madam was weary at heart. She was faint also, for her own dinner had consisted of little more than the refreshment of secing the child eat. Now she was straining her ears to learn the extent of the mischief.

"I'm so hungry," said little Agneta pitifully.

"Yes, dear, we are both hungry," replied the mother gently.

There was a fierce altercation going on behind. Madam's own conveyance was too far ahead of the foremost of the others to allow her to hear distinctly all that was said, but she caught words that, mingling with the beating storm, were not calculated to strengthen her courage.

It was long before the driver returned.

"What is it?" asked madam anxiously.

"Horse fell in a hole. The man is wilder than a hungry wolf," replied the driver slowly. "He had a narrow escape of losing the beast. It was an ugly hole."

"Will he drive on?"

"Not he. Declares he will risk his neck no more. He will seek the cover of the trees—there is good shelter beneath yonder hill—and camp until sunrise. The rest will follow him."

'And you?" asked madam, her voice not quite firm.

"I agreed to take you to the house of Axel Bonde," he replied. "I will abide by my bargain, unless, indeed, you bid me stay and try to save the stuff, which will be none the better for lying in the mire."

"What, has harm befallen the chests?" exclaimed madam.

"Heard you not the thumps as the boxes fell from the side of the wagon, hastened, I doubt not, by a thrust of the fellow's foot?" asked the driver.

"Surely I heard the sounds," said madam. "Are the chests broken?"

"Two of them lie with their contents strewing the road. The men of this region are honest, aye, and the men of this company also," said the driver, "yet does it look wiser to gather up the goods from the ground. The storm will not respect your property, and an angry man is perchance as little to be trusted."

"What will you do?" asked the lady.

"Gather together that which is scattered around, and put the broken chests in my wagon, leaving the uninjured one until morning," was the reply. "But my horse is well-nigh spent. If I put behind him this load, it will be at the expense of your legs."

"You mean that we must walk?"

"Nay, madam, there is no 'must' about it," he said. "I will carry you according to my promise, if you so will it, but then will the chests have to take their chance. My horse can do no more than journey yonder once. He is almost worn out."

"How far are we from the house we seek?" asked Madam Botorpa.

"If we go not faster than of late, it will take nearer three hours than two," replied the man, "yet could I myself reach it on foot in half that time."

Madam hesitated.

"I will go back with you and examine the chests," she said at last.

The result of the examination was decisive. The broken chests contained wearing apparel and personal effects, and madam saw more than one case of jewelry lying in the mud of the road, in imminent danger from the wheels of wagons in the rear.

"I will risk the journey on foot," she said, "and trust to you to bring these things in safety."

"It is good, madam," he replied. "They shall reach you—if not to-night, then after daybreak."

A lantern was procured, and Madam Botorpa stooped and lifted the little Agneta in her arms.

"The track should be plain enough all the way," said the driver.

His words were almost drowned in the shrill shrieking of the wind. Madam pushed forward, over the brow of a hill, and down again into a valley. Then she was completely and fearfully alone. A feeling of utter detachment, of belonging neither to that which lay behind nor to that which stretched out before, overpowered her. Somewhere in that region behind was the castle, the old house she had learned to call home, the place to which her child belonged. In the dim distance before her was—what? Shelter, at least, and rest and food. The weary body called out feebly for these, and refused to let the mind go further. And towards the rest and the warmth Madam Botorpa set her thoughts, and walked on, the weight of the child growing more burdensome as her overtaxed strength diminished.

The road led through lower lands as she proceeded, where the wind had less power. Before she had well begun to rejoice at its weakening, however, she wished herself on higher ground again, for setting her foot on what looked like an innocent stretch of snow-covered road, she felt the treacherous surface give way, and plunged forward into water above her ankles. She saved the child, but not the lantern. It fell with a crash, and with it madam's hope of speedy deliverance from the loneliness of the way.

CHAPTER VI

Half stunned by the calamity that had befallen her, Madam Botorpa scrambled on to level ground, and stood bewildered, till the frightened waking of the child in her arms aroused her to fresh effort. To go on without light was impossible. The shelter and the rest with which she had cheered her failing courage receded into the black distance.

She peered round her anxiously. A denser darkness on one side suggested trees and possible cover from the storm. Feeling her way carefully towards the shadow, she found herself in what seemed the blackest night. Here the force of the wind was broken, and madam's extended hand touched the trunk of a tree. A low, weary sigh told of the relief of abandoned effort as she seated herself on the protected side of that tree. She wrapped her cloak more closely about the sleeping child, bent over it until her head rested on her breast, and slept from sheer exhaustion.

How long she remained asleep Madam Botorpa did not know, but suddenly a sound smote on her ear and brought consciousness with it. She lifted her head and listened—intently, eagerly. It came again—the deep, far-reaching voice of a dog. At the same moment she became aware that the steady rattle of frozen snow that before had been striking pitilessly upon the further side of the pines had ceased. The wind also had lost its fury, having exchanged it for a mood of alternate blustering and wailing. Madam Botorpa looked up, and through an opening in the trees saw a star. She could even dimly discern the road.

The bark of the dog was heard again, a sound more blessed than music It changed for her the desolate, storm-possessed solitude into a place of habitation. The house she sought could not be far away. It would be better to try to reach it than to wait for daylight, which might be many hours distant.

The road once gained, madam found it not impossible to pick her steps. Somewhere behind the clouds a young crescent moon was rising, and from the rifts a few stars did their best to set a limit to the power of darkness. Better still, the next rising ground revealed a very earthly light, the unmistakable glow of blazing pine. It could shine from nowhere but the window of a dwelling. That light was the cheeriest thing that Madam Botorpa had seen for many days. It set the chilled blood flowing through her veins again. Her footsteps perceptibly quickened. The rest and warmth and food which had receded into the dim distance came very near now. She gathered the little Agneta closer to her. The child shivered in her sleep, and the mother felt rather than heard the low sob, of which the little girl was herself unconscious. She bent her head over the sleeper.

"Poor little one!" she whispered. "Everything for thee behind, and here—? Well, thou shalt at least awake amidst light and warmth."

The light that had served as guide proved, upon Madam Botorpa's approach, to proceed, not from the dwelling house, but from an outbuilding that formed one side of a great quadrangle, about which all the farm structures were grouped. It was a long building of squared pine trunks laid one upon another, and as she neared it madam heard the sound of voices. Passing round to the side from whence the sound proceeded, she approached a window, just as a merry snatch of song made itself heard. A girl's figure at the same moment came between the light and the casement, and then Madam Botorpa stopped to look within.

It hardly seemed possible that that homelike inside scene could be in such close proximity to the lonely, storm-swept road, abandoned of everything but desolation, along which she had groped to find the half sheltered spot where she had slept from utter exhaustion. In the centre of the building a royal fire blazed and crackled on a hearth, sending leaping flames around the huge cauldron swinging above it. About that cauldron the hands of the singer busied themselves, while three or four other maidens, bright-faced and strong-armed, ministered to the wants of the remaining—and in point of numbers, most important—occupants of the place. These were ranged along the outer sides of the house, the firelight gleaming on horned heads, and revealing the big friendly eyes of oxen and kine looking forth on the girls.

The maidens and the cattle were the best of friends. Why not? They spent the short summer months on the mountain side together, and when winter came, the ladugård, or cattle-house, spread its broad, generous shelter over cattle and herd girls alike. There was no lack of company. Bold goats and timid eyed sheep were ranged along the comparatively dim outer stretches of the big, friendly dwelling place, and from some vantage point overhead a cock crowed shrilly. The girl standing by the iron pot stopped her song and turned to a companion.

"Toss in another handful or two of meal," she said. "I want no lean cattle under my charge, nor will I make the Tomte Gubbe my enemy by treating other than well the beasts that look to me for food."

And into the big cauldron, where forage was prepared for the cattle, went more meal. Beret Andersdotter was acknowledged to have no superior in the art of milking and cow tending, or in the general work of the cattle-house.

As she spoke she shifted her position, and the face and form by the window became visible to her. She uttered a sharp cry.

"What ails you, Beret?" asked her companion. "You look as if the evil eye had fallen on you."

The girl made no answer. Her own eyes were staring wildly. Then her companion also turned, to seek the cause of her strange fear, and immediately lifted up her hands in dismay.

" 'Tis the face of no mortal woman," she said. " 'Tis whiter than a snow shroud on a grave."

But to the face and figure by the window belonged a voice, and at that moment it was raised sufficiently to reach the ears of the girls, terror-stricken at the fancies their imaginations had conjured up.

"My girls, I would see Axel Bonde at once, and I know not where to find him. I pray you send one of your number to act as guide, or to bid Axel come to me here."

The words reached the interior faintly. Madam Botorpa intentionally spoke in a low voice, partly from anxiety lest the little Agneta should be awakened, partly because she divined that her sudden appearance had aroused the fears of the girls.

She had stood gazing into that comfortable interior longer than she knew. The warmth and homelikeness of it had a fascination of their own. There were the beds, or rather, cribs, raised above the floor in the wide open space where the firelight shone. On them the herd girls passed nights of slumber as profound as that of their charges. She had slept on worse beds since she left the castle. Axel Bonde must be a prosperous man, she mused, else would he need fewer herders. It was not every peasant who required five maidens to tend his cattle. He had grown richer since she saw him last—and older, for that was more than ten years ago.

When no answer came to her summons, Madam Botorpa spoke again.

"I pray you hasten," she said. "The night is cold for those who stand without."

Thus admonished, one of the girls hesitatingly opened a door and peered out into the darkness.

"The master is within the house," she said, and with more than one backward and fearful glance into the face of the stranger, led her across the quadrangle to the side on which lay the dwelling house. Into this, without the formality of knocking, the girl admitted herself.

"Axel Bonde," she cried, "there is one without who calls for you, saying that she is in haste."

An old man, tall and meagre, clad in the long coat of the peasant class, answered the summons.

"One without!" he said. " 'Tis little wonder such should be in haste. Without is the wrong side of the door at so early an hour."

Madam Botorpa crossed the threshold.

"Axel Bonde," she said, "I come to thee a stranger, perchance, in face, yet to the foster brother of Eric Dahlbo should Eric's daughter not hesitate to turn in her need. I bring you Eric's grandchild. Father and grandfather—both good men and true—lie in their graves."

The old man's hand was already on her arm. He drew her into the full light of the kitchen. Though over the fire preparations were being made for breakfast, no one but himself was in the room.

"The child and the grandchild of my brother Eric

will ever be welcome to claim aught that my house affords, or that this arm can do for them," he said. Then looking into her face, he added gently: "You are weary as well as sad."

"We are hungry and cold," she said, with a smile as wintry as the chill morning without.

"Give me the bairn," he answered, gently placing his guest in a chair by the fire. "And before you tell me what you desire of me, remember that the blood from these veins—it was young blood then—was once set flowing till it mingled with the blood of Eric. He boasted of connection with a noble house, and I was a peasant born, but that mingling of blood made us of one family. Living or dead he is my brother, and his bairn is mine. Eric's daughter, thy wishes shall be as the wishes of thy father. What wilt thou that I do for thee?"

"Give me shelter and safety," she said. "My father is dead. My husband also lies in the grave. All that is left to me is following somewhere upon the dreary road where this night I fought alone against the storm."

"Stop!" he said. "You have told enough. All else can wait. A night spent without, and such a night as this, calls for that which my house can furnish. Katarina!"

He raised his voice sharply, and a woman, who, judging by her age, might have been one of the younger of his daughters, but who was in reality the wife of his only son, stepped into the kitchen.

"Katarina," he said, "the daughter of my brother

Eric has come to me. Set food on the table, and tend her as a guest to whom your father would fain do honor."

He kept the little Agneta in his arms, carrying her tenderly, and himself led the way into the big living room, the heart of the house. Here, though it was but four o'clock in the morning, the sound of the spinning wheel was to be heard, and a girl of sixteen stopped in her steady walk back and forth, to look wonderingly at the intruders.

It was then that the child opened her eyes, and fixing them on the fire, which, here as in the kitchen, greeted the strangers hospitably, and which had in it a suggestion of Brita's generous hearth, said sleepily:

"Is the journey over? Have we got home?"

"Yes, my bairn," said the old man, looking down into the sweet child face, "you have got home."

And then he busied himself with attending to the wants of his guests, bidding the girl go on with her spinning, and keeping his daughter-in-law employed in furnishing the best the house could offer. She herself said little, and asked no questions. But her eyes followed the movements of the strangers, and she drew her own conclusions.

"Put a fire in the guest chamber," said Axel, when the meal was finished. "One who has traveled all night needs rest. And you, Anna," he continued, addressing the girl, "go, give your mother your aid. Let the spinning wait."

When they had gone he turned to Madam Botorpa.

"Is there aught that is necessary to be told before you sleep?" he asked. "You spoke of goods upon the road. Of what do they consist, and how far are they from here?"

Then madam told him of her journey, of the train of wagons somewhere on the way, and of the chests that were left by the roadside. With a very few questions he possessed himself of all necessary details.

"While you sleep I will attend to the safety of your property," he said, "and when you wake you shall tell me what you will."

"I will tell you now," replied Madam Botorpa.

The old man stooped and lifted the little Agneta to his knee. The blue eyes, very grave now, had long been studying his face. At last a small hand was laid gently on his knee. It was then he bent over and lifted the child into a close embrace. Holding her thus he listened while madam told of her husband's death, and of all that had followed.

"And was there no provision made for this little one?" he asked, interrupting her for the first time.

"None, for the present, and for the future, worse than none," she replied.

He looked at her inquiringly.

"He who by legal right claims her father's lands, claims also her father's daughter," she said, in answer to that look. "He would call the child his own as well as the estate. Axel Bonde, I came here, driven, not by poverty, but by fear—fear for the future of my child. There are relatives with whom

I could have sought a home, but none who would see with me that it were better to lay that little one by her father's side than to give her into the keeping of a man who has made other mothers blush for the girl bairns they once rocked in their arms. To such a man I will never yield up my child, though she were a thousand times betrothed."

"God forbid," said Axel reverently, and madam, whose voice had at last lost its composure, remained silent.

"We might have stayed in the old home," she continued at length. "Monsieur Pors was generous. Everything would have been left without change, had I willed it so. He pleaded hard. It was not to be loss to the child. When she was eighteen she would rule in her father's house again—as his bride. It was her father's own arrangement. He himself would hold her interests sacred. So he spoke, and to do him justice he appeared sincere. But to give him his will would have been to put the little one at his mercy. In the thirteen years yet to pass before the carrying out of the betrothal promise, sin might eat as a canker into his life—verily it hath not the tendency to purify itself, or that which it touches—and withal she would still be his. Do you wonder that I gathered together everything that could be called mine or hers, and journeyed to the most distant, as well as the most safe refuge? Of money there was little, but in those chests is much that will bring money. I ask you for a home, but I ask it not without recompense."

The hand of the old man was lifted.

"Stop!" he said peremptorily. "You are Eric's daughter, and you speak of Eric's grandchild. Is it meet in such connection to bring money between her and Eric's brother?"

A smile illumined the lady's face.

"Because I am Eric's daughter," she said, "I must even speak of money. We have not much, but our wants will be few. That which we have will last us long."

"Yes," he said, "that which you have will last you long," and in his eyes there was the light of a smile that did not reach the lips.

After that, Madam Botorpa repaired to the guest chamber and slept, and before she awoke the greater part of her property was safely housed. To accomplish this had been Axel Bonde's first care.

The old man was a peasant, one of the proudly satisfied class who tilled their own land, and called no man master. His arable lands lay somewhat scattered, but they were well cultivated—else would they not have owned Axel Bonde for master. Whatever Axel Bonde undertook was perforce well done, and though he lacked not two winters of having seen the earth threescore and ten times wrapped in snow, there was little done upon the farm that did not come beneath his hand or his personal oversight. His son, being of a less energetic character, had never shown desire to supplant the old man, and if his daughter-in-law was not of quite so accommodating a disposition, she had sufficient faith in Axel's management to leave it undisturbed.

Madam's first waking vision was of the little Agneta, bright, winsome, satisfied, standing before her.

"Mother, grandfather's brother Axel says this is home, and that we are to go in the wagons no more. Is it so? It is not like the castle, but—I like it. Is it home?"

And when madam said yes, the little girl wondered why her mother's eyes were misty and she turned her head away. To the child, grandfather's brother Axel, as he had taught her to call him, was very good, and the farm was a pleasant place.

On the afternoon of that day the wind stopped moaning, and left the land in peace. Above the pine forest that lay over beyond the farm the sun was setting red, and full in its light stood the little Agneta, quietly surveying the situation. The big cobble-paved quadrangle surrounded by house and farm buildings lay beneath her feet, and her eyes were just now contenting themselves with the sight of two sheep and a goat, that, more adventurous than their neighbors, had climbed by a long and circuitous route of outbuilding roofs, to the comparatively high elevation of the house roof, there to regale themselves with the luxuriant grass that covered the almost level surface of the same. Beyond the house lay the cultivated fields of the valley, and outside them all the encircling hills. The sun dipped suddenly down behind the trees, and the air grew chill. An old man, tall, calm, and commanding, though he was a peasant, appeared on the scene.

"Come, my bairn," he said, "it is time to go in," and Agneta put one hand in his, and with the other pushed open the low, heavy door that yet swung easily on its long wooden hinges, stopping a moment to trace with her small fingers the quaint designs which in hammered-out iron embellished and at the same time strengthened this barrier against outside evil. Then she and the old man passed in and the door swung to.

CHAPTER VII

The sea was very quiet and gracious on a morning in July, nearly seven years later than the time when Madam Botorpa turned her back on the stone castle upon the hill. Old ocean had proved a good friend to the vessel, that, with all sails set, and a fair wind, came proudly into the bay, heading for the point where the distant, tree-covered shores drew together. She carried a Swedish flag, and light-hearted passengers, for the hazardous sea voyage was behind her, and the land in front looked a right pleasant country to the travelers.

It had been a prosperous voyage. The ship's guns had not been forced to open fire on an enemy, nor the sails to be reefed because of violent storm. Scarcely seven weeks ago the passengers and crew gave a last ringing cheer for Old Sweden as they left her shores, and now New Sweden was in sight. They had large expectations in connection with the land that lay in front of them, a place where the vine grew as freely as in Italy, and fruits and flowers were to be had without cultivation. It presented no iron-bound shore, but a sweeping bay, that welcomed them with open arms.

"Sail ahead!" sang out the watch, and the passengers turned from their eager scrutiny of the shore to catch a sight of the vessel.

She was well ahead of them, but as the day drew on they succeeded in overhauling her, and passed her where the shores began to approach each other. She was a Dutch ship, making her way, like themselves, to the River of New Sweden, or, as the Dutch called it, the South River. It was the great South River, forming a highway for trade, and opening easy communication with the Indians, that made both the Dutch and Swedish nations so ready to claim a share in this particular part of the new western land, a land that was broad enough to hold many peoples, and was yet being quarreled over by a handful of men who could neither fill it nor use it.

"She is in no hurry to reach the fort, else would she crowd on more sail," said one of the officers of the Swedish vessel.

"She'd crowd it on fast enough if her own Fort Nassau stood guard over the river, instead of being well up stream," rejoined the captain. "She's in no great hurry to heave to and pay toll."

"We may thank our lucky stars that our Fort Elfsborg stands at this end of the river, instead of their Fort Nassau, for then would the boot be on the other leg," was the answer.

The two vessels kept their relative positions for the rest of the day, the Dutch captain slowly falling behind. After Fort Elfsborg came into range the Swedes had little time to watch the stranger. To them the sight of human habitation on this strange shore was more engrossing, and the fort, the symbol of their country's sovereignty over a part of the western land, was a brave show. They cheered lustily when they came near enough to distinguish the Swedish flag waving over the land that their good king, Gustavus Adolphus, had planned to give to Sweden for a possession.

By this time they were fairly in the river, and had the opportunity to distinguish its separate features, the stretches of sandy beach, the deep coves, and the rich low-lying meadow lands where the eye of the Swede fell approvingly on the rank grass waiting to furnish food for his goats and cows. More than one shout of surprised satisfaction went up, when, from some marshy stretch by the river bank, swarming wild fowl rose in the air, hovering for a minute over the reedy reach, and then dropping out of sight again.

"This is a land of Canaan," quoth a short, thickset Swede. " 'Tis worth crossing the ocean, and saying farewell to the dear old Sweedland, to leave a good broad share of such a country as a heritage to your children."

Among those who stood on the deck of the Swedish vessel there was one whose voice was not once heard. He looked on the new land earnestly, persistently, but his face did not brighten. And yet it was an intelligent face, and there was enough along those shores to awaken interest. The countenance was grave to sadness, far too grave for the age of the young man. He could not have been more than nineteen years old, but there was a manly dignity of bearing calculated to make the world deem him older. When his eye brightened, and his lips relaxed, men had been known to think him younger. But his eye did not brighten, nor his lips relax, while the ship, aided by a friendly breeze, sailed up the river.

He had not changed his position for hours. He stood back from the group of eager Swedes, his eyes scanning the bank nearest to him, instead of looking ahead in impatient anticipation. He was bound, like the rest, for the new land, but he seemed as one who had no interest in it—to whom it offered no prizes. Only once, when the fort came in sight, did he lift his eyes and look far forward, with a long, sweeping glance that took in fort and river banks and the whole surrounding country. For a minute he stood thus, drawing a long breath of admiration of its beauty and promise; then the momentary animation left the face, the hand, half raised to shade the eyes, went down again, and the eyes, that had lifted but not brightened, dropped to the nearest bank.

It was a good land, an excellent land—for all but him. As they swept on, the words of the great Gustavus Adolphus were ringing through his brain. The king had designed to plant here a colony where the laborer should reap the fruits of his toil—blessed laborer! Would that he were in his place!—and where the rights of conscience should be inviolate. The lips took a closer pressure as he mused. No slaves, decreed the good king, should burden that soil, for "slaves cost a great deal, labor with reluctance, and soon perish from hard usage. But the Swedish nation is industrious and intelligent, and hereby we shall gain more by a free people with wives and children."

He knew the words by heart. They had appealed to him in the old days when he too could claim a heritage among "a free people." He had never expected to come to the colony for which the good king planned, and lo, he was here, amidst the free people who were to inhabit it, and he was not free. Before night all his fellow passengers would set foot on the free land promised to them, and he—he might or might not be permitted to go ashore, but ashore or afloat he would still not be free. The land knew no slaves, but it knew prisoners, and he came to it a prisoner, sent thither by his country as an outcast—he who belonged to an ancient burgher family, and who had never dreamed of aught but upholding untarnished the family name. It was little wonder that the beauty and promise of the new country brought no comfort to his heart. Its promise was not for him.

The brave little fort was so fully in sight now that the travelers could distinguish her guns, and discern the figures of men moving around her. The ship had been seen, and the twelve men of the garrison, all as eager for news of the old home as were they themselves for knowledge of the new, were watching her approach. Presently boom! boom! came the Swedish national salute. The guns of the fort were welcoming the home vessel. In answering salute their own guns spoke promptly, and amid the shouts of the ship's crew, and the happy bustle of preparation for landing, the vessel dropped anchor before the fort.

Though none of them intended to stay in the neighborhood of Fort Elfsborg, most of the passengers hastened on shore. They wanted to see the little fortress, with its four brass and four iron guns, and to make a closer acquaintance with the land they had viewed from the vessel.

The fort stood at the mouth of a creek, at a place where the South River was still broad, though not so broad that the guns could not sweep it. Perhaps the Dutch vessel, that, as she neared the fort, crowded on sail, would have shown a different front but for those guns. It looked as if she hoped, in the confusion of the double arrival, to run past the fort, for she made no preparations for coming to, as the Swedish vessel had done. If so, she made a false reckoning. Those in charge of the fort were on the lookout for her.

"Looks like a runaway, don't she?" remarked the lieutenant, viewing the swiftly moving ship with an amused smile.

"Aye. It goes against the grain to have to strike her flag to our colors," replied his companion.

In truth it was a standing grievance that the Swedes had laid claim to the jurisdiction of the river, and had built their fort so as to command the same, exacting recognition of every passing vessel, though the vessel might belong to the great Dutch

West India Company itself, or to private merchants carrying on their trade under the protection of the company, and though it might be proceeding to the Dutch Fort Nassau further up the river. None the less for these things must it lower its colors and pay toll to the Swedes, who claimed the right to control the navigation of the stream.

The present vessel, a merchant ship proceeding up the river for the purpose of trading with the Indians, seemed disposed to set their pretensions at defiance, for it kept on its course till well abreast of the fort, bearing towards the opposite shore, and running before the wind.

"Means to give us the slip," said the officer, and a minute later a shot went across the bows of the Dutchman, a gentle reminder that the garrison was not in a mood for any playful liberties.

The stranger did not take the hint. The Dutch flag flew defiantly aloft, regardless of the expectations of the Swedish colors waiting to have their supremacy recognized, and the ship held on her course.

But if she was in earnest, so was the garrison. Once more a shot fell across her bows, but the next cut a hole in a sail, and a third swept her deck. Then she sullenly hove to, lowering her colors, and waiting for the Swedes to come aboard.

They came promptly, a little triumphant over the quick termination of the contest.

"Didn't see the fort, captain, did you?" remarked the lieutenant, with a derisive smile.

He was answered by an oath.

The smile disappeared, but there was a mocking tone in the voice that said: "Come now, captain, it's we that ought to do the swearing. You cost us four good cannon balls by your blindness."

"We yield to might, not right," replied the other savagely. "Our West India Company's vessels sailed up these waters before you knew there was such a land, and years before ever a Swede set foot on what you have had the impudence to call New Sweden."

The lieutenant laughed.

"That's an old tale," he said, and proceeded to examine the ship's papers, and to exact toll.

She went on her way the same evening, for the sun was not yet down, but the Swedish vessel stayed till morning.

"Who is that young man on your deck, standing as stiff as a figure-head?" asked the lieutenant, as his boat passed the home vessel, and the captain came to her side.

"Which? Ah, yes. He's a prisoner; sent here for burning down a house, or something. He has no pleasant prospect before him, poor fellow. Doesn't feel very lively, and no wonder," replied the captain.

"Better look out after him, sir," said the officer, in a lower voice. "He might easily get ashore, and then you'd find yourself in hot water with the Governor. He's set his face like a flint against having any such in the land. Says there are plenty of good settlers ready enough to come to New Sweden, and the country shall not be polluted with men that might with more wisdom be put off the face of the earth than kept on it to cumber it. He's for sending them all back whence they came. It would be safer to put irons on him. Such as have been sent here before work in irons. But Printz will have no more of them. I doubt you will have to take yonder specimen back with you."

"Not we," said the captain; but a few minutes later the young man, who during all the encounter with the Dutch ship had not shifted his position, felt a touch on his shoulder.

"You are ordered below."

The voice was that of a soldier on his way to join the Governor's forces at Tenacong, further up the river.

The prisoner obeyed without question or protest, and the deck saw its silent occupant no more during the journey.

CHAPTER VIII

It was the afternoon of the day following that on which the Swedish captain dropped anchor before Fort Elfsborg. Within the walls of a goodly mansion, the pride of New Sweden, sat a man of soldierly bearing, engrossed in the perusal of a paper, the seal having been just broken. He was a man great in a physical sense, with features heavy and imposing. Just now he looked ill pleased, and the seafaring man by whose hand the communication had been received, notwithstanding that his dress proclaimed him of captain's rank, had not been invited to be seated. The Governor of New Sweden showed unmistakable signs of being in no pleasant mood. As a consequence he stood rigidly on his dignity.

John Printz was not by nature a mild man, and when his anger was aroused he was the reverse of gentle. For every man who loved the Governor of New Sweden there were ten who feared him. He had large ideas of his country's greatness, and he deemed it essential that John Printz, formerly lieutenant-colonel of cavalry in Her Majesty's forces, now Governor of New Sweden, should both exalt his office and be exalted by it. His estimate of the importance of John Printz the Governor was only equaled by his estimate of the importance of

John Printz the man. The man and the Governor were equally irritated at the present moment.

"Why didn't you come up the river last night?"

The loud tones broke the stillness with a suddenness that made the Governor's companion start visibly.

"The day was spent when Fort Elfsborg was reached," he said, after a momentary pause spent in recovering his scattered senses, "and there was business to transact with the garrison. It was too late to proceed further. I knew not, beside, that your Honor desired haste."

"It is a lie!" broke in the stentorian tones of the Governor. "A rascally Dutch sloop found her way up here almost by daybreak. The sun showed no favoritism, I'll warrant. He would have shone as well on you as on her. And hark you! The business of the Governor of New Sweden always demands haste. You bring stores for the Governor's service, and ammunition for the garrisons. By what right do you delay their delivery?"

"I meant no delay," said the captain deprecatingly, but he was cut short.

"Meant! I care not what you meant. It is what you do that affects me, and that, in the present case, is ill enough. Get you about your business of unlading the vessel, and think yourself fortunate if I complain not of your negligence to those who sent you hither."

The captain turned away discomfited, but before he could reach the door the Governor spoke again.

"Stop!" he called authoritatively. "What do you mean by bringing the scum of the old land to contaminate the new? This is no sink-hole, into which to pour the filth of a country that, good as she is, hath yet a share of scoundrels, else would she not so easily lay her hand on captains such as you."

"You speak of the prisoner sent out by Her Majesty's officers of justice," said the captain. "Truly I had no hand in the business. He was delivered into my care to be conveyed to your Excellency's domain, and by you put to any service that might be deemed most expedient. For the matter of that, he will do no great harm in your land. The lad comes of a rare good family, and to my mind should never have been sent hither at all, and that not lest the land should suffer."

He spoke somewhat hotly.

"What! You take part with criminals, and dare to question the actions of your superiors?" roared the Governor. "Get you gone, before I clap you in irons as well as your prisoner."

Nothing loth, the captain turned to obey, but while he was yet on the wrong side of the door, another at the further end of the room opened, and a lady stepped within. With proud carriage and haughty look she advanced towards the Governor, her eye the while fixed on the unlucky visitor, who was making desperate efforts to put, in the smallest possible time, the outer walls of the mansion between himself and the irate ruler. From the sailor the lady's eyes turned towards the Governor of New Sweden. The signs of anger did not escape her, nor, to all appearance, overawe her. She came and stood by the table near which the Governor sat.

"So the expected ship has arrived," she said, the hard, cold ring of her voice contrasting strangely with the tones in which the Governor had last spoken. "I am in haste to see whether the articles which I ordered to be sent me are to my liking. This is a gala day. Ships come not from Sweedland in every moon. Therefore you, my father, should, methinks, show a less troubled face."

He turned from her impatiently.

"You women are ever pleased with trifles," he said. "Stores are useful enough. I deny not that we can ill cope with the savages without them, and while the Hollanders sail in with goods in plenty to tempt the Indians' fancy, we too must be awake. But soldiers would be better than Indian stores. If Her Majesty would but send me men, I would show this Dutch West India Company and all its representatives where they were. Reinforcements there are none, beyond a paltry soldier or two sent hither because he desired to throw in his lot with the new land. I tell you this country is worth struggling for, whatever they at home may think."

"New Sweden has all odds in its favor while John Printz is its Governor," said the lady quietly. "More soldiers are desirable, truly, yet have the Hollanders fewer than ourselves, and with the

Indians our friends we have more to hope than to fear."

"Aye, could we keep everything in our favor we might do well enough," returned the Governor. "The natives are our friends, surely, and will be till the Hollanders tempt them with rum and trinkets. But how long will they be true to us now that the rascally interlopers are established in their new fort on the Schuylkill? Would their Fort Beversrede ever have risen in the place where the Minquas resort if the savages had been as staunch as of old? What safeguard have we, with a Dutch fort in their midst, and a Dutch vessel but now sailing up the river, in haste to reach the trading place before new stores of ours find their way thither? The rascally Hollander will pervert more savages with his powder and his rum than can be induced to trade with an honest government in a twelvemonth."

"Nay, croak not so loudly," said the lady. "Verily we have the lion's share of the trade, and are like to have, if we keep ahead of those insolent Dutchmen, who, though they have established their fort on the Schuylkill itself, will yet find that they have to deal with the Governor of New Sweden as well as with a few greedy Indians. It is your place to see that they learn what that means."

"Aye, that is it," replied the Governor. "Let the trade with the Minquas fall into the hands of our rivals, and little will be left to us save the tilling of the soil,' a right good occupation for our peasants, and one which a man of other rank than they may well use as an auxiliary, but not that for which our good Queen sent out the Governor of New Sweden."

"The trade will not fall out of the hands of my father," said the lady calmly. "It is a danger little to be feared. In the meantime, what news brought the captain?"

"None, to me," said the Governor testily. "I talked not with the fellow."

"The chance is not lost," replied his daughter quietly. "But at least he brought you a communication from home."

He put the paper in her hands. She read it through, and replaced it on the table.

"This prisoner of which it speaks," she questioned, "what more have you learned of him? He is of good family, and before the committal of the crime was considered a youth of promise and parts, and ought therefore to be of use in a new land, saith the writer. Truly I am curious to see him. Have you required that he should be brought hither?"

"Not I. I am in no hurry to deal with him. Did I have my will, no convict should set foot on these shores."

"You are right," was the answer, "but since this one is here, we may as well see what can be made of him. His crime is serious enough, in all truth. The burning down of dwelling houses out of malevolence is a record little calculated to make him a welcome addition to any settlement."

"I am inclined to ship him back," said the Governor, "and let those who condemned him see that he is duly punished."

"Nay, act not hastily, my father," the lady replied. "The influx of such has almost ceased. Your action has already brought the evil well-nigh to an end. Better send for this one and hear what he has to say. There may be special reasons for relaxing your vigilance on the present occasion. Shall I dispatch a messenger to the vessel and demand that the prisoner be brought?" she persisted.

"As you will," replied the Governor.

Half an hour later the Governor was informed of the attendance of a soldier from the vessel lately arrived.

"Send the guard and his prisoner in here," directed Printz, and the soldier entered, accompanied by a young man who bore himself respectfully yet proudly in the presence of the Governor of the land. To the surprise of the latter no fetters bound the prisoner. He walked as free as the soldier at his side.

"Soldier, what mean you by bringing this fellow here without irons?" demanded the Governor sternly.

"The captain spake not of irons, your Honor," replied the man, "and none were necessary. He told me to bring my prisoner, and here he is. He'll no more attempt to escape now than he has done on the journey; that I'll warrant."

The Governor frowned.

"The captain is a fool!" he shouted, and this

meeting with no contradiction, he relapsed into silence.

The young man, after saluting the Governor respectfully, stood to all outward appearance calm, though the tumult in his heart found outlet in a noticeable pallor of the face.

"Bring the prisoner forward," commanded the Governor, after a pause.

The young man advanced, walking erect, with eye undaunted, but with such an absence of boldness that even the Governor could find no fault with his mien.

"Your name is Eric Helm?" he asked.

"Yes, your Excellency."

The voice was low, but under perfect control.

"You are sent here for having burned down the outbuildings, and having attempted to burn down the dwelling house, of one Oscar Bure," continued the Governor.

"I am sent here accused of that crime," was the reply, the slight stress on the word "accused" making the answer almost a denial.

"What mean you by that?" inquired the Governor sharply.

"That it is of this men accuse me," said the young man, in the same low, respectful tone.

"And you would claim, falsely, eh?" questioned the Governor severely.

"Nay, your Excellency, I say not that," replied the prisoner.

"Then you own that you are guilty?"

"No, your Honor, that do I *not.*"

The words were emphatic. They had an irritating effect on the Governor. He grew red in the face.

"Do you take me for a fool?" he roared. "You are not innocent, and you are not guilty. What are you, then, you idiot?"

"Your Excellency," said the young man, "of a truth I know not whether I am innocent or guilty of the crime laid to my charge. I was beside myself with passion. This much I know, that I threw down a lighted torch. Verily I thought that my foot afterwards extinguished it, but I know not. My enemies say that it burned yet, and that the loss which befell the owner of what was once my uncle's home was by deliberate act of mine. It may have been by act of mine, yet was it surely not deliberate."

The Governor frowned savagely.

"Those better able than myself to judge have deemed you guilty of more than being mad with passion," he said. "But were that all, he whose sole excuse is that he was beside himself with rage, might well be accounted a dangerous citizen, fit only to be bound with chains."

"Your words are just," said the young man sadly. "To the giving the reins to passion I plead guilty Of aught else I have as little definite knowledge as your Excellency."

"You would have me believe you strangely innocent," sneered the Governor. " 'Tis the kind of innocence that will avail you little now that the law has laid her hand upon you."

The prisoner made no answer, only his lips set themselves together, and a sadder look came to his eyes.

"May it please your Honor," said the soldier, speaking for the first time, "the captain has sent a letter to be delivered to you. It concerns the prisoner."

"Why was it not given to me sooner?" snapped the Governor, taking the packet and tearing it open.

"Oxenstiern!" he ejaculated, after examining the signature, and then he relapsed into silence.

The prisoner stood straight and motionless, his eyes fixed on the table near him. From the opposite side of that table the lady of Printz Hall regarded him curiously. Prisoners of his stamp were not often seen in New Sweden. To her he looked little like a dangerous character. If the young man were a criminal, he was strangely unlike his class.

When her scrutiny had been carried sufficiently far for her own satisfaction, the lady rose, and passing round the table came and stood behind the Governor, letting her eye run down the page his hand held. A few minutes later her voice broke the stillness.

"Soldier," she said haughtily, "take your prisoner to the further end of the room."

The soldier obeyed, and the lady turned to the Governor and spoke in a low tone.

"The lad is a young fool," she said bluntly. "I

dare swear he is no worse. We may perchance be the better for his folly."

"In what way, I pray you?" asked the Governor testily.

"Why, see you not that the youth is one to be useful?" she asked. "The Queen's minister says here of him that he has the reputation for being a good draughtsman and for being able to carry out as well as plan the construction of buildings, also that he can survey land, and that he knows somewhat of the principles of fortification, that he has withal considerable mechanical skill, and that he might even be made to serve your purpose in exploring the land for minerals. Do I not even now exceedingly desire an addition to the pleasure house in the grounds, and are there not forts and strong houses to be built to keep our neighbors, the Dutch, from crawling into the best trading places? What better can we do than set this young prisoner to work, and make of his folly a benefit to ourselves and New Sweden?"

"I want not the music of clanking chains about my premises," growled the Governor.

"Chains!" quoth the lady, with a laugh. "I will forge you a chain that will bind yonder youth securely, and yet leave the fetter invisible. Nay," she added more seriously, "I wonder at you. With the colonists giving you reluctant service, you should rejoice to get a pair of hands to labor for you without remuneration. Shew the lad a little kindness, and I swear you will win his gratitude, and secure a devoted follower and helper. 'Tis a better fetter than one of iron."

"It is folly," said the Governor, but his tone was less positive than before. "Oxenstiern knows not the youth himself, but relies solely on the word of one who was acquainted with the boy's father. He denies not that justice must take its course, but bids me avail myself of the young man's services, which in this land may well be of value, and, where it is possible to do so, temper justice with mercy."

"Exactly," said the lady triumphantly. "The boy is a prisoner, and a prisoner he must remain, but he may as well be a useful prisoner, and he need not be an ill-used one."

"Who talked of ill-using him?" asked her father.

"Not the Governor of New Sweden," was the diplomatic answer, and that it pleased not the hearer ill was attested by the lifting of the cloud upon his brow.

"Well, well, I might do worse," he said. "Prisoner, stand forward."

The young man advanced a few steps, and stood attentive.

"Advance to the table," commanded the Governor.

The prisoner obeyed.

"I have here," continued the great man, "a letter from a minister of Her Majesty. He writes from information given by one who knew your father in Sweedland. He speaks well of your family. Would that he could speak as well of you! To disgrace an ancient name is a sore offence, yet for your father's sake would I show mercy to his son. By the sentence imposed upon you I should, were I to consider you as a common transgressor, put irons upon you, and apportion your lot among those who are outcast, and dwell apart, performing toil for the benefit of this new land as some measure of reparation for their crimes. But I am told that there are in your case extenuating circumstances. I would willingly believe it. Be it true or false, I will give you an opportunity to shew yourself a man worthy to live among respectable and loyal citizens. I shall therefore put upon you no fetters, nor assign you a place among the other convicts. A soldier will be appointed to act in some measure as guard, though I expect not treachery of you. To him you will render obedience. Your orders will come from myself. If you shew yourself worthy of the leniency I am about to display towards you, it will be well with you; if not, I shall know how to act."

"Your Excellency shall not find me ungrateful," said the young man, and at a sign from the Governor, prisoner and guard withdrew.

CHAPTER IX

The metropolis of New Sweden lay baking beneath a July sun. It was hot, even for the land of the South River. The rosy bloom seemed hourly to deepen on the cheeks of the peaches that were coming to perfection in the orchard of Printz Hall, where the Governor of New Sweden, and the Governor's daughter, walked daily with much secret delight and self-gratulation.

The Governor was passing beneath those trees at the present moment, on his way to the pleasure grounds. His step, albeit it was heavy, was not slow. For a man who weighed over four hundred pounds the Governor was active. He had not gone beyond the trees when his eye took in the meaning of the movements of some half dozen men grouped round a building in the grounds. The partially raised foot found a resting place on the earth again, and the Governor stood still to watch. The massive face relaxed its sternness the while. To Governor Printz the Island of Tinicum—Tenacong the Swedes called it—was the centre of New Sweden, and Printz Hall was the centre of Tenacong.

Tenacong had been an uninhabited waste when John Printz set foot on that part of the American soil which is to-day called the mouth of the Delaware. The island lay further up the stream, separated from the western mainland only by a creek, and the keen eye of the new Governor at once took in the capabilities of its bold, high shore. Its natural features, at that time unmodified by the hand of man, appealed as strongly to him as do the altered forms of them to the people of Pennsylvania to-day, when, in the beautiful site of the Pennsylvania Lazaretto, where vessels bound for Philadelphia are quarantined, they admire anew the old Tenacong that recommended itself to the Swedish Governor. The island, too, was but a short distance below the Dutch Fort Nassau, and Governor Printz, taking all its advantages into consideration, passed by the old established Fort Christina, with its little town behind it, and journeyed on to Tenacong, to turn it into the metropolis of the new land. Here rose the Governor's town and fort of New Gottenburg, and here was built Printz Hall, a mansion worthy of Old Sweden. Thither also were drawn, by the attraction of the Governor's presence, the chief men of New Sweden, who built for themselves houses and started plantations on the island.

It was the pride of the Governor to make Printz Hall worthy of the builder. The appearance of the Governor's dwelling should at least suggest the dignity of his office. More than one murmur of dissatisfaction was heard when the settlers were called upon to leave their own concerns to lend a hand in making and keeping the residence of the Governor exactly to that Governor's taste.

The Governor's daughter was possibly yet more interested in the perfecting of the Hall and its surroundings than was the Governor himself. But for her suggestion he would never have thought to utilize the coming of the young prisoner to carry out an improvement to the pleasure house in his grounds. To-day, as he stood looking from a distance at the workmen, he congratulated himself on having listened to his daughter's counsel. The planning of the addition to the building had been placed entirely in the stranger's hands. Now, as the structure rose, the Governor was more than satisfied.

"It was well that I did not carry out my first intention, and send the young man back, as I have done others thus indiscreetly brought to these shores," he mused. "Verily he is of another stamp than they. Those who moved Oxenstiern to write to me in his favor did not err. He is a young man of parts. Judging by his energy, and by many tokens of character, I am ready to believe with the writer of the letter that he had enemies, else would he not have got into so serious a scrape."

By which decision it will be seen that the way to the heart of Governor Printz lay through the carrying out of the Governor's schemes. Eric Helm had proved himself useful—very useful—and all thought of sending him back whence he came had been abandoned. The Governor felt no inclination to be too severe in the case of a man who could be turned to account in so many ways; one, moreover, whose talents lay at the Governor's disposal, and could be drawn upon without expense.

As for the young man himself, he worked persistently and intelligently, bringing his best knowledge to bear upon the business in hand, throwing all his energies into it, and trying to believe that in the good fortune which had removed from him the hardest features of a convict's life he had cause for both rejoicing and hope, but at heart never for a moment forgetting the shame of it all, but when night came, and in the soldiers' quarters to which he had been assigned the men joked and laughed, and at last slept, going back in thought to the old Swedish land, and living over again the days when he had big hopes for the future, and when he would have laughed in the face of any who told him he would ever sit, an outcast among men, with them, but not of them.

The dear old land! He loved her yet, though she had done him a wrong. Aye, but had she? Was she or was she not right in sending him from her shores as one unfit longer to tread them? At one time his heart would cry out bitterly against his country's decision. There was not a man on her soil who loved her better, or had more desired to be worthy of her. He had had great hopes of what he would do in her and for her. His architectural studies, his mechanical and engineering efforts, had been mingled with aspirations of the good to be achieved by them in and for the dear old Swedish homeland. He had believed that every son of

Sweden should make her richer by his toil; and now she had banished him from her shores as unworthy of her—turned him out among those who had become to her a curse. Had he not a right to accuse her? Was ever son truer to her, and was ever son more harshly judged?

At this point the iron hand of logic invariably came in, remorselessly crushed back the tumultuous upspringing of passionate protest, and forced the heart to cease its outcry and let the head face hard facts. What had the country to do with men's aspirations? It was their actions with which she had to deal. If a man's deeds were the deeds of an enemy, it mattered not to her that he claimed to possess the heart of a lover. Eric Helm did not deny that his actions had been unworthy of her or himself; he only pleaded, like a weakling, that he had lost control of himself; that when the act of which he was accused was committed, his power of self-government was in abeyance. What was the admission but a vindication of his country's action? What did she want with men who could not stand under the pressure of temptation? A man is none the less a menace to society that he eschews evil except under strong pressure.

And yet, if the rule the good Gustavus Adolphus had laid down for the new land had been carried out in the old, if the rights of conscience had been so fully respected that a Calvinist might stand side by side with an orthodox Lutheran and be regarded without prejudice, would his rash act have been so harshly judged? Well, the question was foolish, for then would the act never have been committed.

It was nothing but a weary circle of reasoning, round which Eric Helm went ceaselessly, finding no end, and turning from it resolutely at last to court sleep, that he might be fit for the next day's labor. It was only when he let his thoughts stop at one point in the history of the past months that the hopeless round of accusation and extenuation and counter accusation would cease. Then, indeed, the torturing endless circle opened, and released him from its enchanted course, where his thoughts were kept on the stretch and forced to go round and round without end. No evil enchantment could hold before the clear blue eyes and sweet questioning face of the child who stood forth at this point of the past history.

A child? Well, yes, a child, of course, and yet she hardly seemed to him of ordinary human origin. She was part of a night scene full of snow, and glistening ice crystals, and pale, clear moonlight, and cold—intense, benumbing cold, sufficient to quench the fever in his veins. The fever had reached its height then, and it died out that night. It was not the cold that killed it. It was the child's face. Of course she was human, and must have lived an ordinary, every-day life in the old farmhouse that loomed up dark in the background of the picture. The house had been all dark on that night, except for a light shining from one window—a softened light, pale, like the light of the moon.

He was fleeing from his fellow men, blindly running from the consequences of his own deed. He had not felt weariness until then, though he had traveled far. Then it came suddenly upon him, with the numbing cold, and the heavy weight of his feet, and the burden of the only thing left to love him, a burden under which he tugged and toiled, and panted in the bearing. Yet he dared not put it down. The dog's tongue licked his face, and once, he remembered, he laid that face on the faithful head. It was a relief to stop for a moment, and hide his eyes from the sharp cold, and feel the warm body of the animal writhing in an effort to express sympathy and love. But it was a dangerous experiment. It made the creature struggle to free himself, and necessitated a short, sharp conflict before the foolish animal's mad impulse of love could be dominated by the stronger will of his master.

Hunger and exhaustion were telling upon Eric Helm. He had felt as if he could go on for ever in his one unreasoning determination not to let his enemies have their will in his public humiliation. And until now he had known no fatigue. Now it came upon him with increasing force. He tried to remember how many days he had traveled and hidden and traveled again, doing more walking than hiding, but the effort was too much for the weary brain. Until the maiden appeared. Then things grew clear.

But before then he pushed on and on, his arms

threatening every moment to give way beneath the weight of the dog, and his feet taking to strange tricks of stumbling. Even his eyes began to play him false, and he mistook the way, and wandered round in a circle, and found himself back again by an old farm dwelling that he had passed an hour ago—or perhaps it was only minutes, though it seemed long to him. And then she appeared, the young maiden, tall and straight, and lithe like a growing sapling, with a face that in the moonlight glowed with a warmth of life and beauty bewilderingly fair and sweet to him.

She was only a child—just a child, of course—and she lived in the farmhouse he had passed. And she was not afraid of him, though he was wandering about the country like a thief, under cover of the night. She bade him stand forth in the moonlight, and she looked into his face, and then her own lighted with a smile as she said:

"I saw you come past the house a few minutes ago. You staggered, and I thought you had drunk too much brandy, but you lifted up your face, and I saw your eyes, and knew that you were not drunken."

"No," replied the wanderer, half wondering, and half stupid yet, "I am not drunken."

"But you do not walk as you should. You nearly fall as you go," persisted the child. "I think you need some one to aid you. Are you tired?"

"To the point of death," said Eric, "and yet I may not rest."

"Why not?" asked the maiden.

"Those from whom I flee would find me. I must press on," he said.

"You will go none the faster for wandering round and round, too weary to go forward," she said, with quiet wisdom. "Come, I will show you where you may rest and none will see you," and she led him to a ruined outbuilding where the moonlight shone in through the broken roof, and where there was yet shelter in the further corner.

"Is the dog hurt?" she asked, looking at the animal in his arms.

"No, but if I let him escape from my arms, his footprints by the side of my own will tell those who brought him from afar for the purpose of tracking me that he has found his master," he answered.

"Is he your dog?" she questioned.

"Aye. The only thing left in all the world to care for Eric Helm."

She looked at him for a moment, and then, ignoring his last words, said in a practical tone: "Are you hungry?"

He smiled. In spite of what lay behind, and what was yet before, the smile came. He could not help it. The quiet, practical wisdom of the question struck him as an incongruity amidst the high pressure of excitement under which he had been traveling.

"Yes, little lady," he replied, "I am hungry. I think, though I am not sure, that I have not eaten for days. But that is of small moment."

"My name is Agneta," she said. "And hunger is not of small moment. You cannot travel without food. To attempt it is folly. Sit down there in that corner, and put your dog from your arms. Tell him not to stir. He will obey you, because you are his master. I will bring you food."

After that there came a blank. Eric must have slept, for when he opened his eyes the dog was standing by him, keeping guard over the food that lay at his side. And when he had eaten, the same girlish figure stood suddenly before him, and the young voice asked if he felt rested.

"For it is six hours since you came in here," the child said, "and if there be need for you to depart before daylight, you must even be going on your way."

As he rose to go, and tried to thank her, she stopped him.

"I wish I could have told my mother about you," she said. "She would have known what to do. You do not. You are not in a fit state to act wisely. But she is very ill," and here the voice lowered and the eyes dropped for a moment, "and I may not disturb her. You could have told her all about the trouble you are in, and she would have told you what it was best to do. It is no good hastening, and going nowhere. Are you going anywhere?"

Eric Helm hesitated, and then looked earnestly in her face.

"Whither should I go?" he said. "I am an outcast, fleeing from those who pursue."

"You cannot flee for ever" she said. "From whom do you hide?"

"To tell you that would take long," he replied, "and I know not whether you would care to listen."

She stopped to think before she answered.

"Yes, I will listen," she said. "And I think you had better tell me. It is of no use to wear yourself out with running you know not where. Tell me all. I cannot advise you as my mother would, but perhaps I shall know better than you, because I am not too tired to judge."

It was then, when he tried to put into speech the story of the foregoing months, with the eyes of the child Agneta studying his face, that the mists began to roll away, and he found himself able to discriminate more fairly, and to bring back facts and words more clearly. When it was not so she interrupted him by question.

It took few sentences to tell of his earlier life in a Swedish city, and of his removal after the death of his parents to the home of an uncle who had purchased an estate near a small town. His father, a rich and well respected merchant in the boy's earlier days, was a well respected merchant to the day of his death, though not then a rich one.

"His son never loved him better," said Eric proudly, "than when he made himself poor that none might suffer poverty through deed of his. His name was untarnished—until now."

The last words were spoken bitterly.

"Who has tarnished it now?" said the little maid,

and her eyes searched his face gravely as she waited for the answer. It did not come quickly.

"His son," said the young man at length, and there was a depth of sorrow in the tone that for the moment brought an answering shadow into the child's eyes.

"Would he have thought so?" she questioned, almost immediately.

"Truly I know not," said Eric. "He was ever gentle in his judgment of me, and would believe that I intended not that which sprang from my act. Yet would he warn me, as often before, that to give the bridle to anger is to court ruin."

The maiden nodded gravely.

"You gave way to anger," she said. "What else? Was there just cause for the anger?"

"Aye, that was there, if just cause ever existed," he replied. "Could a man see a woman, old and helpless, dragged from her bed and thrust out of doors on a night when the very dogs should be housed, and that for no crime but that her faith tallied not with the creed of the ruffian who laughed at her helpless protests, and not grow angry at the outrage?"

"Nay, surely," said the child. "And is it for this that you hide? Truly I would face the tyrant and justify my act."

"Ah, but you know not yet how far anger led me," he said. "My uncle's barn to-day lies in ruins, and the house itself was partially destroyed, through mad passion of mine. I regret not that I attacked the perpetrator of that deed of cruelty, though the attack was surely illegal, nor that I drove him from the cottage—his own property—and compelled him to give the woman until the morrow to remove herself and her goods. Had I stopped there, I should have had naught to charge myself with. And yet," he said, his voice rising as memory brought back the scene of that night, "how could I hold back my passion? Was it not enough to arouse it when he dared to revile my uncle, the man to whom he owed all he possessed? He had heaped abuse on me, and on that which was sacred to me; now he turned his tongue to vile words in reference to his benefactor."

The hand of the young man clenched itself, and a light that had not before been there burned in his eyes. The child saw it, and wisely passing over all that was most important in his words, asked:

"Was your uncle yet alive?"

Her question recalled him to the present. The fire of passion died from his eyes.

"Nay, else would my position have been different," he said sadly. "While he lived the old man loved me well, though with a love different from that of my father. Had I been, like himself, a staunch Lutheran, I think my uncle would have seen no fault in me. He was orthodox through and through, a Lutheran to the heart's core, and I— Will it shock you to know that I am not?"

"That you are not a Lutheran?" she asked.

"Yes."

"No. What are you?"

"A Calvinist," he answered.

"Do you think it right to be a Calvinist?" she questioned.

"Yes, or I should not be one."

"Then what else could you be?" she said. "My mother says that every one must do what conscience bids him, though he must be sure he is following conscience and not self-will. Of course you must be a Calvinist if you think it right. Go on, please. Did your uncle think you were wrong to be a Calvinist?"

"Ah, that did he," said Eric. "He could never quite forgive me the offence of thinking otherwise than he himself thought, though in those outside his own family he would tolerate a difference of creed. He even, contrary to the custom of many around him, allowed Calvinists to live on his estate. But he abhorred their faith, and it always stood as a barrier between us that I was not a Lutheran."

"But it did not rob you of his love," said the child.

"No. And he led me to believe that the estate would one day be mine," replied Eric. "I staked not my future on that, however. I deemed that my father's son should by his own exertions win competence for himself, and I studied hard that in either architecture or engineering I might some day find a field for my efforts."

She nodded approval.

"Before my uncle died," continued the young

man, "the influence of one who lived with him—the sister of his wife who was dead—told upon his affection for me. She was the most bigoted Lutheran I have ever seen. She hated all who differed from her by a hair's breadth, and she never rested until, when my uncle's brain was weakened by disease, she induced him to change his purpose."

"Was it on your uncle's estate that the poor woman lived whom they would have turned out in the night?" asked Agneta.

"Yes, and her sole offence was that she was a Calvinist," he said bitterly. "She had been warned to depart, but she was old and helpless, and knew not whither to go. I bade her stay. It was folly on my part. I know that now. But my uncle would never have sent her away."

"To whom did the estate then belong?" questioned the child.

"To the father of the young man who committed the outrage," said Eric, "and he owed all that he possessed to my uncle. He might at least have respected his memory."

The words were spoken sadly.

"Yes," replied the maiden. "It was very wrong of him. Will you tell me how you came to burn the barn down? You did not mean to do it?"

"No. My passion went not thus far," he said. "But it raged fiercely, and left me without sense to turn away from the man who, I see now, sought to provoke me beyond bounds. I bore it while he taunted me with being a hanger-on about my uncle's estate—a beggar now as I had been in his lifetime, and a beggar, moreover, who consorted with those who had yet to learn that their cursed creed should not take root on that soil. But when he went on to add that no roof on that property should shelter the heads of such pestiferous vermin, however much the old fool that was dead had been cajoled into letting them remain, I forgot all else, and followed the speaker, bent only on proving to him by strength of arm that it was not safe thus rudely to criticise his benefactor's actions in the hearing of his benefactor's nephew. He went into the barn. It was full of hay at that time. I saw that lights burned inside. He slammed the door in my face with an insulting laugh, and a word that will not bear repeating. And I—I was wild with passion."

He stopped, and she waited for him to proceed.

"I forced open the door, running at it like a mad bull," he continued, "and there went up a shout of derision as I entered. The fellow had three of his associates there, men of like mind with himself. Exactly what happened then I do not know. I was beside myself. I know that I tried to reach the man after whom I had come, and that others stepped between. They had lanterns there, but one had foolishly brought in a torch. He came leering at me, and thrust the torch in my face. Then I seized it and flung it from me. There was an outcry that partly brought me to my senses. I sprang forward. They tried to hold me, but I fought them off, and reached the torch. It was burning near the hay.

I trampled it under my feet. Verily I believed that every spark of fire was extinguished."

"And was it not?" asked Agneta, when he stopped.

"If it had been, how could the barn have been burned?" he said wearily. "I turned and went away, when, as I imagined, I had beaten out the fire. The danger from the torch had diverted me from my purpose. They shouted words at me that I only half heard. I understood later that they were accusing me of an attempt to burn down the barn. I walked far that night, my passion too hot to allow me to stop, but long before the day broke I turned my face homeward. Then I saw a light in the sky that was caused neither by sun nor moon. All was over when I reached my uncle's house. The barn was burned to the ground, and one end of the house was in ruins."

"And was it the torch that did it?" asked Agneta.

"It could have been no other," he replied. "And yet, I could have sworn that every spark was extinguished."

"Did they say you burned the barn?" she questioned.

"Not to me," was the answer. "I was going towards the house, for as I neared the place I saw the red glow from the still smouldering hay, but the tenant with whom I had stayed since my uncle's death met me. 'Stop, stop, sir!' he said. 'Go not there as you value your liberty. They are boasting of what they will do to you when you are taken.'

'To me!' I cried. 'Yes, sir, for the torch you threw among the hay set the barn afire,' said the man. 'Sir, take my advice, and get as far as possible from here before daylight, for they vow you shall see the inside of a prison.'

"I was stunned—bewildered," continued Eric, "but I still persisted in going on. Then he told me that he had overheard them exulting in the expectation of humiliating me by marching me a prisoner through the streets of the town that had known me as my uncle's heir. 'I would never give them that satisfaction, sir,' he said, and that decided me."

"You ran away?" said Agneta.

"Yes," he answered. "I knew that I had few friends among the influential men of the neighborhood. Those who would judge me would not forget that I was a Calvinist. In that district to be a Calvinist is to be suspected—at least. The advantage was all on the side of my enemies. I started that night. I have never stopped since, except for short snatches of rest."

For a minute the child did not reply. When she did speak, it was not in answer to his last words.

"I think your father would be sorry that you gave way to passion," she said gently, "but I do not think he would say that you had been all wrong, or that the loss of the barn was entirely your fault."

Somehow the words lifted a load from his heart. It came back later, but just then the maiden's verdict seemed like an acquittal.

And now, whenever he thought of them, the words seemed to make his judgment of that which was past clearer, as they did that night, when the feverish excitement departed from him, and he found himself able to think calmly again.

He had been quite prepared for her next question when it came. In truth, his own thoughts were already busy with the problem it suggested.

"Where are you going next?" she asked.

He had never, before this, intelligently planned his next step. Now he was trying to do so. His first blind impulse had been to deprive his enemies of the satisfaction they desired. Then, when he found, as he did find, that he was followed, he had doubled, and turned, and tried solely to throw those enemies off the scent. Now, for the first time, he looked to the future.

"I do not know," he said. "Two days ago the man I least desired to see passed my hiding place. He had got upon the scent, and was hunting me down. For the time my refuge was a safe one. I was in a tree beneath which he passed with a companion. Then I learned that he had formed the plan of tracking me with my own dog, Jupiter. The animal was not with him then, but by his words I knew that he was close by. That he would find me I doubted not, for many a time he had traced me miles from home. It must have been an accident that saved me. Yet the accident has cost me dear."

He looked down at the dog at his feet. The

animal answered the look with an attempt at a caress.

"That night Jupe broke loose," he continued. "He came to me with a frayed rope dragging behind him. There was snow on the ground then. I knew that the track of the dog would betray me. But more snow began to fall. It covered the prints. Then I lifted the dog in my arms, and his feet did not again touch ground, except under cover. He was an additional burden, and yet—I was not altogether sorry to bear it. The world was not all hostile while he was with me."

There were tears in the maiden's eyes.

"Do you think you can carry him always?" she asked.

"No. But—I cannot kill him."

"Shall I take care of him for you?" she said.

"Would you?"

His voice was eager.

"Yes. And you? What will you do?"

He looked at her for a moment.

"If you will take care of Jupe, I will go back and face the worst," he said. "I will go of my own accord. That fellow shall not have the satisfaction of dragging me thither. I will elude him, and go back to the neighborhood of my uncle's home, and take the consequences of my act."

And she said: "I think your father would say 'Go.'"

Eric Helm went. His enemy laid no hand upon him. He delivered himself up to justice. If he had not been a Calvinist, the justice would have been more impartial. To be a Calvinist in that country of Lutherans was to be suspected, and ofttimes harshly treated. Men who knew him were prejudiced against him, and those who did not know him caught the prejudice as soon as the fact that he was a Calvinist was revealed to them. He found himself accused of wilful destruction of the property of his uncle's heirs, in revenge for having himself lost the estate. The chief witnesses against him were the young men who had been in the barn on the night of the fire. The elderly lady who had lived with his uncle had also much to say. The case looked black against him. And the end was New Sweden, and a convict's life.

But whenever Eric Helm thought of the night on which he decided to face the consequences of his own act, the eyes of the child Agneta seemed again to look into his, and his judgment of himself and his deed grew clearer.

CHAPTER X

"That is the second rascally Dutch vessel that has sailed up the river in less than six weeks, to come back loaded with skins. Verily this half-hearted work is the rankest folly. Where is the sense in authorizing me to curtail the privileges and resist the encroachments of the Hollanders, while yet I cannot bid them stay out of New Sweden altogether?"

The Governor's voice was loud and angry.

"Yet methinks the Hollanders themselves find their movements somewhat impeded."

The words rang through the room in the cold, sarcastic tones of the lady of Printz Hall. The Governor gave no heed to words or speaker. His heavy footsteps shook the floor as he crossed it, and the slamming of the door that fell to behind him on his departure was suggestive of the crack of doom for all Dutchmen daring to trade in New Sweden.

"Ha, ha! Well spoken, my sister," laughed the only other occupant of the room, a young man whose resemblance to the Governor suggested the relationship between the two. "Ask that Dutch fool, Hans Jacobsen, what he thinks of Dutch privileges on the Schuylkill. I would that you could have heard him 'protest against such unwarrantable and unjust treatment of a subject of the great Dutch West India Company, and their High Mightinesses the States General,' and stand wringing his hands and swearing by turns while we tore down the walls of his half-built house, and, lest any should find the ruins a stumbling block, set a torch to the pile. The whole went off in smoke, I assure you, but the question of the privileges secured in New Sweden by the rascally Hollanders would hardly have filled your mind with apprehension had you witnessed the rage of the builder."

The Governor's son laughed loudly over the exploit which a few weeks before had taken him to the neighborhood of the Schuylkill. While the dwellings of intruding Dutchmen could be thus easily tumbled about their ears, the future of New Sweden looked to the young man safe enough. A power that was able to oppose fifteen men to every soldier the Dutch Commissary had at his command, seemed in a sufficiently enviable position.

But to the Governor himself the matter did not present itself in so simple a light. He desired to hold New Sweden for the Swedish crown, and he proposed to hold it without division of power. That the Dutch should attempt to trade on the west side of the river was in his eyes a grievous affront to Sweden. John Printz felt the honor of his country at stake, the more so as there was much money involved in the controversy. That powerful quickener of national eyesight had been at work upon the vision of John Printz. Where thousands of beaver skins were the point at issue, it behooved the Governor of New Sweden to keep his eyes well open, and to be quick to discern any infringement of his country's rights. Forty thousand beaver skins would annually find their way into the hands of the Swedes could the Dutch be kept from the west bank of the river. It was little wonder that the honor of Sweden grew particularly dear to the loyal Swede at such a crisis. To uphold the sovereignty of Sweden in this valuable tract of land, and in so doing to uphold the authority of John Printz, was just now to the Governor of New Sweden a vital matter.

It could not be said that he had ever been lax in respect to the widening of the Swedish power and the curtailing of that of the Dutch. From his first landing on the shores of New Sweden this energetic governor had had one object in view. For the attaining of this object Fort Elfsborg rose near the mouth of the river, and the great waterway which the English called the Delaware was practically closed to the Dutch, since none could pass up it without the permission of the Governor of New Sweden.

That he was not quite at liberty to refuse that permission altogether troubled John Printz much. The Dutch Fort Nassau had stood far up on the eastern bank before Peter Minuit took the first Swedish ship up the river, and it stood there to-day. To that fort the Dutch must be permitted to pass. The two powers, Holland and Sweden, were at peace with each other, and the two colonies, or rather the rival claimants to what was virtually one colony, nominally divided the shores of the South River peaceably between them. But there was no peace in the heart of John Printz, and possibly little more in the hearts of the Dutchmen, who, equally with the Governor of New Sweden, saw the advantages of the trade to be carried on with the powerful tribes of Indians whose hunting grounds lay back in the woods about the South River and its tributaries.

The balance of power was at present in the hands of the Governor of New Sweden, though the Dutch had that summer achieved a victory in the shape of securing land for a fort on the Schuylkill, at that time the very centre of the Indian trade. It was this achievement that rankled in the mind of John Printz, and rendered him especially disposed to treat with severity any Dutchman bold enough to try to erect a dwelling in the territory on the west bank of the river claimed by New Sweden, while yet he owned allegiance to the Dutch West India Company's Colony of New Netherland.

It was this achievement also that caused the passing upward of a Dutch trading vessel to anger the Governor so seriously. While the anger was yet hot within him he came across the young convict, Eric Helm. The addition to the pleasure house had some time since been completed, but the Governor's daughter had discovered more than one improvement about the house and grounds in which the services of the young man could be turned to account, and he was still daily to be seen in the precincts of Printz Hall. The Governor beckoned to him.

"What do you, idling here?" he asked testily.

"Your Excellency's order to alter the style of yonder gate is all but carried out," said Eric. "It will take but a short time to complete the work."

"What care I about the style of a gate?" said the Governor angrily. "It pays well, surely, to bring you from Sweedland to waste your time over such child's play. If you could contrive a gate that would shut out those thievish Hollanders, then would your achievement be worth the labor. Hark you!" he added, as a sudden thought struck him. "How is it that with all your boasted skill you have yet done nothing to justify me in giving you the liberty you enjoy? I require of you that you do something to shew that I was not a fool in virtually setting you free from the sentence imposed upon you. Why should I let you walk this soil like an honest man, if you justify me not by exerting yourself in the interest of the land that might well have refused you a footing upon it, or given you at the best but the lot of a common convict?"

The blood rushed hot to Eric's face at the Governor's words. Hitherto, though, like all who had dealings with John Printz, he had more than once heard sharp speech from the Governor's lips, no direct allusion had been made to his peculiar position. It was true the soldiers had not been as considerate, but the novelty of having among them a prisoner who was practically a free man was wearing off, and Eric's powers of self-control were not as severely taxed as during the first days of his residence in New Sweden. This immunity from the annoyance naturally attending his circumstances made the Governor's unexpected attack the more disconcerting.

For a minute the young man was at a loss for a reply. He stood looking at the speaker, and fighting back the sense of injustice which was urging his tongue to the utterance of words that would have been simple madness on the present occasion. To reason with the Governor of New Sweden when he was angry was a proceeding peculiarly dangerous to the reasoner.

Eric Helm, albeit he was a convict, felt himself ill used. He had begun by putting all his energies into the task in hand. Every whim of the Governor or the Governor's daughter had been carefully considered, and the young man had taxed himself to the utmost both to plan and to carry out the improvements desired around Printz Hall. In point of actual labor he had the consciousness that he had performed as much as any two of the men under his direction. He had not spared himself, and he had hoped that the Governor would see in his zeal his real gratitude for the opportunity given him to shew himself something more than a common prisoner. That the Governor was dissatisfied had not occurred to him—nor to the Governor, until the present moment. John Printz was in a rage, and a man in a rage is a little less likely to be amenable to reason than the same man under ordinary circumstances.

"What's the use of standing staring at me like an idiot?" he shouted.

"I am sorry, your Excellency," began Eric, but he got no further.

"Sorry! So am I," roared the Governor. "I'm sorry that I thought such a fool—or knave, more like—worthy of anything but a convict's chain. Get you to your gate, since you are fit for nothing better than to saw a board in two."

Eric's voice was certainly not quite steady as he answered. He felt as if his breath were fairly taken away.

"What does your Honor require?" he asked, bringing out the words hurriedly, lest he should be cut short. "Whatever it be, I will do it."

"Oh, you will, will you?" retorted the Governor. "You are ready enough at promises, young man. What do I require? Well then, listen. I require some plan of defence that shall put those overreaching Dutchmen at a disadvantage, and make them wish they had chopped their right hands off before they used them to try to get the better of John Printz. That, my fine fellow, is what I require. Now go to work on that, while you get that miserable gate into the shape your fool's head has planned."

Eric turned away. His head, whether a fool's or that of a wise man, was in a whirl. Was the Governor in earnest? Did he actually expect of any man the carrying out of so unreasonable a command?

For the moment the young man was more angry than afraid. But as his blood cooled, and his brain cleared, he began to see the danger in the situation. John Printz was by nature an arbitrary man, and an unreasonable one. His power in New Sweden knew practically little limit, and his power over a convict was of necessity almost absolute. That he was asking an impossibility would not materially alter the situation in the eyes of John Printz. The demand had been made in a fit of unreasoning rage, but it was more than probable that when the rage was over the Governor would refuse to retract his words.

Eric's work that day received but a small share of his thoughts. Never since he began his improvements at Printz Hall had he worked with as little interest in the outcome of his labors. He worked swiftly—it was an outlet for his indignation. When the indignation had been worn threadbare, his thoughts almost unconsciously followed the lead of the Governor's, and he began to consider the situation, especially on the Schuylkill, and before he realized it he was grappling with the problem the ruler of New Sweden had hurled at him that morning.

In the midst of sawing off a post he stopped with a suddenness that sent a jar clear up to his shoulder. Then, not knowing what he did, he drew out the saw, and let it fall with a clatter to the ground. For many minutes thereafter Eric Helm stood staring into space, his face wearing that look of distance from present surroundings always both suggestive and tantalizing to a beholder. Presently he stooped, picked up the saw, and inserted it in the saw cut.

That the gate was not a failure as to style or workmanship was due to the fact that Eric Helm had carefully considered its details before coming to the actual performance of them. He certainly did not consider them after. In a purely mechanical manner he finished his task, gathered up all rubbish, and left the grounds of Printz Hall.

That evening the soldiers found Eric for the first time a talkative companion. He asked more questions in one night than he had done during all his previous residence in New Sweden, and showed particular interest in the new Dutch fort on the Schuylkill.

"The youngster's waking up," commented one soldier in an aside to another.

"Waking!" was the response. "How he can hang round Printz Hall and not get an awakening beats me. I tell you thunder's nothing to the Governor's roar since the Dutch Beversrede's been built. Thought my head would be off my shoulders to-day, when I was up at the Hall. If the devil journeyed upwards as often as the Governor calls on him, New Sweden would have another ruler than John Printz, I'll swear."

The next morning saw Eric in the Governor's presence.

"What do you want?" demanded New Sweden's chief magistrate peremptorily.

"Permission to go to the Schuylkill and inspect the Dutch Fort Beversrede," replied the young man calmly.

"Ah! To be sure! Shall I order a transport, when I am about it, to carry you to other points of interest in this and adjoining lands?" asked the Governor sarcastically.

"Your Excellency knows best where I can be of most use," replied Eric quietly. "At present your commands have extended no further than the Schuylkill."

"What, you fool? Do you mean to tell me that you can do anything worth wasting time over up there?" shouted the Governor.

"I intend to try, your Honor," answered the young man.

"Oh, you do? I pray you in what direction?"

The Governor's curiosity was getting the better of his temper. He waited for an answer, and when it came he listened to it.

"I know not the exact position of the Dutch Fort Beversrede," said Eric firmly, "but from what I can learn, it stands not as near the river as might be. That a building could be placed in front of it that should cut it off from the stream, and be the first seen by the savages coming to trade, seems to me a possibility. To learn whether my suppositions are correct, and whether, if they be so, your Excellency would deem it advisable to erect such a building in which to carry on barter with the Indians, I have ventured to trouble your Excellency this morning.

To me it seems not impracticable thus to deprive the Dutch fort of its advantage of position. Could the savages be diverted from trading with the Hollanders, the new fort would be of little service to its owners."

The Swedish Governor stood speechless, staring at the speaker. When Eric would have spoken again he held up his hand to command silence. He was pondering the situation, and he pondered long. Before his cogitations were ended his face cleared. It was the first intimation Eric received that his proposition had struck the Governor favorably. He breathed more freely. Presently the Governor advanced, and laid a heavy hand on his shoulder.

"Young man," he said, "say to no one else what you have said to me. Do you hear? As you value your liberty breathe no word of this. You shall go to the Schuylkill to-day. I will send Sergeant Van Dyck with you, but even with him keep a still tongue. I shall tell him I want you to make a rough map of the shore in the neighborhood of Beversrede. Go, and use your eyes and your time to some purpose."

The Governor's tone was friendly, nay, almost cordial. In the proposition he saw an opportunity of retaliation that set his warlike heart thumping to a battle tune. To render comparatively inefficient as a trading centre the Dutch fort that ever since its erection had been an aggravation and a menace to the Swedish Governor, was worth an effort.

"The Hollander shall yet learn that he cannot catch John Printz napping," he chuckled. "Go ahead, young man. Do your best, and remember that the Governor of New Sweden has his eye on you."

That very afternoon, when the tide came in, a small yacht set sail from before the blackened ruins of Fort Gottenburg on the island of Tenacong. She was bound for the mouth of the Schuylkill, a short and easy journey when the tide was high, for then four or five feet of water covered what is now meadow land, and she could sail straight across from Tenacong into the Schuylkill, and drop anchor before a rocky island in that river, within gunshot of its mouth. Here she was once more under the protection of a Swedish stronghold, for on these rocks Governor Printz had erected a fort, hoping by it to close the river, and all the country it commanded, against Dutch traffic. The building of Fort Beversrede further up the Schuylkill had upset his plans.

Two full days were spent by Eric Helm in the vicinity of the Dutch fort, and then the yacht returned to New Gottenburg, the metropolis of New Sweden, and the young man gave in his report to John Printz. When the interview was over, the Governor was observed to be in good spirits.

CHAPTER XI

Upon the day when Eric Helm left Tenacong, to inspect the Fort of Beversrede, and for the first time in New Sweden felt himself something more than a convict, a horseman was riding along one of the loneliest of the roads of old Sweden, passing through a district so thinly peopled that, but for other features, it might well have been mistaken for a section of the new land. Horse and rider were evidently strangers to the locality, and as evidently not strangers to each other. The driver looked about him curiously.

"It is no wonder I found her not," he mused. "The ends of the earth could scarce be more remote. Verily I appreciated not the strength of a woman's will. Seven years of such solitude as this, while the old castle stood empty, with naught to hinder her occupancy of it save—myself! 'Tis the sorriest compliment to me, I vow."

A light that was not of pleasure leapt to his eyes, and unconsciously he allowed his heels to touch his horse's sides. The animal started, and responded to that impatient movement. For a minute or two fields and trees flew past, and the feet of the horse seemed barely to touch the ground. The rider at first made no attempt to check the animal's speed. He gave himself up to the race, riding with an easy grace that showed him to be well at home in the saddle. Presently he leant forward and allowed one hand to stroke the glossy neck of the horse. It was the touch of the lover as well as the master. The beautiful black head was lifted higher, and the dilated nostrils quivered in response.

"Gently, my beauty! That stab was not meant for you."

The voice was low and clear. The ears of the horse moved responsively. Gradually his pace slackened till he settled down to a quick canter. The hand of the master still caressed the quivering neck. He had not drawn rein, nor intimated, other than by that gentle caressing movement, that he willed a slower pace.

"So, my beauty!" he said "Must you also judge me harshly, even as does another? Will soothing words avail me here, I wonder," he added, "or must I have recourse to arguments of stronger mould. Seven years of such a life may well have worn my lady's resolution to a thread weak enough to snap at a touch. And yet—'twas as a chain of steel when I saw her last.

"The little witch is well-nigh a young maid now," he added, this time not aloud. "A rustic maid, I trow, brought up in such solitude, yet dare I swear 'twill be the rusticity of innocence and want of knowledge of the world, and that alone. 'Twould go hard with a very boor if he found not his manners in madam's presence. Well trained the child has been, I'll wager."

He let his hand rest again on the neck of his horse.

" 'Tis a question which is destined to give out first," he said, "this road or our patience."

As he spoke, a loud, eager whinny sounded from a clump of trees near by. The horse lifted its head, sniffed the air, and made answer. There was a minute's silence, and then a soft call, inarticulate, but sweet as the voice of a bird, with a long concluding note that rang musically through the stillness. It startled the rider even more than it did the horse, though the latter tossed his head and began dancing beneath the restraining hand.

"Gently, gently!" said the rider, in a low voice, bringing the animal to a walk.

"Anders, is that you? I've caught a splendid basket of fish. They are biting so well that I'm going to stay. I think I'll send these home by you."

The words were uttered in the ringing voice of a young girl, and sounded very pleasant to the traveler. The speaker was evidently on the other side of the belt of trees that here shut in the road. The rider sprang from his horse.

"If that be the voice of a peasant maiden, commend me to the peasants of this region," he said. Then in a louder tone: "I have not the good fortune to be the Anders whom you seek, yet would I fain entreat you to make use of me as though I were."

Holding his horse by the bridle, he led it through

the trees in the direction from which the sound had come. It is not to be denied that his gaze was eager as he emerged from the cover, and his eyes sought the speaker. She stood by the bank of a stream, her back to the water, and her attention fixed upon the strip of woodland. His face brightened as he came upon her.

"A veritable wood nymph," he said, in an admiring tone.

She was a very young maid. He would have called her a child, had it not been for a certain gentle dignity of bearing that was more suggestive of the woman. A child he *did* call her later, when he had time to study her more carefully. She stood waiting his approach, a slight flush on her fair face. The blue eyes looked at him fearlessly.

"Pardon me, sir, for summoning you," she said gravely. "I thought it was Anders returning to the farm."

"Nay, it is I who should ask pardon," he said, "for presuming to suppose that I might be permitted to take the place of the more fortunate Anders."

"There is neither fortune nor misfortune about it, sir," she said simply. "I did but want Anders to carry home my basket as he returned. Yet can it as easily wait."

"Why should it?" he asked, and there was a smile on his lips. "Is not my arm as strong as that of Anders, or do you fear that the fish would offer temptation to a hungry traveler?"

She looked at him questioningly.

"Sir," she said, "if you are going near the farm you need be hungry but a short while longer."

"What?" he answered lightly. "You will take pity on me? Fair maiden, I proffer you my thanks beforehand."

"My grandfather will tell you that it is a pleasure to entertain strangers," she said.

"Your grandfather?"

"Yes, sir."

"But I thought, little lady—nay, I am sure that I mistake not when I assert that you are no peasant maiden."

She drew herself up a trifle proudly.

"Grandfather Axel is a peasant," she said, "but my mother says that the noble by birth and the noble of heart represent two forms of aristocracy, and that grandfather Axel is of the highest."

"Your mother, little maid, must, I think, represent both," he said.

To his surprise the blue eyes filled with tears. The child made him no answer. He watched her with a curious satisfaction, noting approvingly the entire absence of constraint or awkwardness in her manner.

"The lady, your mother—will she also welcome a traveler?" he asked, after that minute of waiting.

Then the face of the maiden was turned quickly from him, and for a moment there was an unexplained silence. It was but for a moment, however.

"Sir," she said, and this time her voice was not quite clear, "my mother refused welcome to none while she was here. Now—the angels have welcomed her."

"What? I am too late? Madam—" He checked himself. "Pardon me, dear little friend," he said gently, "I dreamed not of this. I thought to grasp her hand again in friendship. Now—"

"You knew my mother?" asked the child, and her face was turned to him again. Tears glistened on her cheeks. He held out his hand.

"Will you let me comfort you?" he said. "I knew your mother well, therefore can I appreciate your loss."

She placed her hand in his readily now, and her eyes looked up at him through the tears.

"Come and see grandfather Axel," she said.

She had forgotten the fish. He picked up the basket and rod, and turned again to her.

"You did not walk?" he said.

"No, my pony is here."

She led it forth, and vaulted lightly into the large wooden saddle, bowing her head in acknowledgment of the hand that would have helped her had there been time. The pony was of no choice stock, but it was well groomed and cared for, and the lithe girlish figure lost nothing by the change of position. Her companion thought the maiden made a pretty picture as he mounted and placed himself at her side.

"I was looking for my friend and her little daughter," he said. "Fortune has been good to me in sending me to one of those whom I sought."

The face that was turned to him was very friendly, but it was questioning also.

"Little one," he said, "did the gentle mother never speak to you of one who was your brother's friend, and to whom your father accorded a son's privilege?"

A startled look came to the grave eyes. Those of the stranger were bent upon her. He noted the quickened flow of blood to the delicate cheek. She hesitated a moment.

"Nay," he said, smiling, "surely my little playmate has not herself entirely forgotten. We were the best of friends in the old days."

Was it fancy, or did the girlish figure draw itself a little straighter, and the hand take a firmer hold of the bridle?

"My mother forgot none of her friends," she said.

"And you?" he asked.

"I think I see those days with my mother's eyes," she replied. "She has told me so often of everything that pertained to the time after my father died, and the days when we left our home, that the things I remember of the castle, and those of which she has told me, are blended. I know not one from the other, but I can see them all to-day."

"And the old friends also?"

The blue eyes met his squarely now.

"I was too young to know aught but that all were kind to me," she said.

He smiled.

"Has the world changed since?" he asked.

"No, sir, not in that respect," she replied.

"I think I may safely promise that it never will —to you," he said.

"And so you will not say one good word of our friendship in the old days," he added, after they had ridden for some time in silence.

Her smile was a very open one.

"The little girl of the castle has a lively memory of pleasant frolics with Monsieur Pors," she said. "But—she was a very little girl, and—"

"Now she has become a fair maid. Fear not, little one; I am in no danger of forgetting the distinction," he said.

The bright tint was upon face and neck again. Her ingenuousness pleased him not ill.

They were passing well cultivated fields. Monsieur Pors regarded them with the eye of a landowner, recognizing the value of the tract of country upon which he had come. He noted it carefully. This was no poverty-stricken domain. What was the child doing here, now that her mother was dead?

"Little maid," he said, "you spoke of your grandfather. I understood my gentle friend your mother to say that her parents were no longer living."

"True, sir," replied the child. "Grandfather Axel is the brother of my mother's father—his fosterbrother."

"And not of equal rank?"

"Nay, sir. Grandfather Axel is, as you surmised, a peasant."

He looked at her scrutinizingly.

"Pardon me," he said, "but is there no other to assume guardianship over you, now that the best of all guardians has left you? Believe me, little friend, I ask not from curiosity."

There was no mistaking the pride of her tone as she answered him.

"Sir, think you not that my mother knew what was best for her child?" she said. "Her daughter has not a doubt of the wisdom of her judgment."

If she looked for answering pride in his face, she found it not. Whether her words angered or pleased him did not appear.

"Her daughter is right," he said. "Yet may circumstances change, and the wisdom of one moment become the mistake of another. I would that I could have spoken to her before death put a seal upon the past. Will the kindly Agneta think it presumption if I ask on what footing she remains in a peasant's house?"

"Here comes grandfather Axel," said the young girl quietly. "He stands to me in the place of my mother. He will answer for you all questions that —it is right for you to ask."

Monsieur Pors bowed, but he seemed in no hurry to lift his eyes towards the approaching figure. They were fixed upon the face of the girl. A flush that was deep enough to be painful suffused it, and there were tears in the blue eyes.

"Forgive me," he said, in the gentlest of tones. "I meant not to throw a doubt on the mother's wisdom. Little one, I knew her too well not to accord to her the fullest admiration and respect."

The eyes met his again. There was in them a light that shone through the tears.

"Thank you," she said simply.

The advancing figure could no longer be ignored. The child's companion looked up. The old man who was coming towards them was tall and erect. He carried his seventy-five years lightly. The dignity of age was his, but its weakness had as yet passed him by. The face of the maiden brightened as he drew near.

"Grandfather Axel," she said, "I bring to you Monsieur Pors. He was my brother's friend."

The old man bared his head. Instinctively the horseman followed his example.

"You are welcome to my house, sir," said Axel Bonde, and to Gustavus Pors it seemed that there was the slightest possible stress on the word 'house.' Was the old man thinking of a treasure to which the stranger was not welcome?

The house in question was not in sight, but Agneta turned to her escort.

"I thank you for troubling yourself with the fish," she said. "While you talk with grandfather Axel I will take them to the house."

He yielded the basket to her with a courtly bow, and watched her as she rode away. His eyes had in them nothing but approval. The perfect grace of her every movement commended itself to him. Whatever lay in the future, she was as yet unspoiled.

He turned about to become aware that another pair of eyes had been fixed on him. He met them, and the question in them.

"You would ask me of my business here," he said. "I came to learn of the welfare of the little lady yonder."

"The bairn is in safe hands."

Axel Bonde's face was grave even to sternness.

"I doubt it not, friend," replied Monsieur Pors, "yet would I have given much to have been able to talk with Madam Botorpa ere she died. I cannot but flatter myself that she also would have desired it."

"Upon the ground that your ministrations afforded her comfort in the days that are past?" asked the old man.

For a moment the face of the younger changed color. He recovered himself quickly.

"I would that I had had opportunity for the ministrations," he said. "I lost sight of my friend when sorrow had for the time made her doubt if the friendship of any were real. I sought her anxiously, tracing her to the point where her carriage left her, yes, and a day's journey beyond—even to a spot where she came, wet and weary, seeking rest for herself and her little one. Beyond that place no sign could I find, though I scoured the road for days. A month ago I came upon a flagon, the sight of which brought back the days when I clasped hands with my dear old friend, the father of yon little maiden, and when he gave me the privileges of a son. I had seen it last upon his table. I followed the clue, and it brought me here."

"And now?"

Gustavus Pors hesitated.

"Now—I will be frank with you," he said. "It was a matter of moment to me to find this place. Yonder gentle maiden is my betrothed."

"Aye. I know it."

"Madam told you of the relation between us?"

"She told me *all*. It was necessary. The bairn was to be in my care."

Undoubtedly the younger man winced at that "all." His tone was a little more haughty as he said:

"Then it will be needless for me to explain. You understand my interest in the maiden. I came that I might learn of her welfare and inquire of her future. It is my right."

"To inquire—yes."

"To control, if necessary."

The old man smiled. That smile had an irritating effect. Gustavus Pors dismounted hastily.

"Let us understand one another," he said. "Your guardianship over the maiden—is it legal, or simply friendly?"

"As legal as law can make it. And it will be upheld."

The voice was quiet, very quiet, but the old man's attitude was firm as the rock that cropped through the earth at his side.

"And you intend to bring her up here—in these wilds?" asked Monsieur Pors.

"I intend to bring her up in the safety of my own care, wherever that may be."

The younger man stood holding his horse. He was visibly annoyed.

"It is the maddest folly," he said. "You will make a peasant maid of her."

The shadow of a smile played about the old man's lips. It was a tender smile, and it was not intended for the speaker.

The two men talked long. It was fully an hour before Axel Bonde brought his guest to the farmhouse. He extended towards him the most ungrudging hospitality. As for Agneta, she was very quiet and gentle, but Monsieur Pors found no further opportunity for converse with her. He left the farm at early morn. Axel Bonde walked for some distance by the horse of his guest. When he returned, his face was graver than usual.

CHAPTER XII

The entire garrison of the Dutch fort at Beversrede stood by the gate, looking up the river. There was nothing to see. Not even an Indian canoe broke the monotony of river and shore. The garrison would have been glad of a diversion other than the inevitable pipe, sole solace of the long days between the visits of expectant Indians carrying bundles of skins. The broad face of the soldier leaning against the post on which the gate swung presently divested itself of a portion of its aimless look, and his lips opened lazily.

"Times have grown dull since our friends the Swedes departed," he said.

Whereupon the soldier whose back was supported by the post on the opposite side of the gateway slowly brought his mind back to present surroundings.

"Aye, and that's more than a week ago," he replied. "Soon tired of hanging round here, didn't they? I tell you, though, Fort Beversrede's giving John Printz as much as he can swallow. Sticks in his crop, this little trading house does."

The garrison chuckled.

"I wonder what they were up to," remarked the soldier by the first post, which, as the garrison had already talked the subject bare, was not an original remark.

"Up to! Wearing their hearts out with envy at us," responded the soldier by the other post.

Then the garrison relapsed into silence.

"Yonder's a sail!"

Half the garrison had been looking the wrong way, the other half having lately taken to gazing down stream. The less fortunate half shifted its position, and the garrison watched the oncoming vessel.

"Swedish!" ejaculated the soldier nearest, by the width of the gateway, to the approaching craft.

"Aye, she's no Dutchman," said the soldier farthest away.

Thereupon the garrison with one accord stepped outside the inclosure.

"What does she want this time?" asked the larger half of the garrison, the man who had first descried the sail. He was taller by a head than his companion, and in point of breadth had a yet greater advantage.

"Come to see if by good luck our fort's been blown up in the night, like the Swedish New Gottenburg," hazarded the other and smaller half of the Dutch forces at Beversrede.

The wind was unfavorable, and the Swedish sail approached slowly.

"She's well manned," commented the garrison, as she came nearer.

She anchored before the fort, and four men came ashore.

"Are you all there?" asked the officer in charge of the party, derisively coming to a stand before the little garrison and saluting. "You look dangerous. Don't be too hard on us. We are no match for you in point of numbers, whatever we may be in courage."

The Dutch garrison looked fierce, while from the vessel half a dozen more of the Swedes stood watching.

"Right you are there, friend," said the bigger of the two Dutchmen. "Fort Beversrede *is* dangerous, and her garrison is all there, and very *much* all there. Two Dutchmen and a fort may well count for more than a dozen Swedes any day."

"That's good news," replied the officer coolly. "We're coming to camp right under your shadow for protection. Come, Eric, we're ready for business."

The last words were spoken in a louder voice, and were meant for the ears of a young man just stepping on to the river bank.

"What are you going to do?" demanded the Dutch garrison, both halves speaking at once.

"Wait and see, friends. Wait and see," responded the officer.

And since there was nothing else to be done, the garrison waited, while the Swedes fell to work, and unloaded good hemlock logs from the vessel. The young man, Eric Helm, was in the meantime engaged in levelling the ground about twelve feet from the gate of Fort Beversrede. It was not long before the men were at work under his direction, and before night the foundations of a long building that would reach fairly across the front of the fort, and shut it off from the river, were strongly laid.

The Dutch garrison stood for a time speechless. Then, when the full import of the proceedings became apparent, the hearts of both halves of the same grew hot within them, and words rushed to their tongues.

"In the name of the great West India Company, and our noble lord, Petrus Stuyvesant, we protest against this outrage," shouted the stronger voice of the two.

"Their High Mightinesses the States General shall hear of this," chimed in the weaker, with a roar a tone less frightful.

The Swedes placidly continued their labors, but upon the face of the officer there was an amused smile. As for Eric Helm, he took little heed of the menaces of the Dutchmen, or the jests of the soldiers of his own party. He was very much in earnest. He had planned this reprisal, and he was intent on carrying it to a satisfactory completion. His object was to place in front of the fort a strong house that should effectually screen the Dutch fortress, and should catch the eye of all Indians passing down the river. He had designed the building to form as complete a cover as possible, and he was engrossed in the business of making the foundations strong and sure. Only when the Dutch garrison, with a burning desire to show these Swedes that the Dutch power was not to be trifled with, drew together, and with drawn swords advanced upon him at a moment when his assistants had withdrawn to the shore, did he seriously consider the Dutch side of the question. Then he drew back a step, picked up an axe, and confronted the enraged garrison.

"Better take things quietly, friends," he said, and his tone was not derisive, as that of the officer had been. "Even brave men may well give in to a superior force. Those to whom you must account will see that there has been no lack of courage on your part. As for this house, his Excellency, the Governor of New Sweden, claims a right—by virtue of the district being a possession of Her Majesty, the Queen of Sweden—not only to the land on which it stands, but to that also on which your fort is placed. In his estimation it is you who are encroaching on our domain, and surely we may come and put up a house on our own land."

"The Governor of New Sweden is a liar!" roared the bigger Dutchman, but his eye falling at that moment upon the returning Swedes, discretion got the better of valor, and he headed the procession back to the gate of the fort.

"He is a liar, I say," he shouted again, from that safe vantage point. "The land our fort is built on was this summer solemnly made over to us, for the second time, in the presence of the honorable members of the high council of New Netherland, La Montagne and Van Dincklagen. Aye, and their honors visited your lying Swedish governor, and stood up to his face and told him so in his house of Printz Hall. He told not the same tale to them, I dare swear."

"You've sworn enough, friend," retorted the officer, and a shout of laughter went up from the Swedes as the two halves of the garrison made good the words by a burst of language more effective than choice.

The Swedes worked with a will, laying in place the logs they had brought with them, and fetching more that earlier in the year had been conveyed to the Schuylkill. In two or three days the house stood completed, a building thirty feet long and twenty broad, and the gate of Fort Beversrede had become almost inaccessible. Eric Helm stood contemplating his work, his face expressing more decided satisfaction than it had shown since he landed in New Sweden.

"That was a good idea of yours," said the officer in charge of the party. "The Dutch will at least find themselves compelled to share the spoils, and if we get not the biggest share it will not be our fault."

Within the fort the garrison fumed and swore, and longed for the presence of Andries Hudde, the Commissary of the South River. But the Commissary was at the Manhattans, laying his case before the Dutch Governor, Stuyvesant, and there were but six soldiers, all told, in the Dutch garrisons of New Sweden. Therefore the garrison of Beversrede dealt solely in wordy missiles, and wasted enough strong language to have dealt death to their rivals if a thousandth part of the energy of that language could have been turned into effective power.

Eric Helm returned to New Gottenburg with a fair amount of apparent satisfaction, and a large amount of hidden exultation over the success of his plan. The strong house on the Schuylkill was an accomplished fact, and the Dutch fort was put effectually in the background. Governor Printz listened to the officer's report, and then sent for the young engineer.

"Eric Helm," he said, "you have done well. The rascally Dutch have had to admit once more that John Printz rules in New Sweden. Let them depend *now* on their good friends, the Indians who sold them the land. With my traders on the spot they will learn to their cost that the savage has as keen an eye for an advantage as has a beggarly Dutchman. You have made of your building a good strong house in every particular, have you?" he added.

"It is strong enough for a fort, your Honor," replied Eric.

"That is well, though I doubt not the Dutchmen have the fear of John Printz too fully before their eyes to attempt any treachery," replied the Governor. "You have done a piece of work that will be of lasting benefit to New Sweden. I am very well satisfied with your efforts."

Eric took the words for a dismissal, and turned to leave the Governor's presence, but before he had moved many steps the Governor spoke again.

"Stop, young man," he said. "I told you before you started upon this expedition that my eye would be upon you. It was no idle word. Through the report of my agents I have judged of the work you planned and carried out. I am well pleased with it. You shall not go unrewarded. From this time forth, until you cease to merit the favor, all restriction upon your coming and going shall cease. You shall be free to go whither you will when the day's work is over, always provided that you are back within the soldiers' quarters before they are closed for the night, and that you are in a fit state to resume your labors in the morning."

The warm blood mounted to Eric's face. The outcome had exceeded his hopes. He had expected no reward, and would have been quite satisfied to know that the Governor had been obliged to rescind his harsh judgment, and to admit that in the convict who had been sent to her shores, New Sewden had received a useful addition to her population. His words came less readily than usual. There was honest gratitude in his heart, and it made his tongue falter.

"From my heart I thank your Excellency," he said, and he went out from the Governor's presence with a light step.

To have thus fully propitiated the Governor of New Sweden was a matter of no small moment to one in Eric's peculiar position. The freedom also was very precious. When he sat with the soldiers at night, he had never been able to forget the fact that he was a prisoner among them, at liberty to go and come only with the officer's permission. Now, his evenings were his own. He began to wonder whether it would not be possible to turn them to some account. The land of New Sweden had awakened in him a personal interest since he had planned and carried out the building of the house on the Schuylkill. When he had once served his country in the new domain he seemed not so thoroughly shut out from the bounties of that land. For it *was* a bounteous land. He was more convinced of it the more he saw of the country.

But in spite of its generosity, and the fact that that generosity might yet be extended to himself, his thoughts turned longingly that night towards old Sweden. Of all whom he had there esteemed as friends, he most regretted the loss of the one incorruptible lover and follower who had nearly broken down his resolution by his look of appealing reproach when he bade him stay by the side of the fair haired maiden, instead of following him into the moonlit night. Was the dog happy without him? Had the child been able to keep her promise? The sick lady, on whose consent she had counted so confidently, might not have been of the same mind as the young maid. Yet the maiden had seemed to have no fears.

"My mother will be willing to let me keep your dog," she said. "You can take him no further, and to leave him behind without a home would be cruel. When you are ready to have him again you must come for him."

Would the time every arrive when he could claim his own again, and stand before the young maiden a free man?

The two were always associated in his mind—the dog and the fair faced child. He had seen them last standing in the moonlight, just under the shelter of the ruined outbuilding, the maiden with her hand on the head of the dog, that ever since had seemed to look at him with the same heart-broken reproach in his eyes. To-night, in spite of the Governor's leniency, or perhaps, because by reason of that leniency hope had come again into his life, the memory of the maiden and the dog was especially vivid.

CHAPTER XIII

The waters of the Schuylkill gave back the sun's rays, and the reeds inshore stirred in the breeze. A swan craned its neck to look down at some object in the mud below, and then, too lazy to pursue the inquiry, rested placidly on the stream. On the shore a gray goose moved with amazing swiftness among the tall grass, and overhead sailed an eagle, looking down on that which to goose and swan was yet invisible. Round the bend of the river was presently heard the dipping of paddles, and the gray goose screened herself behind some bushes, and the swan stretched its neck in an inquiring fashion. Four long Indian canoes were what the swan saw, and what the eagle had long seen. They came sweeping round the curve, headed by a smaller one in which stood a single Indian, his eyes turned down stream. He passed the swan without a glance. Wild fowl were common objects there. His paddles never rested till a point was reached from which could be seen a building standing upon the river's bank. Then he extended his arm.

"Yonder lies the fort of the Dutchmen," he said, and paddled on.

A few minutes later he spoke again, turning his head towards those behind.

"The Hollanders' fort changes position with the

sun," he said. "A month ago it held not its present place."

He paddled on again, and the larger canoes followed.

"It changes face also," he remarked somewhat later, as the building upon the shore became more plainly discernible.

In that respect the speaker differed materially from that upon which his attention was fixed. His eyes were often turned to the distant building, but his face did not change. His canoe was steadily urged forward. To the gray goose and the swan the boats soon became objects too distant to excite curiosity. Only the eagle looked down on them still, and followed their course down the river.

The larger canoes lay low in the water, evidence that they carried more weight than the six Indians who made up the crew of each. If further proof were necessary, irregular piles of skins came here and there into sight above their sides. To the eye of the initiated the extra precision of the lines and splashes of paint on the faces of the savages betokened an expedition of some importance. It was evident that each Indian had donned his dress suit of paint. Why not? He was bound for the strong house of the white men. Should he appear before them other than at his best?

The canoes had come from far, their destination being the new fort of the Hollanders who had this year been invited by Indian sachems to build upon the Schuylkill. The savage was not well versed in the underlying principles of trade, but experience had taught him that when more traders resorted to his land a greater variety and a larger quantity of goods came into his possession in exchange for his store of furs. He welcomed the Swede because he brought ship loads of commodities dear to the Indian's heart, and when the Hollander sailed into the river frequented by his tribe, he smoked the pipe of peace with him in turn, and foresaw an increase in the buying power of the skins his squaw had dried and hoarded. The Indians knew no reason why the Dutchmen as well as the Swedes should not build on their shores, and carry goods up their rivers.

To the Dutchmen they were going to-day to test the generosity of the new trading centre, and to make the best bargain that circumstances would permit. Only one of their number, the old man in the smaller canoe, had yet visited Fort Beversrede.

"Yonder lies the point upon which the Hollanders built their fort," he said, as they neared the group of buildings, "but yonder is not the fort they built."

"It is a white man's house, and a large one. Such is the house of the trader," answered one in the next boat.

The canoes were secured, but before the Indians could leave the bank the white trader came out to meet them.

"Welcome, friends," he said briskly. "Our house is open to our brothers."

The old Indian looked him steadily over from head to foot.

"The Hollanders dwelt here a moon ago," he said.

"Oh, the beggarly Hollander is not to be depended on," said the trader loudly. "It is the Swedes who are your friends. Come in, brothers, and see if we do not love the red men."

The majority of the Indians entered the strong house, but the bundles to which the trader's gaze had turned greedily yet reposed in the bottoms of the canoes. Proof of hospitality, in the shape of brandy, was not wanting, and while the Indians drank, their eyes wandered round the house, and rested longest on the corner where certain goods dear to the savage heart were displayed in tempting profusion. There was manifest skill in their arrangement. Articles of necessity and articles of superfluity were ranged side by side. Unhappy must be the Indian whose pile of skins was small, in presence of such attractions.

"Did the Hollanders take their fort with them when they departed?" asked the old Indian who acted as leader.

On the way from the canoe to the house he had carefully scanned the building. Now he spoke for the first time since he stood by the river side.

"Not they," said the wily Swede, a man chosen by Governor Printz to be the factor of the Swedish West India Company's trading post on the Schuylkill. "They would find little use for their fort except where the Indians resort. But the rascals have no business here. It is we who have made a covenant with our friends the Indians, and the Hollander must keep to his own part of the land."

"There is room in our country for all," said the old Indian. "Our land is broad. We will give of it to our brothers the Dutch and the Swedes alike. We will give them much land. Then will they have no need to dwell so near together. The Dutch and the Swedes are brothers. They must love each other much, and be as one, else would not their houses be so close."

He pointed as he spoke towards the wall behind which stood the Dutch fort.

For a moment the Swede looked discomfited.

"Oh, we and the Hollanders get along well enough together while they keep to their own part of the country," he said. "As for our brothers the red men, we look not that they should desert us to trade with the Hollanders. The Swedes were their friends before the Hollanders built their fort in these parts. They love their brothers of this land, as the Hollanders never did. Our Governor has sent across the great sea to procure for them the goods they most desire. Over in our Sweedland our wise men have consulted, and have gathered together that which will best please our good brothers here. Would the Hollanders do as much? They will only bring to you that which the men of their own land will not buy. They call themselves your friends, yet can they never be your friends as can the Swedes. Where are their soldiers to defend you if an enemy should come? They cannot defend themselves. But the Swedes have soldiers many, and strong forts, and our Governor, the Great Sachem, dwells among you, so that he may best know how to be your friend. He lives in your midst, and you pass his house in your hunting expeditions."

"How much will our good friends the Swedes give for a beaver skin," asked the old man pertinently.

The wary Swede hesitated.

"Bring you skins that I may see them," he said. "All that they are worth I will give, aye, and a little more to my brothers to-day."

"We will show our brother the skins," said the old man, and the party returned to the river bank —all but their leader. He passed slowly round to the back of the strong house, and stood before the gate of Beversrede, gravely assuring himself that no feature familiar to him on a former visit had disappeared. He had not stood long before the bigger half of the Dutch garrison espied him.

"Here come our friends the Indians to trade with us!" he shouted. "Where is the benefit of the Swede's trading house? It will not keep the Indian away from us, whatever John Printz may think."

He was already half-way to the gate, which he threw open wide.

"Come in! Come in!" he cried. "You knew where your friends were, if the beggarly Swede did put his house in front of us. We saw not your canoes, else would we have welcomed you sooner. How many are there of you?"

"Four canoes came with me," said the Indian.

"Bring your peltries and come in. We'll find good rum for all," said the Dutchman.

"We must show them to both of our white brothers at once," replied the old man gravely. "The Swede also said, 'Bring in the peltries.'"

"Our goods are better than the Swede can show," said the Dutchman eagerly. "If you put your beavers within grasp of his hungry hand, it is little you will carry away with you but anger in your heart. Bring them hither. Then shall you take back to your castles that which will make all other hunters want to come to Fort Beversrede."

"Very good, friend. Very good," said the Indian. "What will the Dutch give for a beaver?"

"Give? What will we give?" said the Dutchman. "Try us and see."

"How much wampum for a good beaver?" persisted the Indian.

"What has the Swede offered you?" asked the Dutchman, in a quieter tone.

"What the Dutchman offers—promises," said the old man slowly.

The big Dutchman was silent. He stood with his eyes fixed on the Indian. The old man gravely returned the gaze.

"What will we give?" repeated the Dutchman at last, much of the cheerful bluster gone from his tone. "We will give you more than the Swede, whatever that may be."

"Very good," said the old man. "Our hunters shall hear. I go to tell them."

His step was measured and stately as he crossed the inclosure between the fort and the outer palisades. He saw no need for haste, nor for quarreling with the fortune that had made Dutchmen and Swedes so eager to welcome him. His feelings were not shared by the garrison. When the Indian had turned from him, the Dutchman's fears grew apace. Would he ever return? Would the wily Swede let him slip through his fingers so easily? The two halves of the garrison held a hasty consultation, and as a result, the larger rushed to the door of the fort.

"Look out for that Swede!" he called. "He'll have the best of you if you're not as wily as a snake. There are times when a man must keep his eyes open."

"The advice is good, friend," said the Indian impassively, as he passed out of the gate.

It was noticeable that he did not seek the smaller canoe in which his own peltries had been brought, but went straight to the strong house of the Swede. Here the floor was strewn with furs among which the skilled hand of the trader moved critically. His keen eye quickly selected the best skins.

"For each of these I will to-day give a fathom

and a half of wampum," he said, just as the old man entered.

The faces of the Indians showed no change, but the hunter to whom the bundle of skins belonged swept them together with his foot, the movement bringing the inferior skins on top of the selected pile.

"What means that?" asked the trader sharply.

"That the canoe is not too heavily loaded to carry them further, even to the Dutch Fort Nassau," said the owner.

"The Dutch Fort Beversrede is nearer," interposed the old Indian.

The trader glared at him. Then he laughed.

"Oh, you have found the two Dutchmen, have you?" he said. "Powerful friends they'd prove, wouldn't they, if your enemies should show themselves in your land? The truth is, the Dutchman is no good anywhere. He'd fail you as much over your beavers as over the fighting, if you should try him. You'll be too wise for that, though. Our brothers the red men know one thing from another, I'll answer for it."

"The Dutchmen of Fort Beversrede will give more than a fathom and a half for a beaver," said the old man.

"Eh? Who said so?" asked the Swede.

"The big Dutchman himself."

An oath escaped the lips of the trader. The old man stood regarding him.

"How much more will he give?" asked the Swede, after a full minute's silence.

"How much more will the Swede give?" said the Indian.

The trader looked as if he would have liked to make answer in a more emphatic form than was possible in words.

"Oh, I suppose I can afford to give you as much as the Dutchman," he said at last.

"Will you give a fathom and three-quarters?" asked the Indian.

"Yes. It's more than the beavers are worth, but I told you I would give you the best of the bargain," said the trader. "You've got it in earnest."

"The Dutchman will give more," said the Indian.

"The Dutchman's a fool!" roared the trader.

"He may be a fool, friend," said the old Indian. "I judge him not. The white men should know. They are brothers. The Indian is not a fool."

"He is if he trust to that lying Dutchman," shouted the trader. "Go and try him. You'll see what he'll do."

"Yes, friend, we will try him," said the old man. "We must offer our beavers to our brothers the Dutch and Swedes alike, else will they not both smoke the pipe of peace with us."

Calmly and without haste the skins were gathered up, the Swede looking on savagely the while. Then Indians and bundles disappeared round the back of the strong house.

The considerable band of Indians that entered the gate of Beversrede filled the hearts of the garrison with exultation. In the absence of a regular trader the stores were intrusted to the soldiers, and they burned to distinguish themselves. Their triumph over the Swedish factor was in proportion to their former humiliation. John Printz might build strong houses, as many as he pleased. They felt themselves in a position to laugh at his efforts. While Indians poured through their gates, the Swede would not have it all his own way.

The hunters met with something more than hospitality. The Dutchmen were truly brotherly. Packages of skins were in due season opened, and the eyes of the garrison brightened as the superior character of the peltries was revealed.

"You found the Swede readier to talk than to pay for beavers, I dare swear," said the big Dutchman.

"The beavers waited not for his wampum," said the old man. "Our brothers the Dutchmen will pay more. It is their word, and they do not lie."

"Aye, they'll pay more," said the Dutchman, with assurance. "These beavers now, will, in our hands, yield you a fathom and a half of seawan. The Swede would not pay you that."

"The Swede will give a fathom and three-quarters," said the old Indian. "But the Dutchman will give more. The Dutchman does not lie."

"Who told you the Swede would give that?" asked the Dutchman, his face losing many shades of satisfaction.

"The Swede himself," said the Indian quietly. "But the Indian does not lie. I promised my brother that our hunters should know of his offer, and they have brought their furs hither. The Dutchmen will give us more."

"We will give you as much as the Swede," said the superior half of the garrison, his broad face growing grave over such a mighty concession.

"No. The Dutchman will give more, else will he be worse than the Swede," said the Indian.

"How do you make that out? Isn't our seawan as good as theirs?" asked the Dutchman.

"Yes, but it is no better. And the Dutchman promised to give more than the Swede. The Swede did not lie to his brothers. Therefore is he better than the Dutchman."

"Come, now, you ask too much," said the head of the garrison. "We cannot afford to pay our good friends the hunters more than the skins are worth, else should we have to shut up our trading house. We have to send the beavers to our own land to sell them, and it costs much to cross the big sea. Our friends must remember all we bring into their country. What would they do without our goods?"

"The Swede also had many goods," said the Indian.

"But he would only give you a fathom and three-quarters for a beaver."

"Will the Dutchman give more?" asked the Indian.

The broad face of the soldier wore a look of distressing uncertainty. If he should refuse to outbid the Swedish agent, the Indians would return to the

Swedes' strong house, and the advantage over which the hearts of the garrison had but now been jubilant would fall to their enemy. On the other hand, to pay two fathoms of wampum for a beaver was to reduce the profit upon the skins more than would be considered allowable by his superiors. The Dutchman was in difficulties. He pondered, and the Indians waited. They were in no hurry, and if there existed any eagerness beneath the calm exterior of their manner, it was kept very much beneath. They did not betray it.

The garrison removed to a distance to hold a consultation. The situation was critical. If they failed to persuade these Indians to trade with them, the rest of the hunters of their tribe would in all probability follow their example and go to the Swede. Two fathoms of wampum for a beaver skin was a price not to be thought of under ordinary circumstances. But these circumstances were not ordinary. The Swedes had got the better of them in the matter of building. It was insufferable that they should have it also in the matter of trading. And the number of skins in those bundles was large. It was a big trading transaction. The advantage must on no account fall into the hands of their rivals.

"If we secure not the trade with the savages," said the lesser half of the garrison, "this river, aye, and the South River itself, is of little value to us. What care we for the land? 'Tis the peltries we are after. If we get not the beaver and the otter skins we might as well go back to the Manhattans."

"I'll do it, and take the consequences," said the other half valiantly.

And while his courage was at its highest he approached the Indians.

"Brothers," he said, "you ask much of us, more than we can afford to give. We cannot always give two fathoms of seawan for a beaver, but that you may know that the Dutchman does not lie to his brothers of this land, we will to-day give even that for a good skin."

"The Dutchmen are our friends," said the Indian, and the piles of beaver skins began to change hands rapidly.

The stores of the garrison were soon drawn upon by the red men. Wampum also was in demand. Some of the hunters were desirous of carrying back a supply of the Indian money, instead of expending all their furs in the purchase of the tempting articles displayed by the white men. The strings of beads which the Dutch styled seawan were accordingly brought to the fore.

"Two fathoms of white or one of black seawan for a beaver, friends," said the big Dutchman. "Here you are. Who shall say we do not treat our brothers well?"

The old Indian motioned to a lithe, long limbed savage, the tallest of the party. He stepped forward, and held out his hand. The Dutchman looked aghast at the length of his arm. It boded ill for the wampum.

"Two fathoms for a beaver," the savage said,

and extending his long arms to the utmost, measured off upon the string the greatest length he could stretch. This was a fathom.

The Indians watched him with unmoved countenance, and the Dutchman with growing apprehension. Two fathoms for each beaver skin, and every fathom the length that man could stretch! Truly it was buying success dearly.

The wisdom of the old Indian's choice became then apparent, as did the value of long arms. Three ells' length went to every fathom as that Indian measured it, and yet there was nothing of which the Dutchman could complain. The length a man could stretch was the recognized measurement of a fathom. But it made more than a little difference who was the man that stretched.

The savage performed his task steadily, but with amazing rapidity. The long string of beads tightened for a moment in his grasp, and then, as each fathom was measured off, was lifted swiftly to his face and drawn across his nose. It was the Indian's test for depreciated coin. By and by he threw down a string upon the floor. It had failed to stand the test.

"What is the matter with it?" asked the soldier.

"No good," replied the Indian shortly. "Our brothers should break it up."

The rough edges of the wampum had scratched the savage's nose as they passed over it, proof incontestable that the beads were chipped and worn. Such inferior money was fit only to be broken up and destroyed.

"Nonsense! It is good enough," said the Dutchman, picking up the wampum, and repeating upon his own nose the Indian's experiment. He was careful not to rub too hard, however. "What more do you want?" he added, as the broken edges coming in contact with his nose proved that wear was beginning to tell on the beads.

"Our beavers are good skins. We want good seawan in return," said the Indian.

"The seawan is good enough," retorted the soldier, but he put aside the rejected string and handed the Indian another in its place.

The great packages of otter and beaver skins, and of black fox and fisher skins, had all changed hands at last. The big trading transaction had fallen to the share of the Dutchmen. Not a skin among all that were brought in the canoes that day found its way into the hands of the Swede. Yet the garrison watched the departure of the band with none of the feelings of jubilation with which they had looked on their approach. The Swedish strong house was costing them dear. They had the furs, and the Swede had nothing, but they were not at all sure that the Swede had not the best of the bargain.

It was the beginning of many such transactions, in which first one and then the other of the rivals came off victorious, and the victor and the loser were about equally ill satisfied. The Swede, enjoying the more prominent position, generally secured the peltries, though many a party of Indians passed by the door of his strong house and sought the gate of Beversrede. But whether he left the fruits of his hunting expeditions in the strong house of the Swede or the fort of the Dutchmen, the Indian profited by the competition. He was the only one who was satisfied.

As for John Printz, he rejoiced in the fact that he had made the Dutch Fort Beversrede of little value to its owners, even though he had in the process raised the price of furs for the Swedes as well as the Dutchmen.

CHAPTER XIV

The building of the trading house before Fort Beversrede had altered Eric Helm's position in New Sweden. He was a convict still, but he was in favor with John Printz, and that fact made a material difference in his intercourse with other men. The daughter of the Governor was also pleased to show him some friendliness. She had a certain feeling of proprietorship in him. It was by her intercession that her father had allowed him to remain in New Sweden. She felt that to her sagacity was to be attributed all the benefit that had come, or might yet come, from the young man's talents, and she was inclined to be condescending towards one who had proved her in the right, and at the same time answered her purpose.

She took occasion to explain to one or two of the most favored among the wives and daughters of the leading men in New Sweden that the Queen's Minister, Oxenstiern, was interested in the young convict, and that though the evidence had gone terribly against him at his trial, there were those who deemed that his enemies had painted his deed in blacker colors than was consistent with the young man's previous character and standing.

Her words were not without effect. Eric Helm was astonished to find the doors of good Swedish homes thrown open to him, and their owners willing, nay, a little eager, to extend to him their patronage. A young man of good birth and education, accused of a crime that might easily be considered as purely an accident, and sent from his country to share the lot of the common convict, was in a position sufficiently romantic to awaken feelings of interest. Had the Governor frowned upon the young man, these good folks would possibly never have found out his superior qualities, or the extenuating circumstances in his case. But he had not frowned upon him. He had chosen to treat him with especial consideration, and the Swedish colonists followed his example of leniency, and were convinced that mercy called upon them to lighten his lot by lifting upon him the smile of their countenances, and pressing upon him the hospitality of their homes.

The change, though it proved to Eric that his footing in the new land was becoming assured, was far from being altogether pleasing. Unless he could go among his fellow men without the stain of a convict's name, he would have preferred not to mingle with them at all. He was still Eric Helm the convict, and the fact was ever present to his mind, if not to theirs. He was glad when Governor Printz sent for him, and gave him instructions to go into the woods to inspect the water-mill which the Governor had caused to be built on a creek well suited for the purpose.

"There is something wrong with the machinery,"

said the Governor, "and as the mill goeth early and late, it will occasion inconvenience to those who have brought grain thither if aught interfere with the grinding. Go and see what is needed, and when the wheels can best be stopped that the machinery may be put in repair. The farmers of New Sweden can ill do without the mill that I have erected for their benefit."

The water-mill was one of the Governor's pet projects. It was the first of its kind built in New Sweden, and had proved a great boon to the colonists. The Governor was pleased, on the present occasion, to enlarge upon the benefits resulting from it, and to explain to the young man why he had placed it on the creek where it now stood. He was interrupted in the midst of his discourse by the entrance of a high official of New Sweden, none other than the Governor's Commissary, Hendrick Huygen. There was some excitement visible in his face.

"Well, what is it?" asked John Printz. "Your countenance is solemn enough to forebode ill news."

"It may or may not be ill news, your Excellency," said the Commissary. "I do but bring you tidings that the Dutch are again attempting to get the better of us upon the Schuylkill, and to put the laugh on their side, as they did when Beversrede went up."

"Let them try," said the Governor, frowning at the mention of the occasion on which the Dutch gained a footing on the Schuylkill. "They'll find

John Printz more than a match for a rascally set of tatterdemalions like them. What are they up to now?"

"Commissary Hudde has returned from the Manhattans, your Honor," was the answer, "armed with authority from the Dutch Director General, and has proceeded to portion out land in the region of the Schuylkill to his followers. Even now one Simon Root is attempting to build at the Mastmaker's Point, and others, it is said, are to follow."

John Printz sprang to his feet.

"Simon Root! Who's Simon Root? I'll shew him who he is if he attempt to defy me, the Governor of New Sweden. Aye, and I'll shew Andries Hudde too, if he does pretend to call himself Commissary of the South River. Go, send Swen Schute to me. And you," turning to Eric, "never mind the mill. It can grind a little longer in its present state. You can hold a sword, at least. I desire you to go to the Mast-maker's Point to help teach that Root and his superiors that John Printz, and John Printz alone, rules in New Sweden. It is an insult to Her Majesty, the Queen of Sweden, and an outrage against the Governor of New Sweden, and it shall not be tolerated. Where is Swen Schute? Why has he not come at my order?"

"I think the Commissary has gone to summon him," said Eric.

"Gone! He ought to be back. Go you and tell both that I am in haste."

But at that moment the officer, Swen Schute,

entered, and the Governor's next words were addressed to him.

"Where have you been?" he demanded. "I have been waiting for you, and my business requires haste. Take men and go at once to the Mast-maker's Point. A beggarly Dutchman has presumed to set his rascally foot on Her Majesty's soil. Kick him out! Pull his house about his ears, and if Andries Hudde be there, kick him after the other Dutchman. I care not whether it be the Dutch Commissary of the South River, or any other Dutch fool. Serve them all alike. Now be off, and see that my commands are carried out. And hark you! Take enough men to do the thing effectually. Here is one for you. He can carry a sword and musket as well as the rest."

"Your Honor's commands shall be obeyed," said the lieutenant, withdrawing hastily.

The merry ring of the hammer and rattle of boards went on apace at the Mast-maker's Point. Simon Root was but one of a small band of Dutchmen ready to avail themselves of the opportunity given by the orders of Director-General Stuyvesant to settle the land on the Schuylkill lately purchased by the Dutch. He was blithe at the prospect, for was not Director Stuyvesant himself behind him in this undertaking? The land on the Schuylkill was good, and freemen were allowed by the Dutch to trade with the Indians. Simon Root was looking forward with satisfaction to the gains that would come to him when his house was completed. A small Dutch settlement would ere long rise in this spot, and to it the Indians would resort. Visions of wealth made the hammer swing freely, when the voice of Simon's companion recalled him to the present.

"Yonder are moving figures. Which are they, friends or foes, think you?"

Simon stopped his work and turned himself about.

"Swedes, as I live!"

"And the house more than half up," lamented the assistant, who had himself an interest in this settlement at the Mast-maker's Point.

"Half up! What of that? It's going right up, for all the Swedes. They'll not dare to lay a finger on it when Director Stuyvesant's behind the business," said Simon.

"Don't be too sure," rejoined his companion. "John Printz cares for none, not even for Governor Stuyvesant himself."

The Swedes came on quickly, marching in regular order.

"By what right do you trespass on Her Majesty's domain?" asked Lieutenant Swen Schute sternly.

"I don't," replied Simon stoutly. "I'm trespassing on nobody's land. This land is ours, bought and paid for, and I'm on it by permission of the Noble Pieter Stuyvesant himself. What do *you*, trespassing on the lands of the Dutch West India Company?"

"None of this trifling," said the lieutenant sharply.

"Pull down that house, and take yourself off this land, or you'll find yourself in a bad fix."

"Pull it down yourself, if you want it pulled down," said Simon. "And as for the fix, it's you that will be in it when you have to settle for this with Director Stuyvesant."

"Aye, and I *will* pull it down," said the lieutenant angrily, "and if you mend not your manners, my fine fellow, you shall feel the weight of our Governor's wrath."

The lieutenant would have made good his words, but at that moment a shout was heard from behind, and a Dutchman came puffing and panting up to the soldiers.

"Stop, stop!" he gasped. "Don't fight, any of you. Their Honors the Clerk of the South River and the Deputy Commissary are coming. Wait and hear what they've got to say."

The lieutenant waited. Two Dutch officials, Adriaen van Tienhoven, Clerk of the Court of the South River, and Alexander Boyer, the Deputy Commissary, both of them men who were expecting to build at this spot, were seen approaching, and the Swedes felt themselves constrained to listen to their words. They were weighty, and in view of his instructions from the Governor of New Sweden, embarrassing to Swen Schute. To utterly disregard the protest seemed inadvisable, and yet— John Printz had given very explicit orders.

"At least give us time, until we can send to Fort Nassau and obtain definite instructions from Commissary Hudde," urged the Dutch officials. "You are surely not in such haste that you cannot wait until to-morrow. If Andries Hudde tells us to withdraw, we will move yonder building ourselves."

Lieutenant Schute hesitated. The demand seemed reasonable. On the morrow he would be still at liberty to carry out his orders. In the meantime he could communicate with the Governor. He therefore acceded to the request of the Dutch officers, and Simon Root's house yet stood when the sun went down.

That night Eric Helm was dispatched to New Gottenburg with the unenviable commission of acquainting the Governor with all that had transpired.

"What! That rascally Dutchman's house still standing? And you dare to come and tell me so to my face? You are a set of cowards, every one of you. What did I send you there for, eh?"

"To obey my superiors," said Eric. "Lieutenant Schute ordered me to communicate the fact to your Excellency. I have done so. I am ready to carry back your commands."

"Commands! What's the good of commanding a set of poltroons like you? Let the house stand? Not while my name's John Printz. What care I for the orders of Andries Hudde, that I should wait for him? Pitch them in the faces of his officers, and tear that place down at all hazards. If it stand to-morrow night, you and every man of the company shall answer dearly for its presence."

It did not stand. While the sun was yet low in the sky, Lieutenant Schute hastened to obey the Governor's peremptory commands. The Dutch Commissary had been obdurate. The house must stand, or be torn down by the Swedes.

"Then the mischief be on your own obstinate heads," said Lieutenant Schute angrily. "My course is clear," and he gave the order to advance.

With swords drawn the Swedish soldiers marched to the house at the Mast-maker's Point; the Dutch officials, and all who were interested in the building, followed in solemn protest.

"Once more, before it is too late, I protest against this outrage," said Van Tienhoven. "See, here is the commission of Director Stuyvesant himself. We are not building here without authority."

"I acknowledge no authority in Her Majesty's domain save that of Her Majesty's Governor," said the lieutenant, "and he has bidden me not to allow a stick to be planted in the name of Their High Mightinesses, but to trample under foot whatever has been raised. I have nothing to do with your Government or your Commissary Hudde. He is a rascal and a rogue."

Then the blood of Alexander Boyer was stirred, and he opened his mouth to speak.

"Schute, thou must be thyself a rascal thus to talk," he said indignantly. "Abuse no man, or say it to his face."

Now Lieutenant Schute was a hot tempered man, and to be reproved by a Dutchman was more than he could bear. Almost before the words were out of Boyer's mouth, the hands of the lieutenant were in Boyer's hair. It looked as if the swords of the soldiers might before long find other work than the hacking down of a house. But the calmer onlookers interfered. The combatants were separated with no greater loss than a tuft or two of hair originally pertaining to the head of the Dutchman, Boyer.

"Advance and tear down the building. Leave not the rascal a board or a nail," shouted the lieutenant. "This is a menace to Her Majesty and the Governor of New Sweden."

With a shout the men fell upon the house, using their swords for axes, and the sound of breaking and falling timbers filled the air. When night came no building stood at the Mast-maker's Point, but the breach between the Swedes and the Dutch had grown a little wider.

CHAPTER XV

It was a day in June, and the land was the land of Governor Printz. Very much the land of Governor Printz, for a man of the character of the ruler of New Sweden of necessity dominated more and more as the years went by the country and the people over whom he ruled.

It was almost three years since, by the placing of his strong house before the gates of Beversrede, John Printz had convinced the Dutch that it was to be submission to his will or war to the end between the rival authorities on the South River. The Director-General of New Netherland, harassed by his neighbors of the New England colonies, and being for the present unable to leave his capital of New Amsterdam, was forced, strongly against his will, to let Printz have things very much his own way. New Sweden flourished, and the Dutch traders sailed up the South River in fear and trembling, sojourned in the land in the midst of harassings and annoyances, and occasional violence on the part of the Governor of New Sweden, and departed with anger in their hearts, and beaver skins in their ships, the latter wrested from his domain in spite of John Printz and his agents.

A cloud was on this particular day resting over the South River, not the cloud of the Governor's wrath, but a definite physical cloud, which hung low in the heavens, and from which growls, deep and hoarse enough to resemble the threatenings of the Governor's voice, rumbled and ceased and rumbled again.

The shadow of the heavy cloud deepened the color of a pair of blue eyes that looked straight up into it. Anything but a storm cloud, looking down upon the face to which the eyes belonged, would surely have ceased its grumbling. It was not every day that even a cloud—and in its journeyings it had many advantages—could look upon a face quite as fair. The attraction lay not alone—nor chiefly—in the delicacy of tint and the perfection of feature. There was about the face a subtle charm that mere color and shape could not give It was as much too old for the maiden—she was but fifteen—as it was too young. The simplicity and winning frankness of early childhood had never left it, and the grace and thoughtfulness of womanhood had come to it early. The result was a peculiar charm, that made it hard to turn the eyes away from the childlike womanly face.

The cloud and the maiden and the river, and a strip of sandy beach, had the region to themselves, with a small canoe as a possible servant. The canoe had brought the maiden to her present position from further up the river. From where she stood she could see the stream widening out towards the bay. The tide covered the marshy stretches by the banks, and made the river broad, and at this particular spot deep to its very edge. Her own little strip of sand, narrow and wet, had but lately been washed by the retreating water.

The maiden looked from the cloud to the canoe, and was about to make a step towards the latter, when from the rising land above the sandy shore came a frightened bleat, and the sound of scampering feet. The grassy knoll to which she sprang brought the girl's head level with the bank, and made her a witness of a race for life going on above.

The odds were all against the lamb, that, terrified and desperate, bounded madly across the grass, staggering beneath the weight of a wild cat clinging to its side. The fierce beast of prey had buried it claws deed in the lamb's fleece, and was even now making a vigorous effort to reach the frightened creature's throat.

The eyes of the girl were large with sympathy. She turned to seek a weapon to use on the side of the weaker struggler, but even as she did so the lamb reached the edge of the bank. There was a wild leap that carried hunter and hunted across the narrow stretch of sand, and then a plunge. The terrified cry of the lamb mingled with a warning growl from the storm cloud. The maiden had barely time to turn before she saw the lamb drifting down the stream.

"Poor hunted thing! You shall not die thus," she said, and without another glance at the cloud, which at the moment lifted up its voice in more vehement warning, she stepped into the canoe, and pulled towards the still struggling lamb.

The waters had grown dark as the sky. The face of the maiden as she stood in the canoe looked white and strange against the gloom. Then, in a moment, the storm burst. The flash of lightning, the loud crash of thunder, and the roar of the wind, were almost simultaneous. River and shore seemed for an instant ablaze, and in the midst of the blaze stood the girl, abreast now of the lamb. While the water was lashed into waves about her, she bent over, and with an effort lifted the animal into the canoe.

"There, there! Keep still. None shall do you hurt," she said soothingly, and gave all her attention to reaching the bank.

But the storm, that had uttered warning after warning without being heeded, had now passed the admonitory stage, and was in possession of that little world of river and shore. The waters heeded no more the strokes of the girl's paddle than if it had been a reed. Hurling itself against her and against the water, the wind swept both down—towards the sea, whither the tide had begun to ebb.

The blackness spread fairly across the sky. Then the waters above began to descend towards those below in headlong haste, and were caught by the wind and whirled forward, a tumultuous, broken, rushing sheet, in the middle of which drifted the canoe and the maiden and the shivering, terrified lamb.

The peal of thunder that filled the ears of the young maid in the canoe came rolling and crackling with still more deafening sound about the ears of another to whom the darkness had become almost the darkness of night. Out on the open river the cloud had made the world dark, but here, in the forest, the gloom was deeper. Those ears heard the hollow reverberations of the earth answering to the tumult in the air as branches and trees came crashing down upon it.

They could not fail to hear the response of the earth, for they were very close to it. In fact the head to which they belonged rested upon the earth itself, pressed down upon it so closely that the water which overflowed from a creek some six feet away washed round the face, and set the black hair floating. The rain splashed down over the dark skin, and into the little black eyes, that, in spite of it, looked up and watched the flashing lightning and the rapidly rising water.

It was no wonder the rise was rapid. There was a double source of supply. The rain did its part by sending rivulets hurrying from all points to join the creek, and below, at the spot where the small tributary met the main stream, a dam formed by an uprooted tree arrested the waters of the South River as they descended, and sent a great wave up the creek.

It took but a minute or two to bring the water level with the chin, that again and again tried to lift itself clear of the flood, and every time was held back by a stout hickory limb, that lay within an inch of the forehead over which it stretched without touching. The trunk had fallen across the body of the Indian woman in such a way that its more crushing weight was supported by its own branches, and it failed to press the life out of the form that it yet pinned to the ground. One arm lay broken by the woman's side, the other was fast beneath the tree.

She was old, and lean, and withered, but the black eyes had fire in them yet. They watched the water till it crept up and washed about the closed lips. The head lifted itself then, till the forehead pressed hard against the hickory bough, and the lips gained a temporary advantage over the water.

There was nothing more that the Indian woman could do. No power of movement other than that slight raising of the head was left to her. There was nothing else but to wait till the water crept over mouth and nose, and the eyes that stared upward were the eyes of the dead. For the storm had not long begun, and the clouds had yet much store to pour out.

Along the river the very animals had sought cover, and the region was given over to storm and flood. All but one spot some three miles further up, where a dog stood upon the bank, alert and watchful, yet with drooping tail and wistful eyes.

"How now, good Jupe? Canst find the bairn?"

The dog lifted his head, and gave utterance to a long howl.

With hand uplifted to keep the rain from his eyes, the speaker stood gazing down the stream. He was an old man, but he stood in the tumult of the storm unmoved. There was anxiety in his face.

"Come hither, Jupe," he said, and the dog left the bank and came slowly to his side.

"Art sure she went that way?" he asked, letting his hand fall upon the head of the animal.

The dog looked at him questioningly, almost reproachfully, putting his nose to the ground, and again bounding towards the stream. The old man followed.

"Always the same tale," he said. "And the canoe is gone. Surely the dog is right, and the bairn is further down the river."

He stood by the brink. The waters surged and broke in waves at his feet.

"Agneta! Little one!"

It might have been the voice of a young man, so strong and deep was the tone, but it brought no response, unless the low whine of the dog could be accounted answer.

The old man turned away.

"We must wait," he said sorrowfully. "The bairn will have put ashore somewhere. We can do naught till the storm abate."

He turned towards a farmhouse that stood back from the river. It must surely have been a piece of the old Swedish land brought bodily over to the new. The long low buildings with their sodded roofs, the walls of squared tree trunks, the great paved quadrangle—all were there as in Sweden. Just now everything looked blurred and misty through the driving rain.

The old man passed under shelter, and stood in a doorway, looking down the river. Neither he nor the dog could rest.

And in the wood, some miles below, the little dark eyes of the Indian woman gathered to themselves a look of despair, and the water touched the closely pressed lips, and now and again trickled into the nostrils. A peal of thunder rolled away in the distance, and the despair changed to alertness. Then the lips opened, and a voice, shrill and far-reaching, uttered an Indian call. The cry was prolonged as the thunder itself, and the moment it ceased the woman held her breath to listen. No answer came. Again the lips opened, and this time the call was in the white man's language. There was a sudden momentary cessation of wind and rain, while the storm gathered its forces afresh, and in the comparative stillness the listening ears heard the sound of a voice—the answering cry of a girl.

"Who called?"

"I! Indian squaw! Come! Help!" shouted the old woman, in the same far-reaching tone.

Back at the mouth of the creek, a canoe, whirled into the comparative safety of that opening by the swirl of waters about the overturned forest giant, was urged upward by a young girl's hand. When the voice first came she had been sweeping down the main stream, wondering whether the little canoe would be afloat when the storm ceased. It was when she sought to lessen the fears of the lamb by speaking to it reassuring words, necessarily loud, that the ear of the squaw caught the sound.

The maiden had believed herself alone in that waste of waters. It was a comfort to know that another was near, even though that other was in need of help. It was a comfort, too, to be out of the current, and to feel the canoe obey her will. She urged it forward with rapid strokes.

"I am coming," she cried. "Where are you?"

"Here! Hasten! The water rises."

Just once came the guiding shout, then the voice ceased. To the girl's calls no answer was returned.

She came upon the squaw before she knew herself to be near, and sprang from the canoe with a cry of fear. Water covered the face, and to the maiden it seemed that the woman was dead. At that cry, however, the black eyes opened with a jerk, and made a succession of rapid upward movements, which had the effect of strangely contorting the features, seen, as they were, beneath the water. With ready apprehension the girl attacked the hickory bough. It was too tough for her to break, but she succeeded in forcing it upward. Then the head of the Indian woman lifted itself. She shook the water from her face, and opened her tightly closed lips.

"Good! Good!" she said, drawing a quick breath. "The water rose fast."

"It rises yet," said the maiden, "and the tree is on you. What shall I do?"

"Put your hand down in my belt—there, under the tree. The little squaw's hand is small," said the woman. "It can push in and find the axe."

It did push in, but to do it, it was forced to leave the bough. The face of the Indian woman was again under water. She bore the ordeal with amazing composure, while the maiden wormed and twisted her hand between the tree trunk and the body of the woman, all the while tormented with fears that the squaw would be drowned. The small white hand was bleeding when it drew itself clear of the rough bark, but the girl did not know it. It held the axe, a sharp one lately purchased of the white men. The maiden hastened to push back the bough.

"There, lift up your head again," she said eagerly. "You will be drowned."

The water ran in streams from the brown face. The squaw took the situation coolly. Not till the streams had ceased, and she had taken more than one long breath, did she attempt to answer.

"Now little squaw go to work quick," she said. "Water be up high very soon."

The strokes, dealt with one hand, while the other held up the bough, were necessarily feeble, and it took many of them to make an impression on the tough hickory, but it began to weaken at last, and aided by the strong pressure of the squaw's head, the girl succeeded in breaking it off just as a flash of lightning lit up the forest, and another tree came crashing down almost at her feet. She started back, trembling with excitement and weariness.

"Does the heavy trunk hurt much?" she asked sympathetically, when the crash had rolled away sufficiently to allow her voice to be heard.

"It does not kill. Indian cares not for hurt," said the woman. "That arm no use. Tree broke it. Get the other out. Then it can help."

The girl set to work again to free the squaw's left arm. She chopped away the bark, till, with a great wrench, the woman released the imprisoned member.

"Ugh!" said the squaw. "Get up soon now."

The water was still rising, though not as rapidly. The rain was less violent.

"White squaw get bough, and put it under tree—there," directed the squaw. "Then little squaw bear on it hard—here, close to my arm. That arm help. It not broke."

It helped vigorously, and the bough, used as a lever, pried up the tree. How it was done the maiden hardly knew, but she saw the squaw writhe and wriggle, and then draw herself slowly upward.

"Now press—hard!" commanded the Indian woman, and the girl strained every nerve to make her weight tell. The next moment the squaw was on her feet, her right arm hanging helpless at her side.

"Little white squaw work well," she said, breathing hard after her exertions. Then she felt herself critically over with her left hand. "Indian squaw's bones broke," she added, pointing to her ribs.

"And your arm too," said the girl, her eyes full of pity. "You must come with me when the storm is over. My grandfather is skillful. He will set the bones."

"Indians skillful too," said the woman. "Indian squaw get bones mended among her own people. White squaw stoop and feel for pouch—there, beneath the tree," she added.

The maiden was leaning, white and exhausted, against a tree. Now, at the bidding of the Indian woman, she stooped to search for the pouch, which, in the squaw's effort to free herself, had become detached. It was a bag of skin, and the girl wondered in a dull way what made it so heavy. She was too tired, however, to be actively curious. She had in truth "worked well," how well she hardly realized. As the excitement subsided she found that the past hour had told upon her.

The sky was clearing. Already the thunder sounded distant. The girl carried the bag to the squaw, and watched her as with a grunt of satisfaction she attached it to her belt, first thrusting her hand inside to make sure that nothing was missing. The woman had no inclination to leave behind her any part of the wherewithal to make for herself and her warrior husband many an elaborate toilet.

The contents of that bag represented much personal adornment. There was in it red earth from a creek above Tenacong, that the squaw well knew how to prepare until it made almost as good a paint as the vermilion the trader sold, and white clay from another stream that would make a good substitute for white lead. Black clay also was there, taken from Wolfe creek, far down by the sea. Black as ink would be the paint prepared from it, and frightful in the sight of his enemies would it make the old warrior when he adorned himself in it. Furthermore there was blue earth from the same region, which only needed tempering to render it fit to embellish the bodies of brave and squaw on the most important occasions. It would have taken more than a few broken bones to make the squaw forget these results of her journeying and bartering. The pouch secured, she turned to the girl.

"Storm nearly over," she said. "White squaw want to go back in canoe?"

"Yes," said the maiden wearily, "but I do not think I could paddle yet. I must rest."

"Indian paddle," said the woman. "White squaw get in—squat in bottom of canoe."

"But you arm is broken," replied the maiden. "You cannot paddle."

"Indian's one arm good as white squaw's two," said the woman. "White squaw get in canoe."

The girl looked at her for a moment, and then obeyed. As she stepped into the canoe, however, she possessed herself of the paddle.

"You sit and rest in the bottom of the boat," she said. "I am better able to paddle than are you."

"Ugh! White squaw do as she's told," said the

Indian woman, giving the girl a rough but not unfriendly push. "River too rough for arms that are not strong."

Thus it happened that when the storm cloud rolled away in great masses, a canoe with a white maiden crouching in the bottom, and an Indian woman paddling with her left hand, came up the river against the current.

At the farm-house the dog and the old man had kept their place in the doorway through all the violence of the storm. Now the old man turned into the house.

"Katarina," he said, speaking to a woman within, "I must seek the bairn. I can stand it no longer."

"Nonsense, father! She'll turn up right enough," was the reply. "The girl's not a fool, though she might well be accounted one for staying out when the thunder gave full warning of its intentions. She will have run the canoe ashore, and sought what shelter there is to be had, if, indeed, she be on the river at all."

"Where else should she be?" said the old man. "The canoe is gone, and the dog ever goeth to the river. Had she been on land he would have found her ere this. I will leave it no longer. Harm may have come to the bairn."

"As you will," said the woman, and the old man returned to the river, preceded by the dog.

Before the animal had reached the bank, however, he stopped, with head held high.

"What is it, lad? Didst hear the bairn?"

The dog sniffed the air, listened intently, and then bounded from the old man's side, and went tearing down the stream.

"He hears her. God be praised!" said the old man. Then he raised his voice.

"Agneta! My bairn!" he called.

This time there came an answer in a ringing girl's voice.

"I'm coming, grandfather."

He met her on the bank and held out both hands.

"Thank God, little one! I feared for you," he said.

The girl's voice was not quite steady.

"I also feared," she said. "But—I am glad I was there."

Her hand was in his. He saw the blood on it.

"My bairn, you are hurt!" he said.

"Little white squaw hurt her hand getting Indian from under the tree," said the Indian woman. "She good squaw to work. Indian be dead now, if she not come along."

"Grandfather Axel, the woman is hurt," said the girl. "May she take the canoe further up the river? She will be nearer then to her people."

"Surely," said the old man. "Take it, friend, and send it back when you will," he added, turning to the squaw. "You are in sore need of it."

"Arm get well now," said the squaw cheerfully. "White squaw get it out before the water quite kill. Good little squaw—her."

"Aye, she is good," said the old man fondly.

The squaw nodded, and paddled away, stopping first to push the lamb out of the canoe. The old man turned to the maiden, putting both hands on her shoulders.

"My bairn," he said gently, "you have surely done well, but, little one," and his hand pressed more heavily on her shoulder, "you must take care. The old man's heart would be sore broken if it had to give you up. Your mother trusted you to me. I must look well to my trust—my brother Eric's grandchild."

The girl's lip quivered. She took a step forward, and was wrapped in his arms. Then the tears came.

"There, there, little one! My own bairn!" he said, soothingly.

"I am foolish," she said at last, lifting her head. "I—think—the tree was too heavy for me."

His hand pressed her head back again upon his breast.

"Never foolish to bring your sorrow there, little one," he said. "You have been tried too sorely. You are wet, and over strained. You must go in and rest, and tell me all about it after."

He led her into the house, keeping his arm about her, and when his daughter would have questioned her, he stopped her peremptorily.

"Nay, ask no questions now," he said. "The bairn is overwrought. She has saved a life to-day —and risked one," he added, in a lower tone. "Let her rest. Such a storm is enough to try a stronger than she."

He led her through the big living room to an inner chamber, and put her tenderly in a chair.

"Change those wet clothes, little one, and lie down and rest," he said.

She smiled at him, though her lips quivered yet. That smile was the last thing he saw before he went out and closed the door.

"Well, has she got over it?"

It was a girl's voice, and the speaker, a fair haired, round faced damsel, some two years older than the maiden he had just left, looked up into the old man's face.

"I have told her to sleep," he said. "See that she is not wakened."

"What did she go for?" asked the girl curiously. "Hadn't she sense enough to know that a storm was coming?"

"I have not asked her why she went. She must have started before the storm came," said the old man. "She had sense enough to save a life. Would you have had as much, my girl?"

The damsel turned away without answer, and the old man went out.

CHAPTER XVI

A greater than John Printz was in New Sweden. From the deck of a vessel ascending the South River Director-General Stuyvesant looked out upon the land. The Director of New Netherland had come in state, attended by his chaplain and an imposing suite. It was his first visit to this part of his domain, and it had been long in contemplation. Its object was partly the convincing of John Printz that the principle of unlimited aggression was not altogether a safe one for a ruler to adopt, and partly the official reception of a large tract of land on the South River, which had been ceded to the Dutch by the Indians.

The Director was a soldierly man, of stern and commanding bearing. The fiery eye showed at present its mildest expression as the Director stood talking to Domine Grasmere, his chaplain.

"No wonder Swedes and Englishmen desire a goodly picking here," he said. "It is a land worth having, aye, and worth a little fighting for, if need be."

"The Englishmen have been disposed of, said the domine, but the Swede, in the person of John Printz, is a less easy matter."

"I have yet to see John Printz," said Stuyvesant quietly.

The shadow of a smile played about the domine's lips. The words were significant.

"Where are we now, captain?" asked the Director, when a few minutes later the chief officer of the vessel passed him.

"But a short distance below the Minquas' Kill, where the Swedish Fort Christina stands, your Honor," replied the captain.

"We shall not reach Fort Nassau to-day," said the Director. "The wind dies down. There is a dead calm coming, and the tide is against us."

"Aye, everything is against us," said the captain. "The ship has but crawled for the last hour."

"She'll not do even that much longer," replied the Director, and as if to make good his words, the last pretence of a breeze died away, and the vessel lay becalmed, while the captain fumed and looked furtively at the Governor.

Stuyvesant took the delay quietly. He was in haste to reach the Dutch Fort Nassau, there to confer with his Commissary and to meet the Indians. But wind and tide were at no man's disposal. He turned his attention towards the bank.

"What think you of that for a dwelling in a new land?" he asked, as the domine's eye wandered in the same direction.

The large Swedish farmhouse that stood just beyond the point where the vessel lay looked as if it had been transported bodily from the northern land. The great square of buildings might easily have passed for a fortress, so strong and compact was their appearance.

"It must belong to one who is well-to-do," said the chaplain.

"Of a truth," rejoined the Director. "I have seen nothing to equal it since we entered the river. I will even go ashore and inspect it, since the vessel may not for several hours set sail."

He was as good as his word. With the domine for attendant he stepped ashore, to the great satisfaction of two pairs of eyes pressed close against a window in the big farmhouse. The eyes belonged to two children, and had but lately discovered the vessel.

"Look! Look! Isn't she a big one?" said the younger of the two, a small, thick-set girl of seven.

"Look!" contemptuously repeated the boy addressed. "Do you think I haven't seen her this ever so long? She's Dutch. She's going to Fort Nassau."

"She's not going anywhere. She's standing still," said the girl.

"Standing!" retorted the elder loftily. "That's all girls know. Ships don't—"

But here both watchers at the same moment descried the Director and his attendant.

"Mother! Grandfather!" cried two voices at once. "There's a big ship stopped here, and a Dutch heer coming to this house."

The small faces were excited. The dress of the Governor betokened a person of distinction, and persons of distinction were rare in this land.

An old man entered the room at the children's call.

"What is it, noisy ones?" he said.

"Look, grandfather? The heer and the domine are coming here."

The little girl slipped her hand into that of her grandfather as he came to the window.

"They are coming here, surely," he said, and went to the door to welcome them.

Axel Bonde had grown ten years older since the day he took the little Agneta from her mother's arms, but he had lost none of the dignity of bearing that characterized him then. The Director-General of New Netherland thought the figure awaiting him in the doorway had but a fit setting in the big, substantial house.

"Our ship lies becalmed, my friend," he said. "I was fain to step ashore and see the land, and your house attracted me by the goodly size of its buildings. It looks more fitted for the land from which you came than for this new realm, for, if I mistake not, you are not long from Sweden, and the model of this dwelling is to be found in an older country."

"Aye, noble heer, that is it," said the old man, his eye brightening at the words. "It is built timber for timber after the fashion of the home in the dear Sweedland. If your interest be deep enough to carry you beyond its threshold, I would gladly show you a true Swedish farm-house. I know not to whom I speak, though by your bearing I deem you of soldierly character and of no mean rank, but I think I mistake not in believing that you know more of the Dutch form of dwelling than the Swedish."

"You are right there," said the Director. "I am a true Dutchman, else should I not have been chosen to be Governor of New Netherland."

The stern features relaxed as he spoke. The Director was watching the effect of his words. The old man's manner was unchanged, though his face expressed surprise.

"I knew not your Excellency's rank," he said calmly, "yet will I venture to repeat my invitation. Even the Governor of New Netherland may desire to see that which is unfamiliar to him."

"That do I, truly," said the Director. "Lead on, my friend. That part, methinks, is where you house your cattle."

Axel Bonde led the way to the cattle house, empty now, for the cows were feeding in knee-deep grass in the meadows. There was the same broad open space within that had characterized the ladugârd of the old Swedish home, the same roomy accommodation for the cattle, the same hearth in the centre, where fodder could be prepared. The old habits had not yet adapted themselves to the new surroundings.

"Your cattle must have a good time of it in the winter, if you lodge them in such quarters," said the Governor.

"The Troll will not come to meddle with our cows this winter," ventured the little girl, who had clung to her grandfather's hand, and accompanied him into the cattle house. "There is the Midsummer Qvast."

Her small finger pointed upwards towards a bunch of withered flowers hanging from the roof.

Pieter Stuyvesant was in an affable mood. He looked down upon the child, and smiled.

"Well, little one, and why hangs it there?" he asked. "What harm will the Troll do?"

"Don't you know?" answered the child incredulously "The Midsummer Qvast will keep the Troll away, so that they cannot milk our cows or hurt our cattle. They are ugly evil spirits, who would do us harm, but they cannot come here, for my sister Maria gathered the Midsummer Qvast quite alone on St. Hans' Eve, and she did not speak to anybody. If she had spoken before all the nine different flowers were gathered, the Qvast would have been of no use. Now it will last till next year, and the Troll will not dare to come near our cows. I am going to gather a Midsummer Qvast next Hans' Eve."

The Governor was not listening. His eyes had wandered beyond the bunch of faded flowers, even to the further end of the building, where, framed in a doorway, stood a young girl, tall, lithe, and willowy, the soft bloom of health on her cheeks, and the perfect ease of self-forgetfulness in her manner.

"That is not a peasant maiden," he said, his eyes yet on the girl's face.

"No, your Honor, it is not," said Axel quietly.

Agneta had perceived the strangers, but her demeanor underwent no change. She stepped within the cattle house, reached upward to the top of one of the partitions, and took down a skein of woolen yarn, relic of an evening in winter when old customs had been kept up, and the girls of the household had repaired to the cattle shed with their spinning wheels, there to spin and chat gaily in the light of the big fire, and tell Swedish stories, and grow a little homesick in the telling.

The skein in her hand, the girl turned towards the door by which she had entered, but the voice of the Director-General of New Netherland arrested her steps.

"Come hither, fair maid," he said a little peremptorily.

Agneta obeyed, crossing the building swiftly.

"What will you, sir?" she asked courteously.

"What will I?" he answered lightly. "I will to look upon your face, and to know what such a maiden doeth here in New Sweden."

"My duty, sir," said the maiden, answering the last half of his remark, and ignoring the first, though the lowered eyelids, and the slight increase of soberness in her manner, told that it was understood.

"Nay, nay, veil not those eyes," he said. "Look at me, child. The Governor of New Netherland is wont to be obeyed."

She lifted her eyes then, and a deeper tinge of color came to her cheek.

"I knew not that your Excellency was the Governor of New Netherland," she said gently, "nor that it was the duty of the maidens of New Netherland to look upward when your Excellency approached," she added, with the glimmer of a smile.

He laughed.

"How came you in New Netherland at all?" he said.

"I came with my grandfather to New Sweden, your Excellency," said Agneta.

The Governor thought there was a slight stress on the name, but it was so slight that he could not be sure.

"Your grandfather?" he said. Then turning to Axel: "Is she your grandchild? I thought you told me she was no peasant."

"The grandchild of my brother Eric. We were brothers by adoption," said Axel. "Nay, in the veins of the bairn flows no peasant blood, but that of noble houses."

"I thought as much," said the Governor. "And what does she here?"

"Her mother gave her to me when she died," said the old man. "My brother Eric's grandchild was a precious gift."

"Grandfather thinks Agneta more precious than me and Ian and Maria together," said the little girl, who stood yet by the Governor's side.

"Go into the house and teach thy meddlesome tongue better manners, Kolina," said the old man quietly. "And you, Ian, go with your sister."

The children obeyed, and with a low, respectful courtesy the young maiden turned to follow them, but the hand of the Governor detained her.

"Not so fast, child," he said. "I am curious to know more of a maiden who has no smiles for the Governor of her land."

"Nay, your Excellency," said Agneta, "but Governor Printz claims that title."

"Well, since we are near Fort Christina—for so they tell me—it may be that you are right," said the Director with a smile. "I deny not that your people bought the land about that fort. On this point we shall not disagree."

Then he turned to Axel Bonde.

"How came you, with such a charge, and a good farm over in Sweden, as I doubt not you had, to leave the old land for the new?" he asked. "Doth the new seem to you better?"

A look of sadness came to the old man's face.

"Nay, surely," he said, "for the old heart and the old land go best together. But if a man learn not by the time he is near fourscore that it is ill to put a life almost run out against the interests of those who have yet much time to live in the world, he is strangely slow of learning. Aye, the old farm was good, *very* good, but my son had a desire to come to the new land, and the betrothed of my oldest grandchild was greatly drawn to the farm where he had first seen the girl. He wished much to buy it of me. Anna was a good girl. She deserved to be happy. Therefore, since all were better pleased that it should be so, we came hither."

"All?" said the Director. "What saith this maiden to the change?"

"I go with grandfather Axel," said Agneta. "What he wills is best."

"Will your Honor see the rest of the buildings?" asked Axel.

"Yes, yes," said the Director, but his thoughts seemed not as free as before, and he asked fewer questions. He was thinking of the maiden, who, as they left the cattle house, turned in a different direction.

He saw her again when the old man welcomed him within the walls of the dwelling house. Axel Bonde would have set refreshment before him, but the Director stayed him.

"Nay, I desire naught but a draught of water," he said.

"I will bring your Excellency some that is both clear and cold," said Agneta.

She was gone several minutes, returning with a goblet of silver in which gleamed water cold and sparkling.

"It is pure and sweet, and hath medicinal properties," she said as she presented it. "It was brought this day by the Indians from a spring much thought of by their nation."

The Governor took the goblet, and raised it on high.

"I drink to the health of the gentle maiden who offers it," he said. "May the new land be a land of promise to you, fair daughter. These Indians of whom you speak," he added, as his lips left the refreshing draught, "are they to be relied upon, or does treachery lurk beneath?"

"They are very good to me," said Agneta, simply, though the color upon her cheek had deepened at the Governor's act. "To those who know them well there seemeth no treachery."

"Are there any who are *not* good to you?" asked the Director significantly.

The rosy tint on cheek and brow grew deeper still, but if the maiden saw aught beneath the words, she answered as if she understood not.

"I think not, your Excellency," she said.

He smiled upon her.

"It were a savage land were it otherwise," he said.

CHAPTER XVII

"Verily I am footsore and hungry, yet does this forest show no sign of opening."

The traveler spoke aloud. He was glad to hear the sound of his own voice. The solitude of the forest had become oppressive. He had journeyed in it since early morn.

Eric Helm was no mean woodsman now, but he had lost his way. The region was new to him, and he had miscalculated the distances. He had reckoned upon reaching some Swedish dwelling before this, for his provisions were exhausted, and he traveled fasting. His haste to be clear of the wood was his sole excuse for not supplying the deficiency by means of his gun. Now, as the afternoon advanced, he took himself to task.

"He who goes hungry, with the wherewithal in his hand to supply his need, has little right to complain," he said. "Yonder goes my dinner."

A bird rose before him as he spoke. He lifted his gun, took aim, and fired. The report was loud, for the trees beat back the sound, but in spite of them Eric heard, or thought he heard, another sound for which he could not account.

"A strange cry, that, for a wounded bird," he muttered, and pushed on to pick up his game.

It was nowhere to be seen. A search among the

trees failed to show sign of it, and Eric was forced to the conclusion that his shot had been without effect He went hungry on his way, not being sufficiently in earnest to try again. He believed himself near the edge of the forest, and was more interested in getting to open land than in satisfying his appetite.

"Strange that I hit nothing," he mused. "I could have sworn I heard the cry of some wounded creature."

Had he done so he would not have been far astray. His ears had only deceived him in telling him too little. What he did *not* hear was a snake-like rustling made by a human body crawling into the shelter of the brushwood. He was hunting for the bird too vigorously to notice that stealthy movement, or the former sound might have been explained.

As the young man walked away, a dark head was pushed from behind a tree. Then a young Indian crawled into a freer position, drew off his legging, and from the bared leg extracted a goodly charge of shot, using his hunting knife as a surgical instrument.

"The white men call us brothers, and stretch forth their hands when they meet us near their houses, but when they find us in the forest they make their guns speak for them."

Thus spake the young Indian in his heart, and thus spake the scowl on his face. There was nobody to see the scowl, else would it have been of a more dignified type. The Indian lad was a very young brave, little more than a boy aspiring to the honors of manhood. To have ruffled the studied calm of his face would have required more than a wounded leg, had any been present. The exclamation that escaped him when struck had been called forth by sudden anger rather than pain, and was quickly suppressed. Now, however, there was no one to see, and he allowed his animosity to appear in his countenance.

His rough treatment of the leg completed, the Indian continued his journey, following closely the footsteps of the young engineer. In spite of the wound he gained on the other, and before long was walking abreast of him, though well hidden by the trees.

Once, when Eric paused, an arrow was fitted to the Indian's bow, and the bow-string was between the Indian's fingers. A sudden movement on the part of the white man possibly accounted for the fact that the young brave did not at that time possess himself of his first scalp. There was a dangerous glitter in his eyes, however. The warrior instinct in him was aroused, and he was experiencing the excitement of tracking an enemy. Between himself and the thought of possible retribution was interposed the memory of that wounded leg. The white man was the aggressor, come what would.

"The river at last, and the boundary of this interminable forest!" ejaculated Eric.

Through the trees he caught a glimpse of open

land, with the shimmer of water beyond. His pace quickened till he stood outside the forest, looking upon a broad river, with a settler's home as a nearer object. Why did the sight of that farmhouse take from the young man all power of movement?

As his eye fell upon it, New Sweden faded, and in its place came the old land, dark save for the illuminating power of a clear moon. For the moment he was a fugitive again, hungry and homeless. That house—the very same surely, with its long stretch of low buildings—formed the background of a picture that had never faded. The desolation of utter loneliness rushed over him anew. His arms seemed to bear again the weight of the dog, the last friend left to the wanderer.

"Jupe! Dear old Jupe!"

The words came without volition on his part. They were but the outlet of the yearning of the moment. Many a time his heart had spoken them, now the tongue gave them utterance.

With the voicing of those words the stillness of the scene was broken. Upon a mound not quite within range of Eric's eye a shaggy figure had been standing when he emerged from the forest. Two great wistful eyes had since watched him, while a pair of ears pricked nervously. At the first sound of his voice the whole figure grew animated. A wild determination to annihilate time and space seemed suddenly to possess the animal.

It might be mathematically true that an infinite

force would have been required to place that dog at his master's feet in absolutely no time, but the force of love was well-nigh infinite, and the dog stopped not to reason. An appreciable time perhaps elapsed between that first short yelp and the almost human cry with which the animal flung himself upon his master, but neither Eric nor Jupe knew it. The head of the dog was on a level with Eric's face, the eyes for a moment looked into his. Then the creature fell back, to crouch whining at the young man's feet, in a hopeless attempt to express the long pent up love of his heart.

"Jupe! Blessed old boy! I never thought I should see you again."

Eric was down on his knees fondling the dog, nay, fairly putting his arms about him in his delight, and once again resting his face on the faithful head, as he had done on the night when he and the dog parted company.

A low growl was Jupe's response. What ailed the dog, that his mood had changed so suddenly? The ecstasy of gladness gave place to anger. He seemed to bristle all over his body. He growled, snarled, pushed aside the caressing hand, and broke away, disappearing within the forest.

Eric stood up, bewildered, dazed. How came the dog there, and what meant that farm-house, the exact counterpart of the home of the little lady who had befriended him in his need?

Almost before he had time to wonder, he heard a savage growl, the twang of a bowstring, and a sharp yelp of pain. Eric looked to his gun, and then plunged back into the forest, in time to see a figure dodge behind a tree.

"Who skulks there?" he cried. "Come out and show yourself, or I fire."

There was no response, and the young man let his gun speak for him as a better argument than any he could offer. He fired, not to injure, but to frighten. That he succeeded was evidenced by the cracking of twigs much further away. The enemy, if enemy he were, was retreating.

Eric, however, had little time to spare for the foe. His principal thought was for the dog, that came staggering towards him, whining pitifully. An arrow was bedded deep in his side, in such close proximity to the heart that the young man's exclamation as he saw it was fiercely vindictive.

"Keep still, Jupe, poor fellow!" he said. "We must have that out. Better get clear of the forest, though. This seems a dangerous neighborhood."

The dog followed him to the open land, the wistful eyes, full of pain and longing, fixed upon him. Then the young man knelt, and drew out the arrow. A red stream followed it, and Eric took his handkerchief to staunch the blood. Jupe, meanwhile, uttered no protest, and only a low whine told of the pain. The young man was yet kneeling over the dog when the sound of a footstep caused him to turn. He was not surprised to see the maiden who, since a certain winter night, had occupied a place in his thoughts never yet taken by another. An hour ago he would have been surprised. Now he was almost expecting to see her.

The face was a little more mature, a little less childlike, and the figure had grown taller—for the rest, she was the very maiden of that night. She looked at him for a moment. Then she advanced with outstretched hand.

"You are Jupe's master," she said.

CHAPTER XVIII

Eric was on his feet in a moment. His face lighted up as his hand advanced to meet the one outstretched, but before the tips of his fingers could come in contact with it, he drew back.

"Nay, I may not touch that hand," he said, with proud humility. "Kind lady, you know not to whom you speak. I am a convict."

The light had left his face. A deep red flush took its place. The face of the girl clouded in sympathy. For a minute she was silent. Then she smiled.

"My name is Agneta," she said. "And I do not think that Jupe's master can afford to refuse to be friendly with Jupe's mistress."

Then her eye fell on the dog, and the expression of her countenance changed.

"He is hurt!" she cried, in a distressed tone.

She was kneeling in Eric's place almost before the words were out of her mouth. The pathetic eyes of the animal moved from one to the other with equal affection.

"Who did it?" asked Agneta.

"A skulking Indian," replied the young man bitterly.

She looked at him in astonishment.

"But the Indians have ever been friendly," she said. "Why should they hurt poor Jupe?"

"I know not," answered Eric. "The dog showed much excitement. He ran into the forest. Then I heard the twang of a bow, and was in time to discharge my gun after the retreating figure."

"It is strange," said Agneta, and added: "The blood is staunching. I will fetch a bandage. Then can we better keep this in place."

He watched her as she went, and wondered whether his eyes were playing him false. The three years that had passed seemed wiped out, and all was as on that winter night, except that he himself was no longer a fugitive. A fugitive? Nay; but he was a convict, and as he stood awaiting the girl's return, the bitterness of the fact came upon him afresh. A convict in the presence of the maiden who for three years had occupied a large part of his thoughts! Hundreds of times he had dreamt of meeting her, but always in his thought he was free, with the past wiped out, and the hope of an honorable future before him. His dream was realized. He had met her again, but he was a convict still. That one difference robbed the realization of its gladness.

She returned quickly, and dropped upon the ground by the side of the dog. Two pairs of hands busied themselves about the bandage. Jupe took their ministrations with the utmost gratitude and love. Eric did not need to ask how his old friend had been treated. The dog's affection for the girl told its own story.

He tried to thank her, but his words sounded cold.

He could not forget the barrier between himself and her, and he feared to overstep the bounds that pride or humility set about him. His heart was not cold. It was burning and thumping, and sending the hot blood to his face every time the girl's fingers touched his. This girl, half child, half woman, had so long occupied her own distinctive place in his life, that he could not meet her as he would have met any other.

"There, that is the best we can do for him," said Agneta, lovingly stroking the dog's head, but looking up into the young man's face. "Now you will have to come with him to the house, for I am sure he will not leave you."

"For you I think he would," said Eric, smiling.

"I am not going to try my influence against yours," she said. "I am not fond of being worsted."

She stood up and waited for him to move.

"If we go to the house together," she said, "Jupe will be spared the pain of deciding between us."

Her words were a command. Eric obeyed it.

"Did you come on purpose to see Jupe?" she asked, as they walked towards the house.

"Nay," he said, "I knew not but that the dog and his kind mistress were in the old land."

"Then your coming was by accident," she said. "Truly I am glad of the happening."

"It is good of you to say so," he replied, "but—" and his glance at her was doubtful—"the lady, your mother, may be less willing to welcome one who is yet a convict."

She turned her face fully towards him. He was struck by the sadness upon it.

"My mother is dead," she said, "else would she undeceive you more quickly than I can do."

"Forgive me. I thought not of that," he cried, and now his hand was held out eagerly. "I am a selfish boor, thinking only of my own pain."

She smiled, but there were tears in her eyes.

"My mother heard your story," she said, "and she thought as I did that your judgment of yourself was over harsh. I would she were here to welcome you, yet will grandfather Axel not fail to extend to you the fullest hospitality."

"Nay, I will but put poor Jupe under your kind care again, and depart," said Eric hastily.

He had forgotten hunger and weariness in the excitement of the meeting—forgotten also his intention of seeking shelter at this house. Now, as the thought returned to him, he shrank from it. In any other dwelling he would be known only as one in the service of the Governor of New Sweden, to the inhabitants of this house he must appear in his true character. To take that place in the presence of the maiden at his side was harder than to go away hungry.

"In that case you can be neither hungry nor tired, and you cannot have traveled far," said Agneta.

She was looking at him questioningly. With those clear eyes upon him he could not but speak the truth.

I would journey a little further before I rest," he said.

"That you may sojourn under another roof than ours?" she replied. "Verily you must think ill of us. Grandfather Axel," she added, raising her voice, "here is an unwilling guest, who is, I think, both hungry and tired, but who has such grave doubts of our hospitality that he would seek further for rest and food."

Eric looked up and saw an old man approaching.

"He who comes in friendliness need look no further for either the rest or the food," said Axel. "We can afford him both. Whom have we here, my bairn?"

"Jupe's master," said the maiden, with a bright smile.

"He is welcome," replied Axel.

"Nay, sir, speak not too hastily, lest you repent of your words," said Eric quickly. "Know you that you welcome a convict?"

The old man looked at him gravely and deliberately. The hot blood surged over Eric's face.

"Do I welcome an honest man," he asked, "one who, but for his country's decision in one particular, would be a useful citizen of this land to-day?"

"You welcome one whose aim is to be such though he *is* a convict," said Eric.

"Come in, friend," rejoined Axel. "I ask not for better guest."

The plight of the dog had not escaped the old

man's eye, and when he had assured the stranger of welcome he turned to Jupe.

"What has befallen the dog," he asked.

"He was shot by an Indian," said Eric. "Sir, I would not alarm you needlessly, yet methinks that all the red men around here are not friends. The scowl on yonder sneak's face savored of anything but friendliness."

Axel Bonde looked grave.

"I know not of a single Indian who has cause for complaint against me," he said. "Could his arrow have been intended for yourself?"

"Scarcely," replied the young man, "since I spoke not to human being, red or white, during all the tramp of the day."

Within the dwelling Eric found no lack of hospitality. The housewife herself was gracious to him, and her daughter Maria, a well grown girl of seventeen, was not behind her mother in friendliness. Bacon of the worthy Katarina's own curing, and cheese of her making, were soon set before him, but it surely took less of the good woman's store to satisfy Eric's hunger than it would have taken of the provisions of any other housekeeper. The thoughts of the young man were employed less with that which passed his lips than with the maiden who had looked at him so kindly as she urged him to accept the hospitality of the farm-house.

"And you are engaged on a mission for Governor Printz himself?"

The speaker was Olof, the son of Axel Bonde,

and he sat by his own fireside when the evening meal was over.

"Aye," said Eric, "I am commissioned to rove, and to bring back to his Honor specimens of rock and timber, of nuts that may afford oil, and of aught else that could be turned to good account."

"Well, well, I'm glad you wandered as far as here," returned the good man heartily. "You might be in a worse place."

He was surely in little danger of contradiction from his guest. It may have been because there was for him a central spot to the scene, but certain it was that to Eric Helm that big living room looked a place that might hold its own by the side of many a stately apartment. The month was October, and a fire had been lighted on the hearth. When darkness fell without, it was bidden to stay without, for long lath-like strips of pitch-pine were lighted, and lights and shadows played picturesquely about the great room. The broken spruce twigs that carpeted the floor looked thick and soft in the shadows, and the long wooden sofas sent back an appreciative reflection. The flame lit up the forms of the two serving maids who walked back and forth at their wheels, and fell on the big loom on the opposite side of the room.

At closer range it busied itself with the faces and forms of those who sat immediately round the hearth, bringing into view the broad smile of Olof, the son of Axel, and the keen glances of Katarina his wife. It fell on the buxom Maria, and Eric noticed that the face of the girl was pleasant to look upon, and it played about the fair hair of the little Kolina and her brother Ian. Then it went glancing across to the further side of the hearth, and touched softly the cheek of the maiden who looked strangely out of place and yet at home in the family group. She sat by Axel Bonde, her fingers industriously spinning the flax that had grown on the farm lands without. She did not often raise her eyes, else would those of Eric have been less free to stray that way.

"So the Governor is looking for treasure in the land, is he?" asked Olof.

"Yes. Such are his directions from Sweden," said Eric. "He would learn what trees grow in the forest, and how far they can be of use to send to the old land. And in the earth itself also he would seek for stores of wealth. Minerals plentiful enough to be worth the working are, he thinks, to be found here. Therefore has he sent me forth, that I may go through New Sweden, and report to him my discoveries."

"Governor Printz is no fool," said the peasant appreciatively. "He desires to be ahead of the Dutch Director. Truly he had need bestir himself, for Director Stuyvesant is awake, of that I'll swear, else would he not have built his new fort at this end of the river. Whether it be minerals or trees he is in need of, Governor Printz would do well to make the best of his time in getting them."

"I must be here not far from this same Dutch

fort," said Eric. "I expected to come across it ere this."

"Far?" laughed Olof. "Young man, if you pass yon knot of trees, 'twill be in full sight of your eyes, though it lies somewhat lower down the river. Director-General Stuyvesant came not to New Sweden for nothing. He chose a right fair spot on which to place his fort. Aye, and they tell me it goes hard with John Printz to see it in these parts."

"Yes, he likes it not," said Eric, watching the glint of the fire on a fair head across the hearth.

If he had lifted his eyes, he might perchance have seen that which would have changed the current of his thoughts.

The chimney was large, though not as wide above as a good Dutch chimney of that period, for it tapered off as it rose. It was wide enough, however, to let a pair of small vindictive eyes peer down. The light of the fire was reflected in them, and if Eric, who sat on the innermost seat of the hearth, had looked straight up, he might surely have seen the gleam in those black eyes at the top. He had no time to look up, however. He was watching the play of the firelight on a maiden's hair.

The figure to which the eyes belonged had crept very noiselessly to its post of observation on the roof. Had Jupe been outside the house, instead of resting behind his master, the noiselessness would have availed the Indian less.

"White man shoot into the brush—Indian shoot into the chimney!"

That was what the young brave was saying to himself, as he softly drew an arrow from his quiver, and fitted it to the bow. The black eyes gleamed savagely. The blaze below was dying down. The Indian lad leant further over the chimney, and his fingers drew the string.

Was the hand less cautious, or did the last flash of light before the flame went out show the dog the gleaming eyes above? He was on his feet, bristling, and growling in the direction of the fire, his head uplifted, and his whole attitude one of rage.

"What is it, Jupe?"

Strange that no thought of danger came to the young man as he stepped within the hearth, full in range of that arrow ready to start on its deadly mission.

Twang went the bow-string, and ping! came an arrow against some hard substance.

Then the eyes of the Indian peered into total darkness, and he rubbed them in astonishment and fear. Had the manitou of the white man interfered in his behalf, or was there a devil in the arrow, that had made it bring death and darkness to the whole household of the white man? When the arrow left the bow the young man was fairly beneath it. Now he had disappeared, and the fire itself had gone. What strange and terrible thing had occurred?

Nothing, except that the housewife had taken advantage of the general move to sharply pull the string that hung above the mantel shelf. It sent into its place an iron slide, made to close the chimney when the smoke had all left the wood upon the hearth. The slide fitted across the tunnel and shut in the heat, making the room warmer. It was for this that the chimney, built after the Swedish fashion of the day, narrowed above the mantel shelf. The sharp ping of the arrow sounded at the moment when it struck the hard iron, and rebounded, to fall back upon the slide, and rest, a harmless thing, beyond the reach of its owner or the possibility of doing harm to its intended victim.

"What ails the dog?" said Olof. "His wound has made him savage."

Agneta was already by his side, trying to soothe him, but Axel Bonde rose and quietly left the hearth.

On the roof the Indian shook with fright, and lay crouching, fearing as much to depart as to remain. Then his ear caught the sound of voices, and his terror decreased. The darkness, however, remained. In all his experience he had never known fire to disappear so suddenly, and that without apparent cause. He grew desirous of leaving the dwelling of the white men, and seeking the companionship of men of his own race. He listened long, and then cautiously made his way from the roof, experiencing a sensation of relief when he felt the solid earth beneath his feet again.

As he emerged from the shadow of the building a figure approached him, and the voice of Axel Bonde said:

"Friend, if you seek shelter or food fear not to ask them at my house, but if you seek evil, remember that Axel Bonde and his household are the friends of their Indian brothers, and that the red men deal not treacherously with their friends."

Then he turned and went back to the dwelling, and the young Indian disappeared in the darkness.

CHAPTER XIX

The Director-General of New Netherland had come and gone, leaving behind him two lasting memorials, a fort on the South River a short distance below the farm of Axel Bonde, and a constantly uprising fountain of wrath in the heart of John Printz.

Pieter Stuyvesant had had more than one interview with the Swedish Governor, and if he had not succeeded in convincing him that the Dutch had a prior claim to the South River, he had very surely convinced him that he himself laid present claim to much territory there, and that he had no intention of relinquishing that claim. Worse still, he had held a conference with the Indians in his own Fort Nassau. When John Printz heard of that conference, Printz Hall trembled.

"His aim is to sweep the land from under our feet," he shouted. "What mean those lying turncoats, the Indians, that they thus go over to the enemy? Think they John Printz will stand this? I will appeal to the home government. I will double my force of men. I will show Pieter Stuyvesant where he is. Give in to the claims of a one legged Dutch thief? Not while my name is John Printz."

There was possibly more than ordinary excuse for the ruffling of the Governor's temper. Pieter

Stuyvesant found the Indians disposed to be both friendly and communicative. Not only did they declare that the Swedes had usurped all the land they claimed, except the neighborhood of Fort Christina itself, but they then and there confirmed to the Chief Sachem of the Manhattans, as a perpetual inheritance of the West India Company, the whole territory south of the Swedish Fort Christina, as far down as Boomtjes or Bombay Hook.

Another large tract of country on the eastern side of the river was also during his visit presented to Stuyvesant, and the land around the Schuylkill had already been ceded to the Dutch. The Great Sachem of the Manhattans had on the whole good reason to be satisfied with his friends the Indians of the South River.

His conference with the red men satisfactorily concluded, Stuyvesant repaired in state to Tenacong, and Printz Hall witnessed the spectacle of two rival claimants to the region of the South River sheltered under one roof, in much secret wrath and outward friendliness discussing the vexed question of rights founded on discovery and earliest colonization, against rights established by actual and continued habitation. There was much diplomatic profession of friendship, and promise of abstaining from all hostility, and acting as friends and allies, together with much inward determination on the part of each Governor to further the interests of his own country, and see that his rival in no way gained an advantage over him.

With a remembrance of the superior resources of the Director-General, did he choose to draw upon New Netherland for soldiers, John Printz for the time controlled his anger, but he was very wary about giving the exact boundaries of the territory claimed by the Swedes. "The Swedish limits were wide and broad enough," he declared loftily, and referred the Director to Stockholm for documentary proof of his words.

Then followed a step which proved Pieter Stuyvesant to be a man of action. Fort Nassau, having been shewn unequal to the task of protecting Dutch interests on the South River, by reason of being too far up the same, was by the Director-General condemned to destruction, and in its stead a new fort was begun.

It might have been a desire for friendly intercourse that prompted the Governor of New Netherland to choose the particular location he selected for the new fort. It was but four miles from the oldest of the Swedish strongholds, Fort Christina, on the Minquas' Kill. On the west side of the river, at Sand Hook, near the present site of Newcastle, the walls of Fort Casimir rose. Dutch and Swedes were here, in very truth, near enough for that "neighborly friendship and correspondence" mutually agreed upon by the Governors. It was possible, however, that Governor Stuyvesant was more particularly influenced by the fact that Fort Casimir, being below both Tenacong and Fort Christina, would be far enough down the river to exert a controlling influence over the trade of the same, and near enough to Fort Christina to be a constant reminder to the Swedes that New Netherland claimed a share in the South River.

Against the building of that stronghold the soul of John Printz rebelled, and the tongue of John Printz protested. But with Pieter Stuyvesant yet in the land, and no instructions from the Swedish government, the wisdom of John Printz counselled caution. Therefore Fort Casimir became an established fact, and John Printz, if he did not altogether hold his peace, at least refrained from disturbing the peace of the land.

But when Pieter Stuyvesant had taken formal leave of the Governor of New Sweden, and the territory of the South River, John Printz shut himself in his chamber, and refused to see even his daughter. The ship that carried home the Director of New Netherland was well out on the open sea before he emerged from his seclusion, and when he did appear Printz Hall shook beneath the footstep of the man who, for more than eight years, had held uninterrupted sway in New Sweden. He swore at the servants who waited on him, and the soldiers who came at his bidding. He swore at those who approached him, and those who kept far from him. The deep angry voice of the Governor of New Sweden filled Printz Hall, and those who escaped his wrath for the moment thanked the fates and wondered how long it would be before their turn came.

"Where is Eric Helm?" demanded the Governor

angrily, one day remembering that it was long since he saw the young engineer.

Unlucky was the attendant who reminded him that it was the Governor himself who had given the young man work at a distance from Tenacong. He swore at the informant, and turned his back on him and his news. Thereupon it was deemed expedient to summon Eric Helm.

"Your Honor wishes to see me," said the young man, entering the Governor's presence unannounced.

"How do you know that?" growled John Printz. "You've not been here to ask."

"Your Excellency desired—" began Eric, but the Governor cut him short.

"Little matters it what I desire, with such a set of fools to do my bidding," he said.

Eric was silent.

"Well, what are you waiting for?" demanded the Governor, with an oath.

"For your Excellency's instructions," said Eric.

"Instructions!" shouted the Governor. "Verily, it's a set of idiots I rule over. Is there never a man among you that knows how to make himself useful without being set about it by me? You're fools, all of you. The world's full of fools, as well in Sweedland as here. Don't the Queen's ministers know that New Sweden is worth saving? Why don't they send me men, plenty of them, that I may level that rascally Director's fort, and shew those turncoat Indians which Governor it will pay them best to be friendly with. What are you standing staring there for?" he demanded suddenly.

An answer not being ready on Eric's tongue, the Governor found his own tongue equal to the emergency.

"Get out of here, and do your part," he ordered peremptorily. "The excellent resources of this land must be demonstrated to those at home. Go you and explore the country, and see you don't spare yourself."

Then, as Eric yet waited for further instructions, he added vehemently:

"Off with you, and that at once. Look out for minerals, and especially for the precious metals. And where there are trees, the wood of which would be useful in Sweden, bring me specimens. Get you gone, and see that you bring such an account of the land as shall convince Her Majesty's Government that New Sweden will pay for the outlay of a few soldiers, and that John Printz is not a fool when he asks for aid. And, mind you, rake up the few wits you can boast of, that your errand be not in vain."

"In what direction shall I go, and how far?" asked Eric.

"In what direction? In every direction," roared John Printz, with a sudden access of rage. "How far? Go to the ends of the earth, and beneath it, for all I care."

And at that, Eric started on his investigations, and in the course of them found that for which he was not looking, even Axel Bonde and his charge, the maiden Agneta. That discovery altered the aspect of New Sweden for Eric Helm.

Very much unknown to himself the young engineer had also found a champion. Axel Bonde's granddaughter was loud in her praises.

"It was a downright sin to send him out here as a convict," she said. "The Governor ought to pardon him. I wonder how soon he'll come back again. I'm not so certain that he'll come at all. He did not say he would when grandfather asked him. He was looking at Agneta. She could have made him promise if she'd tried. Why didn't you, Agneta?"

The color rose to the girl's cheeks.

"I think he will come again to see Jupe," she said. "He knows that we shall be glad to see him."

"I'd have been able to do more than think, if I'd been in your place," said Maria. "Truly I think sometimes you have little sense. You are only two years younger than I am, and *I* should have seen that he was waiting for me to ask him."

The flush on Agneta's face deepened.

"You mistake, Maria," she said proudly. "Eric Helm understands that we shall deem his company a pleasure. I certainly assured him of my own wish that he should return."

"Assured him!" repeated Maria scornfully. "A little teasing until he promised would have gone further than all your assurances. He would have kept his word to *you*. I want to see him again, and so, I believe, do you, though you won't say so."

Maria's desire seemed at that moment little likely to be fulfilled. When Eric Helm's hand rested lingeringly on Jupe's head, as he bade the dog go back to his mistress, he meant the caress for a long farewell. He went away telling himself that his return should be indefinitely delayed. He had realized his dream, but the pleasure of seeing Agneta had been more than half pain.

Never, since the first days of his life as a convict, had he chafed so much against his peculiar position. He had become accustomed to his relations with John Printz, and with the daughter of the Governor. At Tenacong also the young engineer was known as a useful man, and if occasionally men made him feel that his foothold among them was uncertain, it was never the better class among the Swedes who were responsible for his annoyance.

Now the old pain of the convict's lot had returned, and with it the weary questioning of the justice or injustice of his fate. Aye, and the key by which he had opened for himself a way out of the endless round of accusation and excuse was gone. The memory of a pair of blue eyes, and of the sound of a soft young voice, could no longer bring relief, or give clearness to the dazed brain. Nay, it was the thought of those eyes that set his brain in a whirl, and raised new questions that went threading in and out among the others, and grew more and more intricate as he tried to free them.

He went out in the morning with a savage determination to let the Governor's business engross all his thoughts, and came in at night, weary in body and mind, to carry on a train of reasoning that the day through had been argued threadbare, and at night was as insistent as ever.

CHAPTER XX

"My son, what ails you? You have traveled far to-day, and you are weary, yet your feet go back and forth across your room as if you were in need of exercise. You have eaten nothing since morn, for so your own tongue testified, and you let a good roast duck stare you in the eyes in vain, and go hungry from the table. Is it sickness of mind or body that thus manifests itself, for of a truth I know that something is wrong with you?"

The stout Dutchwoman came boldly into her guest's room as she spoke, and pushed to the door. She belonged to the Dutch settlers that some years before the time of Governor Printz had put themselves under the protection of the Swedish government, and come to New Sweden to live. They owned no allegiance to New Netherland and the Dutch Director of the same, and even John Printz found no fault with their loyalty to New Sweden.

The business of the Governor had kept Eric Helm for some days in the vicinity of their settlement, and he had gone back and forth to the home of the kindly vrouw, who had not only made him at home in her house, but found for him a place in her heart.

"Look here, my lad," she said, "I'm a mother with two boys of my own laid under ground. I know when another mother's son is in trouble."

The young man stopped in his walk.

"You are perhaps fortunate," he said, and though the words were harsh, the tone was gentle.

She understood him.

"In having them beneath the ground?" she said. "Nay, boy, you are a poor judge of a mother's heart. And you know little more of your own," she added, quietly, "if you think you can ease its pain by making it bitter."

"It is bitter already," said Eric, with a half smile.

"Against whom?"

"Against itself."

She approached him, and laid her hand on his arm. "I've known you for ten days, my son," she said. "It is not over long, truly, yet dare I swear that heart holds no depth of sin. Of folly it may perhaps have a bitter memory. The young are not always wise."

The tenderness of the touch was fatal to the hardening process begun in Eric's heart. He did not shake off the hand that rested on his arm. Instead, he put his own on it.

"Mother," he said, "others judged differently, else should I not now be a convict, with a small fraction of my life in the brightness behind, and the better part of it in the darkness ahead."

She showed no surprise at his words.

"Aye, lad, I know your story, so far as the world can tell it," she said.

He withdrew his hand, and moved back from her, the hard look returning to his face.

"My character has come before me," he said. "I might perhaps have guessed it. 'Tis the kind of news that travels fast. I flattered myself—with how little cause I know now—that in this part of the land I might be regarded even as were other men."

"Nay, boy, flare not up so fast," said the vrouw good-humoredly. "The news did not travel. My man fetched it. He took a boat load of grain to be ground at the Governor's grand mill beyond Tenacong—for truly it grinds fine—and he stopped to see the sights at Printz Hall, and hear all that was to be heard. Aye, and he saw a young man whom the Governor found over and above useful, and heard men speak in his praise. He heard, too, that he was a convict. Verily he came home and told me that it was a thousand pities such a promising lad as you should not be free. 'Twas carrying news, of a certainty, yet if so be that the good man brings his gossip no further than to the ears of his woman, he's not to be blamed too hard as a tale-monger."

She looked into the darkened face with an honest smile, against which the soul of the young man could in no wise steel itself.

"Since the good man has told me a part, you had better tell me the rest of your trouble," she said. "'Twill make the burden none the heavier to share it."

And though he had not deemed himself in a mood to accept sympathy, it was not long before the kind-hearted vrouw had heard the young man's story from his own lips.

"Poor boy," she said. "Truly, there was excuse for saying the future looks black. But, lad, black clouds have a trick of breaking."

He shook his head.

"You think not? Well, to those who are beneath them they ever seem to be made of brass," she said. "Yet does the brass oftentimes turn out to be very thin mist, that floats away with amazing swiftness before a favorable breeze. But this child?" she added. "Have you seen her since?"

A deep flush came to the young man's face. The tone was significant.

"Yes," he replied. "She is at present in New Sweden."

"Ah! And she is—how old? Well-nigh a maiden grown?"

The flush grew deeper still.

"Truly I know not her age," he said. "She is— a maiden apart from all others."

"Yes. I understand," said the vrouw gently. "What next?"

What next? He hesitated. Then the words came in hot haste.

"I will go on my way and forget that there could ever have been a life for me," he said. "What right have I to mourn for it? 'Twas my own mad passion that robbed me of it."

"Nay, you will go on your way and work out of it a life stronger for the one act of weakness, and nobler for the one wrong," she said. "Lad, there's as much cowardice in abandoning hope as in abandoning any other friend."

He started, and looked into her eyes.

"Cowardice?" he said.

"Yes. It is easier to despair than to hope and fight against odds."

"I have no right to hope," he said. "I threw hope away from me that night."

"Then pick it up again," she replied. "You had no business to throw it away."

He was silent, but the dark look had gone from his face.

'My boy," she said, "there is neither merit nor sense in the needless giving up of good. Admit, if you will, that it is beyond your deserts. It might soon be, unless you're better than the rest of us. Yet is a man worse than a fool if he persuade himself that he takes only what he deserves, for verily then must he have little indeed, or he must be a conceited knave."

The smile on the young man's face was met by a motherly glance against which he would have found it hard to shut his heart.

"Go ahead, lad," she said. "Fight your way out from beneath the shadow of the past. And don't neglect friends because you think they are too good for you. That dog of yours deserves a visit from his master now and again."

As one of the results of the good vrouw's words a piece of land in the neighborhood of the Dutch settlement changed hands, and Eric Helm acquired a personal interest in the resources of the South River. He was not without funds. Governor Printz, while he was very glad himself to profit by the young man's services, saw no reason why the settlers should not pay for the same. Perhaps he did not himself remember that it was his daughter who first prompted him to put in the young man's way opportunities of earning money. The lady had not lost her interest in Eric Helm. He was a living proof of her sagacity.

It might possibly have been only fair to attribute also to the good vrouw's words the fact that Christmastide saw Eric again drawing near to Axel Bonde's house. He had been telling himself that he would rather stay away, but it was noticeable—though he did not notice it—that his feet moved faster as he neared the farm buildings.

CHAPTER XXI

"Well, what judge you now of your half-hearted invitation? Will he return after two full months, think you?"

Maria turned suddenly upon Agneta as the two girls were strewing the floor with Jul-halm, the long rye straw that after being dedicated to Christmas-tide would possess strange virtues that would warrant its preservation throughout the year, and its use in time of emergency.

"Of whom speak you?" asked Agneta, the tint upon her cheeks not as suggestive of tranquillity as her tone.

"Know you not?" demanded Maria, flashing a look at her.

"And wherefore should I know?" she said.

"She means Eric Helm," piped in the shrill voice of Kolina, who with her brother Ian was an officious assistant in the Christmas preparations. "Look what you're doing, Agneta," she interposed hastily. "There isn't half enough of the Jul-halm on your side of the floor. We've got plenty of it, and we shall want plenty to strew over the fields if they are unfruitful.'

"All right, little one, it shall be spread thickly," said Agneta, tossing the sweet smelling straw upon the floor, and ignoring the first of Kolina's remarks.

"Maria wants Eric Helm to come. Don't *you*, Agneta?" persisted the child.

"Surely I do—when he wishes it," said the girl.

"Um! He'd have wished it fast enough had you pressed him," grumbled Maria. "I always knew you'd missed an opportunity. Now, it's my belief we shall see him no more."

How far her prophecy was destined to be fulfilled was shewn that night by the appearance of the young man himself.

"You're just in time," cried Maria, beaming upon her visitor. "We are about to start for the cattle house to give the cows the Jul-night supper. You must come with us and help in the good work."

She extended her hand, and drew Eric along with her, chattering with such merriment as she went that he had no time so much as to glance backwards to where Agneta followed with the small Kolina.

"Softly now!" commanded the girl, as the door was thrown open and the party trooped in. "Mark well the position of the cattle, that we may know what kind of harvest to expect next year. Ah, see!" she cried, in seeming distress. "Some of them stand. Then will there be crops that shall be scanty."

"Nay, but those that stand are few. There are more that lie peacefully down," said Eric, making the survey an excuse for bringing himself into a position to watch Agneta.

"Aye, the promise on the whole is good," declared Maria. "Now for the fun."

It consisted in the Christmas Eve visit to each stall, to give the cattle the best forage the farm afforded. At every stoppage the little Kolina tripped up to the waiting animal, uttering in childish voice the usual greeting, "This is Christmas Eve, my little one."

The ceremony seemed strangely pleasant to Eric after the years of loneliness. The big cattle house, with its wondering-eyed inmates, the youthful figures going back and forth, the young pines that had been set up around the house in honor of the season, even the sound of the wind among the trees of the forest, gave him a feeling of Christmastide gladness, a sensation of being welcomed and shut in from the great outside world. Perhaps it was the occasional glance of a pair of soft blue eyes that made the cattle house feel more homelike than the good Dutch vrouw's hospitable kitchen. That was open to him to-night, yet it was the vrouw herself who had said: "The dog Jupe must surely look for his master on such a day. Methinks I have heard that the Swedes make even the watch dogs happy by greater freedom on Christmas Eve."

The horses having been visited and fed, and the chickens given their Jul-grot, or Christmas stirabout of wheaten flour and milk, the party returned to the house, where everything was as bright as recent scrubbing could make it. The Jul fire burned grandly, and the Jul candles were being lighted to replace the usual pine laths as illuminators. The big four-branched candle was Kolina's special pride. She hovered round it till Maria challenged her and Agneta to the game of making small wisps of the Jul-halm, which each as she made threw up towards the rafters as a mode of divining, by the number that lodged there, how many lovers would fall to her share during the Christmas festivities.

"Here goes my first," cried Maria, and sent a little bunch of straw careering up into the air, to fall back at her feet amidst a shout of laughter from Ian and Kolina, joined in by good Olof himself.

"You're out of luck, my girl," he said. "Let Agneta try."

But when the maiden's first wisp alighted upon the rafters and remained there a cloud came to Maria's face.

" 'Tis but one trial," she said, and threw wisp after wisp upward, to find as many back again upon the floor.

"It is a stupid game. I will play it no more," she cried, and noticed not that a gleam of mirth was in the visitor's eye.

The supper table that night was bright with many an article of silver not usually found upon a peasant's table. The light of the Jul fire played on porringer and tankard and cup and bowl of the precious metal, for it was deemed lucky to let the Christmas firelight shine upon all the silver articles in the house. For this reason also more than one silver coin lay upon the table, that after the Jul light had played upon it, it might be fruitful and increase.

"Isn't the table bright?" whispered Kolina to the guest. "More than half the silver bowls are Agneta's. Her mother brought them from the old castle where Agneta used to live."

It was not imagination that made Maria believe Eric's face to be graver, and the laughter in his eye less conspicuous after that whispered confidence on the part of the small Kolina. There was no reason for the access of gravity, except that there had come to him a sense of the exceeding height of barriers raised by circumstance and position.

There was no barrier against mirth and gladness that night. The maiden, Agneta, was very gracious to the visitor, and very gay and winsome to all the rest, and the good housewife looked upon the radiant face of her daughter Maria, and was hospitable.

The table, too, was loaded with good cheer, among which the pig's head occupied a conspicuous place. A great pile of Jul bröd, large and thick circular loaves made of rye flour and baked especially for Christmas, occupied one corner. Its mission was not to feed the hungry—at least on this occasion—but to gain efficacy by association, and later on, when dried and pulverized, to be given to the men and animals on the farm. The horses and oxen that drew the plough would in the springtime receive a portion of the Jul bröd to protect them from disease and enable them to keep together when pastured in wild open land; and the serving men who tilled the ground would be bidden to partake of it that they might agree well with one another. For the rest, it had many virtues, for which some hid it away all the year, to produce it in certain cases of sickness.

Maria was determined that every fitting ceremony should that night be observed, and from the singing of the psalm after the evening meal, through all the performances of Jul night, she was scrupulous to omit no detail. She herself took the lead, and the festivities lost nothing in merriment by reason of the laughing face of the leader.

She made Eric carry the ale for her when they went to give the horses a draught of strong drink that should render them mettlesome for the journey to church the following morning, and she showed him the best place on the barn floor to deposit the Christmas stir-about and the tobacco that were dedicated to the Tomte Gubbe, the little old man of the household, that good, genial elf who was supposed to aid the Swedish farmer in the details of his farm work, and to be especially interested in the welfare of his animals.

She flashed the light of the lantern on the small pines, denuded of their bark and lower limbs, that had been set up around the house, and wished for snow to make them look like Jul time, and she took care that the tankard of Angels' ale put upon the banqueting table before the family retired to rest should be filled to the brim. Celestial visitors should be well treated if they came hither that night, and terrestrial ones certainly found no reason to complain.

Maria carried all before her in house and barn,

until the moment when she proposed a certain dance that was a Christmas amusement in some parts of Sweden.

"I know not the dance," said Eric, "yet if you will instruct me in its measures, I may, perchance, not be too stupid to learn."

"Oh, it is easy enough," laughed Maria.

"Do you also know it well?" asked Eric, turning to Agneta.

"Nay, except by seeing others dance it," she said. "To-night also I will content myself with watching Maria."

The latter turned upon her sharply.

"That will you not," she said. "What whim is this?"

"I know why she won't dance," said Kolina. "He'd have to make love in the dance to either you or her, and Agneta don't like it. She wouldn't dance that way last Christmas. She said she wasn't a little girl now."

The bright color rushed to Agneta's cheeks. Maria laughed contemptuously. From his seat in the chimney corner Axel Bonde saw the flush and noted the laugh. He rose, and came over to the group.

"Dance any way you will, my girl," he said to Maria, "yet be not slow to accord to others the privilege you yourself enjoy. If my bairn desires to rest, tease her not to dance for your pleasure."

He stretched out his hand to draw Agneta to him, but as he did so his sleeve caught against a candlestick and overturned it.

"Ah!"

The exclamation was almost a cry of horror. A Christmas candle had been extinguished, and one and all stood for a moment in silent dismay after that first outcry.

"There'll be death enter the house before this year is over," said Katarina solemnly, and the face of Olof looked disturbed.

"Nay," said Axel, "but if death is to come, it will come none the less though every candle burn until morning."

He relit the candle, and went back to his seat, but there was no more dancing, and except that Maria insisted on trying one other method of forecasting the future, there were no more games.

It was a simple process, nothing more than the pouring of a little molten lead into a bucket of water. Each girl had her bucket—even Kolina claiming one. Then the buckets were set aside to prepare their message during the night's stillness.

This done, the Jul fire was replenished, and the Jul candles examined, that none might go out before morning, for that night the Swedish home must know no darkness.

In the morning, before the drive to church, the buckets were visited, and the lead that had formed into various shapes carefully examined.

"Come and read my future for me," said Maria to Eric, and he bent obediently over the water, and endeavored to find a good omen there. But try as he would he could see no suggestion of bridal coronet, or other pleasant promise, and he declared that the future must hold untold good for Maria.

"I wish it would reveal some of the good then," said the girl, pouting. "Now see what Agneta's says."

"I know! I know!" cried Kolina. "That's a castle. Look there!"

"Yes, and there's a coronet over it. It's her bridal coronet, and the owner of the castle will put it on her head," said Maria maliciously, casting a quick glance at Eric as she spoke.

"You are foolish," said Agneta, and she turned away. "It is time to go to church," she added. "Look, there is grandfather Axel, and I see the big torch already alight."

On that drive in the early morning, long before the sun was up, Eric found himself placed by Maria's side, and as they passed through the crisp air it somehow befell that in a low voice the girl told him the story of the castle and the expectations of the castle's owner. For many a day after, that story was associated in Eric's mind with the flashing of an immense torch on tree and water as they drove past forest and swamp.

That Christmas day was not a success for Eric Helm, or, in an unqualified sense, for Maria. Yet the girl persuaded the young man to return on the last night of the year, and he promised, though, when the words were spoken, he asked himself why he had uttered them.

CHAPTER XXII

There was a new moon waiting to see the old year depart. That was why Maria stood outside the house when the hour drew towards midnight. It was cold and lonely there, and all the rest of the household were asleep. That is to say, Maria inferred they were asleep, since they had all gone to bed, Eric in the guest chamber at the further end of the house.

The girl carried a psalm book in her hand, and a silver coin in her mouth, from which it is to be inferred that she had not come hither to do much talking. The hand that was not holding the book grasped a piece of bread.

Thus equipped Maria stole noiselessly from the door. To let the leaves of the psalm book fall apart where they would, while she herself looked up to the young moon, was her intention, and she was profoundly interested in the carrying out of the same, for from the psalm at which the book opened she could draw an inference of what lay in the future.

But just at the critical moment, when the pages of the book rustled apart, and the girl's eyes should have gone up towards the moon, they were very distinctly bent on the earth, for a sound for which she could not account sent them searching backwards and forwards across the faintly lighted spaces.

It was perhaps well that the silver coin was in her mouth, since it made necessary the suppression of the cry that rose to her lips and would have passed them had it been allowed.

From out of the shadow of the house Maria saw a tall figure emerge. That straight form, only half revealed by the uncertain light of the moon, set the girl's heart thumping.

Had *he*, too, come out to question the future? A thrill of triumph shot through her. Surely the impression she had made was deeper than she imagined. She had not thought that Eric Helm would thus seek to tempt fate.

Ah, but was that tall figure the form of Eric Helm? It was straight enough for the young engineer, but as the moonlight fell upon dress and features, Maria gave a gasp of fear and repulsion, for the face that revealed itself was the face of an Indian.

The girl's momentary exultation vanished. She was disappointed. She was also a little afraid. What was the Indian doing here, and why had he not sought to enter the house?

She had come so softly round the end of the building that he had not heard her. He was not watching for her, though his attitude surely betokened that he was watching. He stood with head erect, and body rigid, waiting for something. A flutter of expectancy passed over Maria, though she knew not what she expected. Certainly not the sound of voices, that rose for a moment in mingled tones, and then ceased. She looked towards the Indian. The rigidity was gone. He stood alert, ready.

Maria turned from him and strained her ears to catch again the sounds that had startled her. It was long before she succeeded, and when the murmur came afresh, and her eyes sought her fellow-watcher, he was gone. Somewhere in the shadows she believed he must lurk yet, but where? And what was his object in waiting there at all?

She peered into the darkness to discover that tall, straight form. It was near to her, she was sure, but she could not discern it. An unreasonable fear took possession of her, a feeling that the darkness was alive with danger.

Hark! Was that a sound? She leaned forward and tried to make her eyes pierce the shadow thrown by the house. The noise appeared to come from beneath the windows of the guest chamber, further along the wall. The thought of the guest chamber suggested another. Was harm to the young engineer intended?

Nonsense! Why should it be?

There would be something tangible to be discovered before long, for now the girl heard distinctly the voices that twice before had for a moment disturbed the stillness of the night. She had but to wait a minute more to use eyes as well as ears. The figures to which the voices belonged were approaching. There were half a dozen of them, and as they came out into the moonlight she saw that they were all Indians.

Then, in place of the intangible fears a definite terror took possession of the girl, for her ears told her that the first words that were spoken came in the tones of a drunken savage. She knew the signs well, and she wished herself safe in the house.

"Yonder sleeps the white man that shoots at his Indian brothers," said the thick, unsteady voice, and an arm was outstretched towards the window of the room where Eric Helm lay.

But while the words were yet in the speaker's mouth, there rose, as if out of the earth, a tall, straight form, that stood for a moment before the window of the guest chamber, and then slowly and calmly advanced.

"And yonder are the hotheads who would draw down upon our people the anger of the Great Sachem," said a low, deep voice.

For a moment the young braves recoiled—for that they were young Maria had already discovered. Then, as they recognized the speaker, anger took the place of fear.

"Why do you meddle with what concerns you not?" demanded the leader, lifting up in the moonlight eyes that once peered down into the farmhouse kitchen through the dark tunnel of the kitchen chimney, and saw the family group about the hearth.

"All that concerns the little squaw concerns Amattehoorn," said the older Indian, and with a start of surprise and relief Maria recognized the name of the husband of the old squaw whom Agneta had saved from the flood.

"Who cares for the little squaw?" contemptuously interrogated the young brave.

"The Big Sachem does," said the warrior, calmly. "His anger will be hot if harm come to his children, and the anger of the Big Sachem reaches far."

"The Big Sachem is in Printz Hall. His eyes see not this part of the land," said the young brave.

"Then Amattehoorn will be eyes for him," replied the warrior. "Amattehoorn will see no harm come to the little white squaw, or anybody in her house. The white men and the red men are brothers, and the white Sachem is the friend of our people."

The scowl on the face of the young brave deepened.

"There is more than one white Sachem," he muttered. "The Dutch Sachem loves not his big brother over much. The enemy of his enemy is to the Dutch Sachem a friend."

"The Big Sachem is here, and the Dutch Sachem yonder," said the old warrior significantly.

The argument waxed hot, though the voices were subdued. Through it all Maria stood in the deep shadow, and listened and trembled. That Amattehoorn had come to the house because he feared that the turbulent excitement of the young braves would lead to some act of violence she now partly understood, and she did not breathe freely until she saw the band of young Indians turn away, and go staggering off in the direction of the forest. As for Amattehoorn, he did not leave the neighborhood of the farmhouse, but withdrawing to a distance continued his self-imposed task. To Maria's sight he was as fully lost as he had been before the braves appeared.

When all were gone the girl crept back into the house. She had forgotten the purpose for which she left it, and her hand shook as she laid down the psalm book unexamined.

"Always Agneta," she murmured, as the words of the old Indian came back to her. Red men and white were strangely alike in some repects.

She fell to wondering how the engineer had offended the young brave, and then her thoughts went further, and freed themselves from the disturbing influences of the night. It was then that she remembered the psalm book, and lifted it to see what message it brought. When she had done so her eyes grew wide with horror.

"Surely it is a death psalm," she said.

She held the book in her hand, her eyes riveted on the words.

"I thought it would have been a bridal psalm," she said, "and that it would prove an omen for me. Verily it is time. I am seventeen now, nearly two years older than Agneta, and yet she——"

She broke off.

"I wonder who is going to die this year," she added, with a shudder.

CHAPTER XXIII

Madam Pappegoya, the daughter of Governor Printz, was apparently looking at her flowers. She stood by a window in Printz Hall, her eyes fixed on the beds where gay blossoms appealed confidently to her for notice. Madam Pappegoya was fond of flowers. She was also proud of her garden. But to-day the garden might have been the property of another, so completely had it lost its power to interest her. The face of the Governor's daughter was disturbed. And it took more than a little to disturb the lady of Printz Hall.

" 'Twill be a terrible pity," she said aloud. "Patience were surely better until——"

She broke off suddenly. The heavy footsteps of the Governor could be heard approaching.

He came into the room, and crossed over and stood behind her, his eyes gazing out of the window with a blank, unseeing stare. He did not swear. He stood long without movement. The bold, blustering energy of the Governor of New Sweden was in abeyance.

His daughter studiously refrained from turning her head. Perhaps she was not quite willing to look into the face of the man who had ruled New Sweden with a hand as strong as his own strong will, and read there defeat. For the success of

John Printz had been the success of his daughter, and his failure was hers. She had ever enjoyed his fullest confidence, nay, she had, far more often than he knew, been the instigator of his acts.

"They'll not get a Governor that will do for them what I have done," he said at last, and he said it slowly and bitterly.

His daughter made no answer.

"What was the land when I came?" he asked, after another long silence.

"What it will be when you are gone," replied the lady, turning suddenly. " 'Twill be a sorry day for New Sweden when you are foolish enough to let a little discontent on the part of the people, and a vast amount of insolence on the part of the Hollanders, drive you to the abandonment of the country."

She was looking at him now, her eyes darting out flashes of light.

" 'Tis not they who will drive me," he said. "I'm weary of waiting."

"Weary!" repeated the lady, scornfully. "And who in all New Sweden is not weary? Yet will one and all have to wait."

"I'll wait no longer," said the Governor.

"Nay," rejoined his daughter, "surely it seemeth to me that you speak truly. It takes a wise man to win success by the hard method of waiting for it."

The Governor frowned, but he neither swore nor shouted. Defeat had come very near to John

Printz, and for the time being his feelings could find no relief by the usual outlets.

He stood with his eyes fixed on the things beyond the window—the gardens he had planted, and the grounds he had laid out. He had thought to make Printz Hall a permanent abiding place, and the name of John Printz a power in the western land. To-day he found himself the ruler of a discontented people, in a country where the Hollanders had encroached on his most carefully guarded privileges, and the fort of the Hollanders stared him in the face whenever he journeyed down the South River.

He had appealed to Sweden for troops, but they had not come. His garrisons had grown small, and he could not reinforce them. His most eloquent protests against delay, and assurances that the colony was worth the expenditure, failed to bring him the desired help from home. He was in sore need of supplies, but month after month slipped by and none came.

The Indians, too, aforetime his friends, could not easily be convinced of the advisability of remaining faithful to a Governor who was able to make them but few presents, and who had not much to sell when they brought him their stores of furs. Better be the brothers of the Hollanders, whose ships came often up the river.

The Governor of New Sweden had not the comfort of knowing that the people over whom he ruled were altogether in sympathy with him in his difficulties. The hand of John Printz had been strong, too strong to secure the abiding loyalty of the settlers in New Sweden. It pressed a little heavily at times. The good Swedes of the South River would possibly have loved it better if they had felt it less. That they did not all love it, nay, that some of them had complained against it, made the heart of John Printz bitter.

He had waited long, hoping for better days. They were still delayed, and the patience of the Governor of New Sweden was exhausted. Therefore, he proposed to return to the home land, and give up a struggle in which active support was denied him.

That his daughter's judgment did not tally with his was very evident to-day. The lady of Printz Hall had no desire to give up her position as first lady in the land, and return to Sweden, the daughter of an unsuccessful Governor. Time had wrought disastrous changes, why should not Time yet undo his work, and turn the scales in favor of John Printz? Madam Pappegoya was inclined at least to give time a chance to show a favorable disposition towards her.

" 'Tis in the power of none to hinder the Governor of New Sweden from making a fool of himself in the eyes of his countrymen, if he so desire," she said, after a long silence. "Of a truth, I think it lieth almost beyond his own power. Pieter Stuyvesant has surely accomplished his desire, since he has sent away in hot haste the ruler of New Sweden."

At the name of his rival the face of the Governor flushed. An oath loud enough to be heard from one end of Printz Hall to the other burst from his lips, and he turned away in a rage.

"What mean you by such words?" he cried. "Do you think I am afraid of that one-legged Director, and his fools of Dutchmen that come traipsing after him as if he were a king at the very least? Surely I have shown them more than once of what kind is my fear. But I will not sit down and be made a fool of in my turn by those at home. If they will not support me, they shall have the colony on their hands."

"He is the biggest fool who gets the worst of the contest," said Madam Pappegoya significantly.

"I pray you tell me who is to get the best," said the Governor angrily.

"You, if you so desire," replied the lady.

"And how, may I ask?" demanded John Printz.

"By bestirring yourself as becomes the Governor of New Sweden, instead of running away like a coward," responded his daughter, in sharp, incisive tones. "What have you done to help matters? Nothing but send a few letters to the home government. Shew yourself in earnest. Send home messengers—men who know the state of the country, and can speak from experience. There are Dutch and English ships ever crossing the sea. Make them serve your end. Then when the reinforcements come you can laugh at the Director-General of New Netherland, and shew the disaffected in this land that John Printz is a man to be conciliated and not calumniated."

With a great oath the hand of the Governor came down upon the back of a chair, making that article of furniture stagger beneath the blow.

"Right you are!" he shouted. "Aye, and so *shall* they learn. 'Tis a good idea, and shall be acted upon. They at home need to be told what John Printz has done for New Sweden. I will send —to-day—this very hour. Swen Schute shall go, and others with him. He knows all that has been done here as well as I know it myself. He can tell them what a Governor they are losing in John Printz."

The floor shook beneath the tread of the chief ruler of New Sweden. Energy had come back to his movements, and life to his face. Madam Pappegoya turned to the window with a smile on her proud lips.

" 'Tis well," she said in her heart. "Patience must yet bring a turn of the tide. 'Tis rank folly to tempt fate."

Printz Hall was not the only home in New Sweden upon which a shadow rested that day. Axel Bonde sat by his dead. The face of the old man was very sad.

"He was my only son," he said. "I thought that it would be he who would thus watch by me."

The body of Olof, the son of Axel, laid on straw, in commemoration of the birth in a stable of Him who robbed death of its terror, was that night watched by Katarina, the wife of the dead man, and by Axel Bonde himself. It was in the middle of the night, when drowsiness had for a season overtaken the heavy-hearted wife, and her head had dropped upon her breast, that the old man bent forward over the dead, and big tears rolled down his cheeks.

"Olof, my son," he said, in low, broken tones, "your strong arm could better have borne the burden of life than can these old limbs, but, my boy, till they lie here helpless as your own, they shall take up the tasks you have laid down. Your father will look after your bairns, my boy—my own first bairn."

He was bending thus over the still form, his own shaking with the sobs that were not allowed to find voice, when a light step crossed the room, and a soft hand stole into his.

"Grandfather Axel," whispered a sweet girlish voice, "I have no right to be here, I know. Only those very near to him should venture to intrude now, but—I wanted to come to you—to you who comforted *me* when my mother died."

Her voice broke. The memory of the clasp of kind arms that closed about her then, and drew her to a warm, loving embrace, was very present.

"My bairn," said the old man, stretching out those arms again, "your place is ever with me," and he drew her to him till her head rested on his breast, as it had done that day in Sweden, when her mother died.

"Little one," whispered Axel softly, "I do wrong to murmur. I have much left."

On Sunday the funeral procession passed through wood and meadow land and swamp to Fort Christina, and more than one eye grew dim, when, in the churchyard near the fort, the coffin was lowered into the grave, and after throwing upon it three shovelfuls of earth the clergyman turned to wait while the nearest male relatives filled up the grave. More than usual solemnity attended the funeral psalm as an old man advanced alone, his head a little less erect than usual, his face drawn and pale. Taking the shovel, he bent to his task, every thud upon the coffin falling like a blow upon the brave old heart that had already taken up the burden of life for his son as well as himself. When all was neatly leveled, Axel Bonde for a moment raised his eyes from the freshly-spread earth to the summer sky above. Then he turned, took the little Kolina by the hand, and stood till the last words of the psalm died away.

In time the farmhouse regained its usual cheerfulness, and the faces of Olof's children grew blithe again, but the face of Axel Bonde was graver than before, and it was noticeable that his gaze more often rested upon Agneta and the younger children.

Nevertheless, upon a certain day in early November, a smile came quickly to his lips, as his eye fell on the tall, well-proportioned figure of Eric Helm.

"Welcome, friend," he said, "and I care not how often I repeat the greeting."

Axel Bonde had come to know his guest well. It was more than two years since he first assured him of a welcome to his house. His greeting to-day depended not so much upon the friendliness of his heart as upon his knowledge of the character of the visitor. The young engineer had commended himself to Axel Bonde, and he was as glad to see him as was his granddaughter Maria.

"Your face speaketh good news," he said, his keen eyes looking straight into those before him.

"For me it is of the best," replied Eric, "since it enables me to call myself a free man."

"I'm *so* glad."

He had not heard the light footstep, nor seen the girl come out of a shed near by. Now she advanced with outstretched hand. The color deepened in his face as her fingers touched his. To Eric Helm this maiden would never be as any other.

"It is good of you to care," he said.

"Is it? I do not think I could help it," she answered, smiling gaily. "I always thought the freedom would come."

"By what means was it wrought?" asked Axel.

The answer would have been prompt, but at this moment Maria arrived upon the scene. Her quick glance from Agneta to the young engineer showed her that emotions stronger than usual were at work.

"Shall the household turn out to hear the news, or will the news come inside?" she asked. "Mother and I feel not like being left out, for that there *is* news the manner of every one of you testifies."

Thus importuned, the young man entered the house. In truth, he hardly knew where he went. The genuine rejoicing that showed itself in Agneta's face had filled his heart with a wondering gladness that left little room for any other feeling.

"Did the Governor pardon you?" asked Maria, bluntly.

"Yes," said Eric. "It must be now or never, he said, since he was about to leave New Sweden. He was desirous of doing all in his power to secure my freedom before he went."

"Before he went!" ejaculated the good wife. "Whither, then, is he going?"

"To Sweedland," replied Eric. "He starts in less that a week."

"To Sweedland? And why?" asked Axel.

"For lack of the patience to wait until evil turns to good; so says his daughter, Madam Pappegoya, and she should know," answered Eric.

"And will he not return?" demanded Maria.

"It seemeth not," said Eric. "Truly, the Governor is not himself. He can ill brook the success of the Dutch, and his own inability to prevent them from trading here troubles much his spirit. Since his messengers have failed to secure for him supplies and reinforcements, he has given up hope. Rumor says he has asked to be recalled, yet can he not wait for an answer. He must go, and that at once."

"And his daughter?" asked the housewife, curiously.

"It goes hard with Madam Pappegoya to see the power fall from her father's hand, though for the time it falls into that of her husband," said Eric, gravely. "She declares the step unnecessary, confidently promises that relief will yet come, and counsels patience."

"And wherefore does not the Governor exercise it?" asked Axel. "Surely, 'tis a better remedy for ill than is hasty action."

"Aye," said Eric, "that is it, for some, but not for John Printz. There are many things the Governor of New Sweden can do, but he cannot wait. He cannot exercise patience, for he knoweth not the virtue, and men learn it not at his age."

"Verily, you speak truly," said Axel thoughtfully. "And so, lad, he has remembered your services, and set you free?"

"Provisionally," said Eric, a slight cloud crossing his face as he remembered that the freedom was not yet altogether assured. "He says my services to New Sweden warrant him in going thus far, and that in Sweedland he will endeavor to have his decision ratified, that the pardon may rest upon a firmer basis."

Eric Helm did not say, perhaps because he did not know, that he owed his good fortune to the daughter of the Governor. When she was assured that her father would stay in New Sweden but a short time longer, she remembered the young engineer, and deemed it unfair that he should be subjected to the caprice of a new Governor.

Through her influence he had obtained a footing among the best residents of New Sweden. She was unwilling to leave him at the mercy of the next ruler, who would have the power to undo all her work, and if he chose, make the lot of Eric Helm, that of a common convict. She had little doubt that the Governor's pardon would be ratified at home.

Maria was jubilant. Her attentions to Eric were both marked and flattering.

"You can begin to make money for yourself now," she said, when the young man took his leave, "and then, I suppose, you'll be wanting a home to settle in like the rest of them."

A light sprang to the young man's eyes, but Maria did not fail to notice that they passed her by and fell on the face of Agneta, who stood behind.

"Yes," said Eric softly. "Liberty means a great deal."

It was Kolina who declared that night that "there were times when Maria was so cross you couldn't tell what ailed her."

CHAPTER XXIV

"Make way, good friends, for one who desires to go aboard."

The voice was not unduly raised, but its clear, well-bred tones cut their way through the confused murmur of voices, the noise of bumping chests and clanking chains, and all the mingled sounds of a wharf, and gained for themselves a hearing. Heads were turned in the direction of the speaker, and the attention of the crowd surrounding a vessel about to set sail was arrested.

"If there's any one of us that's not desiring to go aboard, I'd like you to point him out," growled one of the crowd.

The discontent on the face of the speaker was duplicated on the countenances of his companions. There was disappointment enough on that day upon this wharf in the port of Götheberg to sink it deep beneath the washing waves.

"No use trying to get aboard, sir," said a pleasant-faced peasant woman regretfully. "The ship's got her full list of passengers, and has had it for a week and over, more's the pity."

"Wouldn't have taken her long to fill it twice over," chimed in a short, thick-set man. "Aye, and her captain could have had the best of pay for carrying us across. When a man's sold his farm, and packed up all he possesses in the world, with the intent to go to the new land, he's not like to stick at a trifle to get there."

"So that is the way the wind blows, is it?" said the stranger. "Truly it is an ill wind."

The tall, commanding form of the speaker placed his head above most heads in the crowd. His eyes were fixed on the ship as he spoke.

"You're right there, sir," said the woman, who evidently took him for a companion in misfortune, though he looked not like one to whom misfortune was a near neighbor. "Why, sir," she added, "my good man and me had a farm under the mountain that was a sight better than nothing. Aye, and we were satisfied with it, till the College of Commerce put abroad wonderful tales of privileges to be granted to those who had a mind to purchase land in the new country, and promised them permission to trade with the natives, a thing that has never been allowed before. And to crown all it was a good safe ship to go over in, with plenty of soldiers aboard, and the new Governor there to see that all went well. And now the *Eagle's* crowded, and we're left behind, full a hundred families of us, if there's one."

"What we're all waiting here for 'twould puzzle me to tell," spoke up a man with a group of children clustered about him. "Unless it's the hope that the captain will relent at last, and make room for a few of us," he added.

A half smile was on the stranger's lips, though there was sympathy in his eye.

"Truly it is a sad end to your hopes," he said. "But the College of Commerce will assuredly send another vessel to New Sweden before long, and in it all these good friends may sail to the land of promise. As for me, I must even hurry aboard, for I see the captain is about to start."

"It's no use your trying, any more than the rest of us," growled a surly visaged Swede. "Neither rich nor poor will get footing on the *Eagle*, though they come provided with passports and the best of recommendations. The captain's refused money that he'd snap at on any other voyage, I'll warrant."

"I doubt not you are right, friend," said the stranger. "But it so happens that my passage was taken when the *Eagle* was first chartered to carry over the new Governor. So, with your leave, I will even get on her deck."

A little good-humored pushing accomplished the speaker's object, and he was soon looking at the disappointed crowd across a widening chasm of water, himself one of the lucky two hundred going to New Sweden with the Governor who was to take the place of John Printz.

The fortunes of New Sweden had been at a low ebb, but now surely they were rising. With such an addition to her colonists, and a fair number of soldiers aboard, the Swedish colony would take a new lease of life.

"Gustavus Pors, as I live! Glad to see you here. Going to cast in your lot with us in my new domain?"

John Claudius Rysingh, the new Governor, extended his hand to the stranger. Gustavus Pors turned with a ready smile.

"Not exactly," he said. "Yet I have a notion to see something of that much-talked-of land. I congratulate your Honor on the good character of the territory over which you are to rule. As for me, I would judge for myself whether its vaunted richness be not of a character to change on closer acquaintance. Moreover, there are on its soil those in whom I am interested."

"Ah, say you so? I think I can promise you a flattering reception," said the Governor. "The *Eagle* will want not a welcome when she arrives. We have Swen Schute on board, he who came over to bring a message from John Printz. He can tell you how eagerly the colonists are looking for supplies, and for all the succor the *Eagle* brings."

"Sails he with us?" asked Gustavus, with some show of interest. "He is an authority on matters pertaining to New Sweden."

"The very best. An old soldier and an old colonist is Swen Schute."

It was with Swen Schute that Gustavus Pors was seen conversing before the next day was over.

"Do I know well the settlers in New Sweden?" said the old soldier, in a loud, hearty voice. "Aye, who should, if not Swen Schute? Of which among them do you need tidings?"

"I would hear of the welfare of one, Axel Bonde," said Gustavus Pors quietly.

"Axel Bonde?" replied the soldier. "An old man of eighty, or thereabouts? He is hale and hearty, yet has sorrow come to him in the loss of his son. He has the biggest farm-house owned by any peasant in New Sweden, an exact copy of that in which he lived in the old land, so they say."

"In what part of New Sweden lies this farm?" asked Monsieur Pors.

"In the neighborhood of Fort Casimir, where the Dutch Director left his garrison to be a stopper on Swedish progress," said Swen, with a twinkle in his eye. "We shall pay the Dutch fort a visit on our way up the river, unless I mistake the mood of our new Governor. Then will you have the opportunity to step ashore and see your friends."

"Very good," said Gustavus, and there was a light in his eye also, though it was not called up by the mention of Fort Casimir.

"Eighty years old, is he?" mused Monsieur Pors, as he leant over the ship's side and gazed into the water beneath. "Truly it is time I looked after the little maid. I wonder what kind of a reception the old man will give me."

He had a clear recollection of his last visit to the farm-house, whither he had gone to see the child Agneta. It was made a year after the first, and for aught he could perceive the place was unchanged. But when he presented himself at the low door he saw but one face he knew, the face of Anna, the granddaughter of Axel. He could not complain of want of courtesy. Anna might be stolid, but she was neither rude nor malicious.

"You will come in and rest yourself, sir," she said, "though those whom you seek are all gone away. I'm married now, and me and my husband own the farm. Grandfather has built himself a new house, and taken new land."

"And where shall I find him?" asked Gustavus eagerly.

"You'll not find him at all, sir," said Anna. "Grandfather means no disrespect to you, but he wishes to be left free to carry out the desires of Agneta's mother."

"And you will not tell me where he has gone?" demanded Monsieur Pors, with a sharp ring in his voice.

"No, sir," said Anna, uncompromisingly.

"But I have a right to know," expostulated Gustavus. "This is an unfair advantage to take."

"Grandfather said nobody had a right to interfere with where he chose to live, or how he chose to rear Agneta," said Anna.

"It is ridiculous. What harm could I do the maiden?" said the visitor.

Anna was speechless.

"You're welcome here on the old farm, sir," she said at length, when the silence had lasted long.

"And welcome nowhere else, eh?" he said, and turned on his heel.

What would Axel Bonde say when he presented himself in New Sweden? It wanted still some months to the time when he would have a right to claim the old man's greatest treasure. John Claudius Rysingh had promised him a friendly reception in the new land. Monsieur Pors was not so sure of the nature of that reception.

Swen Schute was right. Governor Rysingh had every intention of paying a visit to the Dutch fort on his way up the river. He and the officer had held many a consultation before the South River was reached, and they understood one another well.

Upon the *Eagle* feeling waxed strong on the subject of Dutch aggression. There was a fairly large contingent of soldiers aboard, and public opinion in consequence leant to the side of sternness. With a superior force it was unnecessary to look at the enemy's side of the question. Such a view of the subject might do when the odds were even, or a little on the side of the other party. But with everything in their favor, the voyagers on the *Eagle* were constrained to assert that the Dutch had but the merest shadow of excuse for their conduct, and that the building of Fort Casimir was an outrage.

"It is an outrage not to be borne," said Swen Schute, when the broad sweep of the bay was entered, and Fort Casimir was not many hours' distance ahead. "The home government is seriously annoyed at the advantage the Hollanders have taken. Our Governor has special instructions to compass, if possible, their removal from the fort. Were it not that they fear the English more than the Dutch, they at home would break with our neighbors altogether. As it is, discretionary power is left with the Governor, and John Claudius Rysingh is the man to know how to use it."

Again there was a twinkle in the eye of the soldier. This time Monsieur Pors perceived it.

"Then we visit not Fort Casimir for naught?" he said.

Swen laughed.

"Well, we stay there not altogether out of compliment to the Hollanders," he said.

There was the stir of excitement on board the Eagle. Some important move was in the air. These good Swedes grew very Swedish in sentiment as they remembered their wrongs in connection with the fact that but ten or twelve soldiers represented the Dutch power in Fort Casimir.

"What say you?" said John Rysingh, linking his arm in that of Gustavus Pors. "Have you a mind to see life in a little more lively form than it presents itself as a rule to the stranger on these shores? In that direction lies Fort Casimir."

His finger pointed up the river.

"And lies the liveliness in the same direction also?" asked Gustavus, laughing.

"Aye, that does it," said the Governor. "I have come hither to carry out the wishes of the government. The government desires to see Fort Casimir abandoned of the Dutch. Very well. The government shall see it. But the government is cautious. So am not I. 'Ask them to step out,' say the wise ones of our land. Verily, I will ask, and they will go. Then will the wishes of the government be carried out."

Gustavus looked amused.

"But spake not your instructions of a peaceable settlement of the question?" he asked lightly.

"And who speaks of bloodshed?" asked Rysingh. "Seems it to you likely that the ten or twelve soldiers yonder will be eager to break the peace?"

"Nay, verily," said Gustavus.

It was afternoon when Gerrit Bikker, the commander of Fort Casimir, saw a ship out in the bay.

"What do you make of yon vessel?" he called to Adriaen van Tienhoven.

"What vessel? Where is she?" was the answer.

"Yonder, in the open."

The two stood watching.

"Is she friend or foe?" asked Bikker.

"Better let me find out," suggested Adriaen.

"Not a bad idea," replied Bikker musingly.

The result of his musing was seen in a small party, with Van Tienhoven at their head, who made the best of their way down the river to meet the approaching vessel.

CHAPTER XXV

"Gerrit."

The voice was the voice of a woman. She came upon Bikker as he stood in the darkness without the fort, his face turned towards the place where the ship should be.

"Aye. What is it?" he answered.

"If yon's an enemy, are you going to fight?" asked the woman, laying her hand upon his arm.

"Plague take the woman!" responded her husband. "What have we got to fight with?"

She came nearer, and put her face close to his.

"There's none too much powder left," she said. "I let some Indians have all they wanted not three days ago."

"The mischief you did!"

"Why not?" demanded his wife. "They paid for it in good beaver. I say it's a sin and a shame to waste powder on the soldiers when you can get anything you like for it of the natives. The men got but three tin spoonfuls each, and that was three too many."

Bikker only grunted.

"What's left wouldn't last long," she continued, "and if it would, a fight would mean the loss of all we possess. A ship such as that is not coming here for naught."

"Drat the woman! Who talked of fighting?" said Bikker. "And why should she be an enemy? The Swedes have been looking for supplies long enough. There they are, or my name's not Gerrit Bikker."

"Friend or foe, don't you forget that it's a right good thing to look out for your country when you can comfortably do so, and a long sight better thing to look out for yourself at every time," said the woman, turning away into the darkness.

"Don't you trouble yourself to give me advice," growled Bikker. "I'm no fool."

If Gerrit Bikker expected Van Tienhoven any time during the night he was disappointed. In the early morning he went out to the sandy beach of the promontory on which the fort was built, and looked down the river. The ship was to be seen, yet a long distance away, and nearer was a small object that Gerrit made out to be the returning boat. It was fully eight o'clock before it touched the beach, and Van Tienhoven sprang out.

"Well, what news?"

"The worst," was the answer. " 'Tis a Swedish vessel, bringing the new Governor and a great crowd of settlers. What, think you, the Governor had the impudence to demand? Nothing less than the surrender of our fort, on the pretext that it was built on lands belonging to the government of Sweden."

Gerrit stared at the speaker.

"Do you hear, man?" repeated Bikker. "He asks *us* to surrender to *him!*"

Bikker only looked contemplatively across the water.

"It was well I went," resumed Van Tienhoven, "it has at least given us an hour or two to prepare."

"Prepare for what?" asked Bikker sharply.

"For what? To show that Swedish upstart the way Dutchmen surrender," said the other hotly.

"What would you have me do?" inquired Bikker aimlessly.

"Do, man? Fight! What else is there to do? Are you mad, to stand there wasting time like that?"

Van Tienhoven had already started for the fort.

"What have we got to fight with?" Bikker called after him. "There's no ammunition, and but a handful of men all told."

Within the fort the garrison and freemen surrounded the returned soldiers. To a man they were eager to give the Governor of New Sweden a warm reception. Bikker, meanwhile, had disappeared. It was some time before they found him in the garret, in close converse with his wife.

"This is no time for dallying!" cried Van Tienhoven, breaking in on the pair. "Give your orders, and there's not one among us that will not risk his life to see them carried out."

"Orders!" responded Bikker. "Where's the use? We can't hold the fort against the men you say are aboard that ship. Better meet the Governor in a friendly spirit. He will scarce show us violence then."

"Meet the enemies of our country in a friendly spirit! Well, it's come to something," quoth Van Tienhoven, and flung himself out of the garret.

The soldiers and freemen below clamored and swore, and watched the river, and while they grew frantic, and Bikker yet delayed to give definite orders, the *Eagle* drew near.

It was Sunday morning, and the hour was eleven. The Swedish settlers along the river had repaired to Fort Christina for the preaching, and the arrival of the vessel was almost unwatched—except from Fort Casimir.

"Now, my men," said Swen Schute, as a boat was lowered and some twenty soldiers took their places in it, "if it be necessary to strike, strike for the honor of the old land and the benefit of the new. Pull away. We'll soon make a change in the colors aloft yonder."

At the fort the men stood by the guns, their eyes and ears as far as possible following the movements of their commander, their fingers twitching to make the guns speak with no uncertain voice, as soon as he should give the word of command. Some of the faces grew purple with rage as the minutes passed, and no orders were given. One or two of the watchers, less easily moved, laughed derisively.

"Gerrit Bikker isn't going to fight, you may take your oath of that," quoth one.

"They're coming ashore," said Van Tienhoven, savagely. "Bikker, what are you going to do?"

"What can I do, save meet them with fair words?"

said Bikker. "If I provoke a fight, I shall get all the blame. If I treat them as friends, they must at least give me proper notice before they treacherously take advantage of my friendship."

There were muttered curses as the commandant went down to the beach, and the last chance to sink the enemy's boat was gone.

The men inside the fort could only watch events. The events were strange enough to cause a few of the more excitable Dutchmen to choke with the curses that could not tumble fast enough over their lips. They saw Bikker meet the Swedes in the friendliest manner, nay, put himself at their head, and side by side with the Swedish officer walk towards the fort. That the visit was not a friendly one on the part of the new-comers was attested by the drawn swords in the hands of the advancing soldiers.

"Traitor!" hissed a Dutchman who stood by a gun. "Verily I would that he were within range of this gun. I would touch it off with the greatest of joy."

"What means that?" inquired another, as a deep boom broke in on the steady tramp of advancing feet.

Again the ship's gun spoke, and before the last echoes had died away the Swedes made a rush for the fort.

"It was a signal!" cried those within.

It looked as if they were not far wrong. No sooner had the two guns been fired over the fort than the Swedes made a rush for the gates, demanding immediate surrender. Bikker offered no protest.

Not so Van Tienhoven. He was not in command at Fort Casimir, but he could not keep still. He advanced to meet the Swedish officer.

"By what right do you enter this fort?" he demanded hotly. "Where is your commission from your government?"

"You hold your tongue, and let your commander speak," retorted Swen Schute.

"Gerrit, why do you stand there like a coward? Let me go to the ship and ask the Governor for his commission," urged Adriaen van Tienhoven, in a low voice. "For your country's sake, man, stir yourself," he added. "Do you want to pass for a traitor?"

"Aye, go," said Bikker, with an air of relief, as if glad to be rid of so troublesome a friend.

Monsieur Pors was standing by the Governor's side when Adriaen van Tienhoven came on deck, eagerly demanding to see the Governor's commission, or any order he might have for thus violently disturbing the peace existing between the Dutch and the Swedes.

There was a derisive smile on Rysingh's lips as he gazed at the excited Dutchman.

"My orders?" he said slowly. "They come from Her Majesty of Sweden. Our good Queen sent her ambassador to ask the States General whether they sanctioned the encroachment of the Dutch on Swedish territory. Our ambassador was referred to the Dutch West India Company. What, think you, my zealous friend, was the reply of that company? Hark you! Not only did they deny all sanction of encroachment on Swedish land, but they added, 'If our people are in your way, drive them off.' We are going to do it. Go and tell your Governor that, my fine fellow."

Baffled rage was in the eyes of the Dutchman. He hurried away, convinced that the turn of the Swede had come. When he arrived at the fort he had to ask permission of the Swedes to enter. Fort Casimir was a Dutch stronghold no longer.

"If any refuse to give up their arms, fire on them!"

It was the command of Swen Schute, and it rang in Adriaen van Tienhoven's ears as he came into the fort.

They did not fire. It was unnecessary.

"Haul down the Dutch flag," said Bikker to his son. "It is of no use up there."

And it came down.

CHAPTER XXVI

It was an unusual thing that only Axel Bonde and Katarina, his daughter-in-law, had gone to the church in Fort Christina. On very few Sundays before had it happened that Agneta walked at this hour with Ian and Kolina beyond the clump of trees that hid Fort Casimir from view.

"Look! Look!" cried the boy and girl both at the same moment. "There's a big ship at the fort."

"It's ours! It's ours!" exclaimed Ian, exultantly, "and it's full of people."

"Is it the new Governor?" asked Kolina.

"Truly it seems like it," said Agneta, her eyes fixed eagerly on the vessel.

A ship from home was a great event, and this one was crowded with people. The maiden quickened her pace. She was curious to see more of the vessel and its passengers.

"What is it stopping at Fort Casimir for?" asked Kolina. "It's not a Dutchman."

Then, a new wonder revealing itself to her excited eyes, she exclaimed:

"Look, Agneta! They are lowering their flag to ours. Why, what means it? It has come down altogether. And—yes—ours is going up. They are surely going to raise it. What are they doing it for?"

"I know not," said Agneta. "It must be in deference to the new Governor."

"I wonder whether he will be as big as Governor Printz," said Ian, "and whether he will swear as loud."

"And whether he will want Eric Helm to serve him as he served the old Governor," added Kolina.

Agneta did not answer. She, too, was wondering whether the new Governor would prove favorable to the young engineer. Had John Printz kept his promise and brought Eric's case before the authorities at home? Would the Governor bring a full pardon, or would the verdict be against the young man? It was possible that even the provisional pardon might be revoked. Then it would matter much to Eric Helm what sort of a man had come to New Sweden as Governor.

"Here comes the Governor himself," announced Kolina, jubilantly. "He's coming up the bank just like the Dutch Director did. Maybe he's coming to our house, too."

"Ugh! Girls are fools," said Ian contemptuously. "He's no Governor. He's just somebody come out of the ship."

"He's not. He's somebody grand. Isn't he, Agneta?"

The girl was not listening. She was looking at the stranger, and her heart was beating less regularly than was its wont. Who was he? She did not need to ask, and for the moment she certainly could not have answered. The quiet, confident mien, the quick footstep, the tall, proud figure —she knew them well. Aye, and she knew too the easy grace with which the head was bared even before a nearer approach.

"He is saluting us. Who is it, Agneta? Do you know him?"

Kolina's voice rang out so excitedly that it reached the ears of Monsieur Pors himself. He listened, a little eagerly, for the reply, but it was of different pitch, and traveled not so far.

"Gently, little one, thy voice is over loud," said the maiden. "Yes. I knew him in Sweedland."

"Good! Good! Then he is coming to see us."

Again the penetrating childish tones crossed the lessening space, and made themselves heard by the stranger. He was near enough now to see the flush on the girl's face, though not to catch the low-spoken reply. The next minute his head was again uncovered, and his hand outstretched.

"Will you welcome me to New Sweden?" he said. "The perils of a sea voyage are behind me, and I would fain receive congratulation."

"New Sweden is ever ready to welcome the new-comer to her shores," said Agneta, the color deepening on her face.

"Who is New Sweden?" asked Monsieur Pors, with a smile. "Will she look upon me with human eyes? It is a personal greeting I crave." Then in a lower voice, while still keeping possession of her hand, he added: "Little friend, why did you run away from me?"

"Why, she didn't," interposed Kolina. "She came on just as straight as she could to meet you."

The shrill young voice was expostulatory. Kolina thought the stranger must have very poor eyes indeed if he imagined that Agneta had shown any inclination to run away from him.

"Did she, little one?" said Monsieur Pors, with a bright smile. "That was very good of her. But what she did not do, you and your brother must do for her. Run away and tell the good mother that a traveler is about to invade her house, even as your new Governor yonder has invaded the Dutch fort. If you will do this for me, then I, as well as the mother, will call you the best of friends."

"Nay, monsieur, the warning is unnecessary," said Agneta gently. "The good mother will need no notice to be ready to entertain a guest, and the farm-house can well find room to shelter another inmate."

"Nevertheless, go, little one, and tell the good wife that we come," said Monsieur Pors to the children.

When they had gone, he turned to Agneta.

"You have not told me yet why you ran away from me," he said.

There was a smile on the girl's lips as she answered him.

"Monsieur, we left all Sweden," she said.

"And it was presumption for one of Sweden's sons to flatter himself that he had more to do with it than any other?" he replied. "Yet, little lady, one of Sweden's sons felt himself aggrieved."

The smile upon the maiden's face broadened, and her eyes looked straight into his.

"There are penalties that attach to presumption," she said.

"And they came upon me? So be it," he answered. "I accept your verdict. Is it also presumptuous, and equally sure to provoke penalty, to ask for a welcome now?"

"No, monsieur," she said. "In New Sweden we are never churlish to strangers. All worthy comers are welcome."

"Conditional, I see," he answered lightly. "And how shall I prove my worth?"

"By telling all the news of the dear home land," she replied.

"Ah! It is the dear land yet. Verily I am glad that you have not altogether broken its fetters from off you. The news? It is sad. The old land mourns for a lost daughter, and especially that part of the land where a castle keeps guard over a lake. There the house stands desolate, and an old woman, Brita by name, asks daily if the young mistress be not on her way to take possession."

He was bending forward that he might get a glimpse of the girl's face. He was not sure, but he thought there were tears in her eyes.

She did not answer, and for a minute there was silence between them.

"Little one, did you think I should not find you?"

His voice was low and tender. It broke in on the

stillness. Again the soft flush covered cheek and brow, but the girl did not raise her eyes.

"It was a long way to come," she said. "It may well be that the object will not prove worthy of the trouble of search."

"I am not afraid," he said.

He did not look afraid—nor dissatisfied—as he neared the house, walking confidently by Agneta's side.

"He's as handsome as ever, and don't look a year older," was Maria's verdict, as she peeped from a window at Agneta and her companion. "And he's as gallant as ever," was her inward comment, as Monsieur Pors greeted her with flattering notice and freedom.

"Surely there has been magic here," he said, as he looked round on the farmhouse and its inmates. "I could swear that this is the very dwelling from which I turned away distraught this four years back. I had traveled far to reach it, only to be told that those whom I had presumed to call my friends had gone from it, without so much as leaving for me a message. I have journeyed across the broad sea to the new land, and to-day I find that dwelling again, the very same, yet richer by far, since the faces of the maidens within it have grown fairer with every day that has passed."

"How did you find us?" asked Maria, blushing rosy red at his words of compliment.

"Ah, how can you ask?" he replied, "when you were cruel enough to cast me off."

"It was neither my fault nor mother's," said Maria, stoutly. "We should not have grumbled if you had come with us."

"Truly you are good to me now," he said, with a look that deepened the roses on her cheeks. "I could wish that I had known that goodness sooner. At least I would have proved myself not slow to profit by your graciousness. And now that I am here, I will even hold you to your friendship."

Not a hard task, since the eyes of the visitor had already set the girl's heart fluttering, and tampered materially with the steadiness of her brain.

"My! I wish he had come to see me," she said, in confidence to Agneta, when the two girls were in the kitchen, on hospitality intent. "You're a lucky girl, if your mother did put fool's fancies into your head. *He* won't be long getting them out."

"Maria, how dare you speak so of my mother?"

The maiden's eyes blazed as she turned to confront the culprit.

"Bless me, don't fire up so," said Maria. "You're all fools, or else you wouldn't take things so serious. I don't mean any more disrespect to your mother than I do to grandfather, and all of you. But I tell you, Agneta, you and him make a handsome couple."

Agneta turned away. It was no use quarreling with Maria. Moreover, at the present moment the girl meant no real harm. Agneta went back to the living room, to meet the eyes of Monsieur Pors.

They had been watching the door ever since she disappeared. They had a more satisfied look in them as she crossed the room.

"Are you curious to hear how the Dutch fort has fallen into our hands?" he asked.

"Into our hands? Did the lowering of the flag mean that?" asked Agneta.

"Truly it did," replied Monsieur Pors, and he would not let her escape again till he had told the story of the capture of Fort Casimir.

"Surely it seems not right," said Agneta, "thus to take advantage of the want of suspicion of our neighbors. Had the Dutch Governor surprised our Fort Christina in such a manner, truly we should have found enough to say."

"Ah, gentle reprover, it would not do to tell the new Governor that," said Monsieur Pors. "There are two truthful sides to every controversy, and each contestant claimeth the balance of truth on his own. It were hard to expect him to spy out the good in his rival's case. The Governor saith, and with some show of reason, that Fort Casimir was erected notwithstanding the protests of John Printz, and in a part of the land that has ever been considered the domain of our Most Gracious Queen. He did but claim that it should be surrendered to its rightful owners."

"And was there no blood shed?" asked Agneta.

"Not a red drop. The knaves knew better than to fight," replied Gustavus Pors.

When Axel Bonde returned, he greeted his visitor

with grave courtesy. However much he had desired to keep this stranger away, he was now under his roof, and hospitality called for a welcome. It came in words at which no guest could cavil.

"In the name of New Sweden I welcome you to its shores," said the old man, "and as a representative of my country offer to my countryman hospitality. Was the voyage a prosperous one?"

They sat talking long that night, for Monsieur Pors had much to tell of the new Governor and his initial exploit, but when Agneta had laid her hand in that of Monsieur Pors, and heard his gentle, "May you sleep well, little lady," and stood at last by the window of her own chamber, the sleep that had been invoked for her seemed far from her eyes. The moonlight plainly showed the river and the piece of woodland that hid Fort Casimir, but in place of the water and the trees the girl saw the hills of Sweden, and in the foreground the snow-covered fields. And instead of the voice of Maria, still to be heard in loud comment in the inner room, she listened to another voice, low, and clear, and sweet, with the longing of the mother heart in it, and the renunciation of one who had accepted death with its partings.

The room had been very still when that voice spoke, for mother and daughter were alone.

"Little one, you are over young to meet the grave questions of life," it said. "They can be really met only by the heart of a woman, yet I must make you look at them to-day. Tell me, dear heart, how much you remember of those you knew at the castle."

And the child answered in surprise: "Why, mother dear, we have talked of them often, of Brita, and Lars, and all the servants, and of those who lived around."

"Think again," said the mother, gently. "Does there not stand out one other form that is associated with your brother Adolf, and with the day we laid him to rest?"

"Yes," said the child, thoughtfully. "I have not forgotten Monsieur Pors, though we have not often talked of him."

"And you remember him—how?"

"As a playmate, I think," said Agneta. "I have a remembrance of being petted and made much of, and—yes, of feeling there was something you did not approve of, either in him or me."

"Do you know what he called you, Agneta?" asked the mother.

"No," said the child. "What was it?"

"Little sweetheart."

The color came into the fair face.

"I was a very little girl," she said apologetically.

"He would have said it with more fervor and significance if you had been older," replied the low, gentle voice.

"Mother!"

"Aye, little one, for he deems that he has the right."

"*Has*, mother? But we have not seen him for so long," said Agneta.

"No. Daughter, did you ever wonder why we left the castle?"

"No," was the answer, "for you told me that it belonged no longer to us, but to Monsieur Pors. I remembered him, and knew whom you meant."

"We need not have left it," said Madam Botorpa. "He wanted us to stay."

"But—it was his house. We could not stay in the house of another," said the child, in a puzzled tone.

"No. But he did not see it that way. Little one, he deemed you as much his as the house, and he saw not why the two should be separated."

"Mother, why?"

The tone was imperative. The suspicions of the child were aroused.

"Because your father gave him the right."

"The right to *me?*"

Anger and dismay spoke in face and voice. The mother drew the child towards her till she knelt by her side, her face close to the white one on the pillow.

"Yes, dear heart, the right to you," she said.

"Why did he? Mother, I belong to you," exclaimed Agneta.

"Would that I could keep my treasure," said Madam Botorpa.

The head of the maid went down on her mother's breast, and for a time there was silence. Then the low, gentle voice spoke again. In loving, tender words Madam Botorpa told her little daughter of that infant betrothal, and something of her disappointment in the man to whom the father had intrusted his child. For the first time Agneta heard the full story of that lonely journey from the castle, taken at a time when Monsieur Pors was far away.

"He has never found us, mother," said the little girl. "He will not find us now."

"It may be that he never will," said her mother. "I think I should be glad to be sure that it would be so. But, little one, it may be otherwise. The time will come when he will have the right to seek you. Gustavus Pors is not the man to relinquish that right if he desire to use it. Perchance he will not so desire. But if he should, promise me that no fair words shall make you do violence to the woman's heart within you, that to that heart you will go for the answer to the question, and not to the girl's head, which, little one, will not have had time to grow wise."

"Mother dear, I can answer now," said Agneta. "You knew best."

"Surely, for that time, dear one," was the answer. "But when he asks again all will be different. He may himself be changed. In any case you will be changed from the little girl of that day. I cannot answer for my daughter, but I can warn her that out of chosen evil good never yet came without terrible suffering and loss. Your heart is pure, little one. Trust to it, and let not the castle weigh anything in the question."

"Mother, whispered the child, fearfully, "can he —can he make me—do it?"

"No," said the mother firmly. "True, the betrothal is binding, yet has Axel Bonde assured me that at word from you he will carry the case to the ecclesiastical courts. It will take money, but the heart of Axel Bonde is true as steel. Money will weigh little with him."

Agneta went back over every word to-night, and remembered her own promise, sealed with a kiss on the lips that so soon after spoke their last words of advice. The time of which her mother had warned her had come. Monsieur Pors was here to claim his bride. Already she had passed her seventeenth birthday. In a few more months the question her mother had told her to ask her own heart must be met.

Nay, it was no question. She had always known what she should answer, though now he was here she was not so sure of the way in which that answer should be conveyed to Monsieur Pors himself. The insistence that was half entreaty and half command, the imperious, deferential manner, the determination to take only the answer he desired, would not be easy to overcome. And even while she thought of how she should make him believe that she was in earnest, and not a willful child who could be argued and petted out of a fractious mood, her thoughts glanced off to the castle, and the words of Gustavus Pors came back to her. "An old woman asks daily if the young mistress be not on her way to take possession." The dear old castle! It was home to her yet.

She stood long by the window, but her thoughts now were of the lake beneath the hill, and the gray old castle keeping ward above.

CHAPTER XXVII

"I wish I could have seen the new Governor before he went up the river."

Kolina was standing by the window, looking at the water, and her remark was addressed to nobody in particular. He who chose to answer her, however, was somebody in particular, being no other than Gustavus Pors.

"What did you want with the Governor, little one?" he asked. "Was there some weighty request you were burning to present?"

"I wanted to hear whether he could swear as loud as Governor Printz," said the little girl.

The visitor laughed.

"I pray you tell me what difference the vehemence of his swearing would make to my little friend?" he said.

"It wouldn't make any difference to me. I was thinking of Eric Helm," said the child.

The eyes of Gustavus Pors had wandered to a golden head bent over some knitting. Was it just now bent a little more determinately than was necessary?"

"Eric Helm?" replied Gustavus. "And who is Eric Helm?"

"He's an engineer, and he built the strong house in front of Fort Beversrede," said Ian eagerly.

"Oh, didn't that house make the Hollanders savage!"

"Eric thought of it all himself," added Kolina. "Governor Printz made him think of it. He had to do just what the Governor told him, because he was a con——"

"Little chatterer, let thy tongue rest while older and wiser lips than thine make answer," interrupted Axel Bonde, who chanced to be passing through the room when the child spoke. "Eric Helm," he added, turning to Monsieur Pors, "is a young man who has proved himself of value, not only to Governor Printz, but also to many in New Sweden. This land would be the better did it possess more men like the young engineer."

"Ah! And he has found a friend in Axel Bonde, I think," said Monsieur Pors.

"He has *given* a friend to Axel Bonde," said the old man, as he passed out.

"Eric Helm," said Gustavus meditatively. "I have, I believe, heard the name before."

His eyes passed lightly over Agneta's face, stopping to note the soft pink tint thereon, and went to Maria's rosy cheeks, resting there very openly.

"Likely enough," replied that maiden. "He is well known here."

"'Here' being this hospitable dwelling?" asked Monsieur Pors. "He is indeed a lucky fellow if that be the case."

"Nay, I meant not that so much as the whole of New Sweden," said Maria.

"And is all New Sweden loud in his praise?" asked Monsieur Pors.

"Nay, monsieur, for surely then were New Sweden a land by itself," said Agneta, suddenly raising her eyes. "Know you any country where there are not to be found men who take advantage of misfortune to call the sufferer a knave?"

"I think New Sweden in any case a land by itself —since a certain little lady set foot in it," he said.

She dropped her eyes over her knitting again.

Gustavus Pors watched her with a half smile on his lips. He had been a week in New Sweden now, and was already very much at home there. Ian and Kolina were his fast friends and allies, and Maria had long since come to the conclusion that if such a lover were the result of an early betrothal, she wished *she* had been betrothed when she was a baby.

Monsieur Pors had made Fort Casimir his headquarters. Not that there was a Fort Casimir to-day, though it had been thus designated when he first set foot in it. The Dutch fort had changed its name with its commander, and the fortress in which the sturdy and jubilant Swen Schute exercised command rejoiced in the name of Fort Trinity, given in honor of Trinity Sunday, the day on which it fell into the hands of the Swedes, and out of the hands of Gerrit Bikker. It was not even the same fort in appearance, for the Swedish engineer, Lindström, who came over in the suite of Governor Rysingh, was already transforming it, and rendering it more formidable than it had ever been when the Hollanders possessed it.

"Is the finishing of that lucky piece of knitting an absolute necessity?" asked Gustavus Pors, bending over Agneta, and speaking low.

"Yes, verily, if she for whom it is designed is not to go barefoot," said the girl, lightly.

"To go barefoot were not such a terrible misfortune were the air always as soft and warm as to-day," he said. "Be good to me, and lay the knitting aside. I want some one conversant with the land of the South River to show me its beauties."

"Kolina is a splendid little guide," said Agneta, looking at him with a mischievous smile on her lips.

"I know a better," he replied, and she put aside her work.

"As you will, monsieur," she said.

"Is it indeed to be as I will?" he asked softly.

She made him no answer, but wrapped a soft silk handkerchief about her head, and waited for him.

"Whither shall we go?" she asked.

"To Sweden," he said, with a look that she could not misunderstand.

She laughed.

"Then must you find another guide, monsieur," she said.

"In that case I will even stay where I am," he answered.

"Will it give you pleasure to know that Governor Rysingh brings good news to your friend Eric

Helm?" he asked, when her hands were filled with the flowers he had gathered for her, and they had walked far from the farm-house.

She looked up at him with a startled light in her eyes.

"I did not think you knew Eric Helm," she said.

"No, but I know Governor Rysingh, and I have heard from him that the best of news awaits the young man."

"I am *very* glad," said Agneta, and then she became aware of the eyes that were reading her face, and let her own drop.

"He is very fortunate," said Monsieur Pors significantly.

"To obtain his freedom?" she asked.

"Nay, but to obtain his friends," he said.

"Yes. Governor Printz has surely proved a good friend to him," she answered. "I thought it was hardly possible that the authorities at home would refuse to sustain his action in the matter. Eric has well earned the freedom that should have come before."

"The intentions of John Printz were in all probability of the best," replied Gustavus, "yet the young man has not the Governor to thank for his present happiness."

"What, the Governor's pardon is not to hold?"

Her eyes were startled, and a little fearful. She lifted them to his face again. It was easy to see that this was not a matter of small moment to her.

"It is not to hold, because it is unnecessary," he said. "The pardon Governor Rysingh brings depends, not on the favor of a ruler, but on principles of justice. New facts have, I understand, come to light, and the sentence imposed upon the young man has been found to be unjust. Hence the pardon."

"And he has been proved innocent?"

"Something like it, I fancy."

She had stopped in her walk, and now stood quite still, looking at him, and letting herself realize the import of the news he brought. If he had intended to gauge the depth of her interest in the young engineer, he ought to have been satisfied. Perchance he was more than satisfied, for his own face for the moment had become sober.

"How glad he will be—and *is*, I suppose, by this time!" she said. "I think you could not have brought better news."

"I am glad I was so fortunate," he said dryly. "Do you always take as much interest in your friends?"

Her cheeks, which had grown pink with excitement, deepened their color. She became suddenly conscious of herself, and of the thoughts of her companion.

"No," she said quietly. "I think not. Happily, few of my friends have been as unjustly treated."

"I think I will get somebody to abuse me a little," he said.

She laughed.

"You must be sure it is unjust abuse," she said.

"Which implies that I am open to abuse that would not be unjust. You are doubly cruel to me now," he answered.

He exerted himself then to make the walk pleasant, and perhaps to divert her thoughts from the channel in which he himself had started them. In the first he succeeded, but the way in which his eyes occasionally searched her face hardly suggested that he considered himself signally successful in the other. She was very bright, and happy, but he could not quite assure himself that a portion of her happiness did not spring from the knowledge he had just imparted.

"I'm so glad! I'm so glad!"

The words ran like a refrain through all that afternoon walk. The world was very blithe that June day, and the girl's heart was blithe too Perhaps there was a little glamour over all. Perchance the flowers of New Sweden never looked quite as attractive as they did when Gustavus Pors plucked them for her with words that were half jest and half earnest. She could not have told, if she had tried, on just what foundation her gladness rested, only she knew that her heart was light for joy at Eric Helm's good fortune.

"He can take his place with the best now," she mused, and then fell to wondering what Monsieur Pors would think of the young engineer, and began unconsciously to contrast the two, carrying on the comparison until she became suddenly aware of her own mental attitude, and took herself to task therefor.

"Why should it matter what he thinks?" she asked, and felt the color rush to her cheeks. It was full time to put a bridle on her thoughts, and to relegate the good news and all it entailed to the background of her consciousness, from whence it lent a warmth and brightness that even the June sun, unaided, could not have furnished.

The girl was chary of sharing the tidings with others. It was not till night that she imparted her secret even to Axel Bonde. He heard it with fatherly joy.

"The lad has had a hard time of it," he said. "Truly I am glad he is cleared of imputations that ill-fitted a character such as his."

Maria pounced upon the news and the news-teller with a vigor that robbed hidden gladness of its touch of romance. *Her* feelings found ready expression in words.

"Well, you must have been either stupid or sly, to keep the news to yourself for a whole afternoon," she said. "My! I should have told it before I was inside the door."

"I don't doubt it," replied Agneta quietly.

"And why not? What is there to be close about?" demanded Maria, sharply. "Isn't one as much his friend as the other? We've all shown him friendship when he most needed it."

"I have no doubt he is duly grateful," said Agneta.

"Oh, he's not one to forget kindness," replied Maria complacently. "I will say this for you, Agneta, you showed some sense when you picked him up for a friend. He'll be able to hold his head above many in New Sweden now, and if I belonged to as good a burgher family as he does, I'd do it too. But he'll not turn his back on those who helped him in his misfortune. It does seem as if things happened just right sometimes," she added. "Here's Eric cleared of all suspicion, and free to make a home for himself as soon as he will, and Monsieur Pors in New Sweden to look after you. It certainly clears the way——"

She broke off, and disappeared in the kitchen, to give the benefit of her experience in the preparing of certain ingredients destined for the morrow's breakfast. From the seclusion of the kitchen hearth her voice burst out in jubilant song, that penetrated to the big living room, and somehow had a disturbing effect on the gladness which all the afternoon had been welling up in Agneta's heart.

Eric Helm was at present in no danger of holding his head above that of any resident of New Sweden. He was in too much uncertainty about his fate to indulge in feelings of pride. For among those who were interested in the subject, almost the last to hear the news of his good fortune was the young man whom it most concerned. Following the instructions of John Pappegoya, the son-in-law of John Printz, whom the Governor had left to administer the affairs of New Sweden when his own impatience drove him back to the old land, Eric had gone far up the bank of one of the creeks, into the country of the Indians, to explore the district, and make a rough map of the same. He started when the fortunes of New Sweden were at their lowest ebb, but a few days before the tide of prosperity began to flow in again. Consequently he was unaware that the successor of John Printz had arrived, and that his own fate was no longer a matter of uncertainty.

When at last he heard that a Swedish ship had come up the river, he turned his face towards Tenacong.

"Better know the worst, and be done with it," he said, but a haunting fear that it might be long before the worst was done with him made the return journey something different from a holiday trip. He had had a taste of freedom, and the possibilities of the future looked darker in comparison with it.

He found the land jubilant. New settlers were everywhere. Much-needed stores were to be had at the forts, and the country was in a stir of gladness. The praises of John Rysingh, and of his energetic righting of Swedish wrongs, were in every mouth. It was New Sweden's time of rejoicing, and she was proportionately elated.

As he neared the island of Tenacong, Eric saw many Indian warriors with their squaws. The original owners of the country were gathering in force.

"Whither are they bound?" he asked of a settler.

"For Printz Hall, to hold a conference with the new Governor," was the reply. "John Rysingh is a man who believes not in dallying. He has ousted the Hollanders, now he would bring back to their first friendship the Indians whose hearts the Dutchmen have stolen. He has for them presents that will prove stronger than all other arguments, and what he has already done at Fort Casimir will teach them that the Swedes are not to be despised."

The young man hurried on. The gladness and stir abroad in the land grated upon him. How much of the increased prosperity would fall to his share?

The conference with the Indians was at its height when he reached New Gottenburg. Had Governor Printz been there, the young engineer would have sought him at once. As it was, he lingered without the Hall, hoping, but half fearing, to learn his fate. He almost expected to hear his name in everybody's mouth.

He found himself very much forgotten. The Indian question was of paramount importance. Would the Indians return to their old allegiance to the Swedes? To be in firm friendship with them was to strengthen the Swedish position materially.

The red men had not been found altogether eager to renew their covenant and vow eternal friendship. They complained that the white men had brought evil to their shores. Since their coming many Indians had died. They did not add that presents had been scarce, but when the Governor rose to talk with them, and freely distributed his gifts among them, they began to be less sure of the advisability of breaking the chain of friendship that bound them to their brothers the Swedes. They retired to consider the situation, and whilst they were considering, Eric Helm arrived.

Governor Rysingh, looking from the windows of Printz Hall, saw the young engineer standing without.

"Who is the young man yonder?" he asked. "He is a right fair specimen of our race. I think I have not seen him before."

"That is Eric Helm, your Honor," replied a soldier in attendance.

"Eric Helm!" exclaimed the Governor. "If such be the case, send him to me. I have a word to say to him."

"The Governor calls for you."

The touch upon his arm made Eric turn hastily. He had taken a few steps away from the building, reluctant to force the interview that he feared as much as he desired. At the soldier's words he followed him into the Hall, his thoughts going back to the first time he entered it. The issue to-day was scarcely less momentous than on the former occasion.

He thought the Governor looked at him with some curiosity.

"Your name is Eric Helm?" he asked.

"It is, your Honor," replied the young man.

"And your position here is——?"

"It *was* that of a convict," said Eric firmly.

"For some time now I have been a free man. Governor Printz, to whom I owe the freedom, deemed that in giving it to me he was justified by more than the goodness of his own heart."

The words were calm, but the face of the speaker had grown whiter since he entered.

"That was, I believe, a provisional pardon," said the Governor. "I have the pleasure of presenting to you to-day a free pardon from your country, together with my own congratulations. The first will, I think, be of the most value to you, especially as it is based on no man's kindness, but upon a simple principle of justice. It is lucky for you that rogues fall out among themselves, seeing that their doing so has in this case brought to light the fact that the fire, which was to blame for sending you to New Sweden, started after you left the barn, and not before."

For a minute Eric stared at the speaker. Then the color came back to his face. He drew himself up as if a weight were taken from his shoulders.

"Then I was not responsible for the loss of the buildings?" he said.

"So it seems," replied the Governor, with a smile. "I will furnish you with a full account of the evidence given by one of the men in the barn at the time when the fire started. Then you can judge for yourself."

The eyes of the young man looked into his.

"I think the assurance that the mischief came through no act of mine is worth more to me than the freedom," he said. "I thank your Excellency for bringing me the knowledge of both."

He did not know how or when he got out of Printz Hall, nor whom he passed on the way. One thing his brain had seized upon and held to. He was not only free to-day, but the shame of the past was swept away. He might have something against the world, but the world had naught against him. And through his meditations there came with bewildering frequency the memory of a pair of soft blue eyes. He let them flash in and out of his thought, and make havoc with all attempt at coherency therein. And when he came to a definite consciousness of the present, he was wondering how those eyes would look at him when their owner heard his story.

CHAPTER XXVIII

"Free at last!"

Eric lifted his head high, and looked up to the sunlit sky.

"Free, and without a stain on my name! Now it will be no more a dishonorable thing to go to her."

The packet he held in his hand shook, and that not with the brisk summer breeze.

Strong excitement had taken possession of the young engineer. The impetuosity, that during these years had been held in stern check, broke its barriers. He was the Eric Helm of the old Swedish days, and not Eric Helm the convict. He was looking life in the face—the life that other men lived. It lay before him as freely as before them now.

As freely? Nay, was there another man in New Sweden, or anywhere else in the world, for the matter of that, who had such a life before him as this, the possibility of which was setting his pulses throbbing and his heart thumping?"

"I will win her if I can," he said, "and I may do it with a clear conscience."

The ground seemed to speed from under his feet, so quickly was he leaving Printz Hall behind him. An irresistible desire to be nearer Fort Trinity than New Gottenburg seized upon him. He could not wait. The years that had passed had been long enough already. Hours had become lengthy now.

He would examine this new evidence which had changed all things, and assure himself that he was indeed free of the charge that had been as heavy on his heart as on his prospects, and then he would leave the past to take care of itself, and begin another life. Agneta had never known him yet—the real Eric, who was not a convict. He had not dared to meet her as he might meet her now. In all their intercourse he had ever remembered that he was under the ban of the law. Now he was free, aye, and cleared of the charge.

He was in haste to read the details contained in that packet, yet they were in his mind secondary to the effects they had wrought. He was not even very angry with those who had so wantonly wrecked his life. He was in too much of a hurry to transform the wreck into a goodly craft, and set sail for the desired port.

He saw, without any intelligent observation, a band of Indian warriors coming towards him. They were on their way to Printz Hall to communicate to the Governor the result of their private conference. They knew that the eyes of the settlers were upon them, and that the white men were desirous of knowing whether the friendship of the natives was to be continued. They carried themselves the more proudly for the knowledge. They were not averse, however, to a little conversation with the white men. Eric Helm found himself confronted by a warrior with whom he had frequently had intercourse in his journeys.

"The Big Sachem comes no more," said the Indian.

The young engineer brought his thoughts back with a wrench.

"No, but the new Governor arrives as the friend of your race," he said.

"The new Sachem speaks fair words," said the warrior. "My people are glad to learn that the white men are in truth their friends. This is a good day."

Aye, it *was* a good day. Eric was very ready to echo the words. A good day! He did not know that he had ever seen a better.

There were others who thought it a good day also. It was the beginning of better things when Naaman, the spokesman of the Indians, chided his brethren for having spoken evil words of the white men, and pointed to the presents that had been given them, to prove how true was the friendship of the Swedes.

"We have already, in the time of Governor Printz, been as one heart and one body," he said, "now shall we be as one head also," and with both hands he grasped his own head, and made a motion of tying a tight knot there. "From this time, if any should attempt to do harm to the Indians, the Swedes shall inform them of it," he continued, "and if we hear of any plot against the Swedes, we will warn them, yes, if it should be in the middle of the night."

"That will indeed be a lasting friendship," was the reply of the new Governor. "If all will agree to it, then shall Swedes and Indians surely be as one."

Upon this the people without heard a loud shout. It was the answer of the red men to the Governor's words, and was the sign of their assent. In quick response the great guns were fired to seal the compact.

"Hear and believe! The great guns are fired," said the Indians, pleased that their league with the white men had been thus honored.

It was a time of general rejoicing. Within Printz Hall the Governor feasted the Indians, setting two great kettles and many other vessels filled with suppaun upon the floor of the great hall, until all had eaten and were satisfied. And in New Gottenburg the Swedes discussed the situation, and were convinced that New Sweden had entered upon an era of prosperity.

"Wouldn't Governor Printz have held his head high if he had seen this day?" remarked a citizen.

"Governor Printz!" was the reply. "Why, man, Printz Hall wouldn't have held him."

The island of Tenacong could not that day hold Eric Helm. Not two hours after he left Governor Rysingh's presence his canoe was racing down the river.

What a world it was that summer day! Surely

New Sweden was a fair land. And yet, except in a general way, he did not see much of its beauty. He was thinking of a girlish face and a pair of soft, gentle eyes. He knew the face and eyes would light up when he told his news. He had an irresistible desire to tell it to her first. The congratulations of the others would be pleasant, but he wanted to see just how it affected her.

The desire grew in force as he descended the river, and it accounted for the fact that he did not go to Axel Bonde's house that day, and that the good Dutch vrouw, Rachel Boyer, was the first to share the joy that was overflowing his heart. It was too late to see Agneta alone that night. All the family would be gathered together in or around the house. He would start early in the morning, and reach the farm before noon. Then, perchance, his desire might be fulfilled.

"Ah, lad, clouds hang not over the sky forever," said the kindly vrouw. "Verily I've heard no better news this many a day."

She laid her motherly hand on his arm, and looked into his eyes.

"What next, boy?" she asked.

He laughed—a light, glad laugh.

"I think I'll see whether the world holds greater happiness for me yet," he said.

"Aye," she answered, " 'twill be your own fault if you let the best things slip through your fingers now."

They had grown to understand each other since

the night when the vrouw invaded her guest's privacy and convinced him that trouble grew no heavier by being shared. That his faith, instead of being of the Lutheran type, coincided with her own and that of her countrymen, possibly made the friendship the stronger. The land owned by Eric Helm, and cultivated in the intervals of his engineering labors, was in proximity to the settlement of the Dutch residents of New Sweden, and Rachel Boyer had seen much of the young man since she first received him into her house. She had liked him then. She liked him better to-day.

"Bless the lad!" she ejaculated, as she saw him start in the morning, with the light of the new gladness on his face. "He looks as if he had but now begun to live. Truly I did not realize what a weight he was carrying on his heart till I saw him set free from it. I fairly believe he stands an inch taller than he has ever done since I knew him."

He went away with a smile on his lips. He was thinking of Agneta, and reveling beforehand in her gladness. She filled his thoughts when he started from Rachel Boyer's door, and he was thinking of her still when the farm of Axel Bonde was reached and he saw a feminine head and—Maria's buxom form. He tried to draw back, hoping that she had not perceived him. It was a vain hope. She came running towards him, with hands outstretched.

"We wondered how long you were going to keep

your secret to yourself," she said. "Truly we took it ill of you that you shared it not with us."

"What? You knew——" he began.

"Of course we did—as soon as you knew it yourself, I should think. The Governor had been here little more than a week before we heard that *your* convict days were over."

He winced a little at the words. They had power to hurt, even now. The light in his face faded. There was nothing left for him to tell. Already Agneta knew all he would have told her.

"You were more fortunate than I was," he said quietly. "To me the knowledge is but a day old."

"A day! Who'd have thought it?" ejaculated Maria. "And we've been wondering what kept you so still. To think we should hear it first! That comes of having friends high up in the world. I doubt if any but Monsieur Pors knew of it," added the girl, with an assumption of grandeur.

"Monsieur Pors?" repeated Eric, inquiringly. "I think I know not the name, and still less can I surmise what acquaintance its owner can have with me."

"Oh, you'll not be here long before you know Monsieur Pors," said Maria lightly. "He's come after Agneta. I suppose he'll take her back to Sweden with him. She belongs to him, you know."

"Ah, I remember."

His face had grown cold. With the girl's words came the memory of a ride to church on a Christmas morning, and of the flash of a giant torch that seemed to accompany and be part of a half-whispered story about a little maid and an old castle.

"He's here, and he's come for her," said Maria, confidentially.

"And what has this Monsieur Pors to do with me, and that which is to me a great gladness?" he asked, in a changed tone.

"Oh, he came over with the new Governor, and he knew all about the pardon, and he told Agneta."

It was doubtful whether, after that, Eric heard much of what Maria was saying. He had hurried from Tenacong to tell Agneta his story. Now it seemed no longer worth talking about. *He* had already told it to her, this prosperous worldling whose touch could not but vulgarize the news he brought. His wonderful good fortune, that had been almost too great to be believed, had become a common thing, a subject that could be talked over to while away an hour.

"She has gone into the woods with Monsieur Pors. He is ever persuading her to act as his guide, and truly she seems to be not unwilling."

Maria had been chattering on unheeded. These were the first words that made their way through to his brain.

"Truly Monsieur Pors is fortunate," he said.

"I should think he is," cried the girl. "Why, he's rich enough to do anything he's a mind to. Agneta will have more than the old castle when she goes back with him to Sweden."

Maria was not looking, or she would have seen an additional shadow sweep over the young man's face.

"Here they come," she announced, a minute later. "Now you will have a chance to see Monsieur Pors."

She turned towards him then, and noticed for the first time the proud look upon his face.

"My! He looks a good match for Monsieur Pors himself," she thought.

The two couples were nearing each other. There was a bright flush on Agneta's cheeks. It did not escape the eye of her companion. When but a few yards separated her from Maria and Maria's escort, the girl turned to Monsieur Pors.

"That is my friend, Eric Helm," she said, in a low voice. "With your permission I will go forward to greet him. I have not seen him since the arrival of Governor Rysingh."

Gustavus bowed, and slackened his pace, a moment later coming to a stand and leaving the maiden to advance alone.

"He didn't know anything about his freedom till yesterday," announced Maria, in a tone loud enough to include the whole company.

Nobody heeded her. Agneta held out her hand, but said no word. She lifted her eyes to Eric's, and he saw that they glistened through a mist. He took the offered hand and looked down upon her. That silent greeting had put his tidings again into the realm of the sacred. Whether the news had first come to her from his own lips, or from the lips of that tall, impassive figure behind her, its contact with the girl's heart had placed it beyond the possibility of being vulgarized.

"You already know what I thought I should be the first to tell," he said softly.

"No. I have heard some of the facts. What you have to tell is more than the outside shell of fact. But—I think I do not want to hear it now," she said.

He understood, and smiled down upon her.

"And I think I do not want to tell it now," he answered.

"Will you give me the pleasure of making Monsieur Pors known to Jupe's master and the friend of Jupe's mistress?" she asked, a minute later. "Jupe is discriminating in his love. He gives Monsieur Pors but a scant measure of it."

The two men glanced at each other for a moment, and each in that moment revised a pre-conceived opinion.

CHAPTER XXIX

"Is Eric Helm coming again this week?"

Maria's tone was significant. It brought the color to Agneta's cheeks.

"I know not. If he should, I doubt not that he will be welcome," she said.

Maria tossed her head.

"You can make him welcome enough now he's no longer a convict," she said spitefully.

"He was ever welcome here, and ever will be," replied Agneta quietly, though the hot color would not quickly leave her cheeks.

"Monsieur Pors wishes he were not," retorted Maria. "I will say you show a most covetous spirit, Agneta. You can't have both of them, though truly it seems sometimes as if you meant to try. If I were Monsieur Pors I'd not wait on your whims. I'd bring you to terms once for all."

Agneta wisely refrained from answer. Perhaps she made allowance for the soreness of Maria's spirit. That damsel was no longer assured that circumstances were conspiring to carry out her wishes. True, there were two maidens and two knights on the scene, and theoretically the result should have been two satisfied couples. In practice the combination usually resulted in one satisfied pair, and an odd man and maiden left to look at the world with discontented eyes.

It could not be claimed that Agneta was one of the dissatisfied. The summer had been to her a happy one. She had not always stopped to analyze the happiness, though now and again she had questioned it. She did so to-day. Maria's words had awakened a misgiving. Would the answer she must before long give Monsieur Pors be the harder to explain by reason of this summer's gladness?"

It wanted but three months to her eighteenth birthday. Then Gustavus Pors would ask the question he had come to New Sweden to propound. Agneta was not as ready to face that question as on the day when she greeted Monsieur Pors upon the bank of the river. It looked less simple than it had done then. Monsieur Pors himself had become a big factor in it. The castle, too, had grown strangely familiar of late. She seemed to belong to it more than ever before. She could almost have imagined that it had been the home of Monsieur Pors himself, so well versed was he in all that pertained thereto. Brita and Lars stood out before the girl's consciousness now as plainly as on the day when she saw the old servant shading her eyes to watch the coach drive away. Agneta felt as if she had a duty towards them all—those old retainers of the family. They were looking for Monsieur Pors to bring her back.

"I have made a promise to Brita," he told Agneta one day. "I doubt not she is in haste to see the fulfillment of the same."

The girl did not ask the nature of that promise.

She was thinking of Brita and the castle to-day, and, it must be confessed, of the castle's present owner also. She had gone out of the house to escape Maria's tongue, which was venomous that morning. She was not surprised, when the trees that hid Fort Trinity were reached, to see Monsieur Pors emerge from their shadow. There were few days on which he did not pay the farm a longer or shorter visit.

"How now, little one?" he said, when his eyes had scanned and his tongue greeted the maiden. "Gravity becomes well that fair face, yet does it please me not to see it thus sober."

"Why should it not be sober, monsieur?" she said. "Life is not all a pastime."

"To you it should surely be, if I had my way," he answered.

She laughed.

"Do you expect always to have your way?" she inquired.

"No. I expect to have it just once, and for the rest of the time to see that you have yours," he responded.

She shook her head.

"The result would be disastrous," she said.

He bent his head until his eyes looked into hers.

"Will you let me try the experiment?" he asked.

"Nay, for it would be no experiment. Your success would be my certain undoing," she said, with a smile that was not quite free from nervousness.

"I am not afraid," he answered gently. "Agneta,

give me permission to prove to you what my success could mean. It shall not be my fault then if your life know aught beside happiness."

"Monsieur, my life has not been lacking in happiness," said Agneta quietly. "Truly I am satisfied with its joys."

"I will teach you to be dissatisfied then," he cried, with a touch of impetuosity.

"Nay, beware lest you find yourself among the teachers who overrate their own powers, or the capacity of their pupils," she said.

"The capacity of my pupil has not yet been gauged," he said, looking into her face meditatively.

"And the powers of the teacher?" she asked, with a laugh.

"Are illimitable," he said gravely.

They walked on in silence. Agneta's pulses were not quite as steady as usual.

"Do you never grow weary of this land?" he asked, suddenly.

"Why should I?" said the girl, looking up at him with a light in her eyes. "They who love me are here."

"And there also, except when they cross the sea to come to you," he said.

Her eyes dropped.

"And so you never tire of life at the farm-house, nor long for a broader outlook?" he said.

"What does one see with a broader outlook?" she asked.

"Men, and things, and the bigger world," he replied.

"Better men and better things than these?" she asked. "Will the big world show me a better man than grandfather Axel?" and she looked up suddenly into his face.

It flushed beneath the clear, penetrating glance.

"Verily, Axel Bonde is a good man," he said, "yet is he but a peasant, with a peasant's narrowness, and a peasant's ideas, that—pardon me if I say it—must have a reflex influence on one who——"

He hesitated, not quite sure of the wisdom of completing the sentence.

"Who thinks him well-nigh perfect," said Agneta. "Perchance they do. It is truly possible that my ideas are also 'narrow.' Seem I so very rustic to you, monsieur?" she added, with a touch of mockery in her tone.

"Nay," he said, smiling down at her, "shall I tell you what to me you seem? Will you let me?"

"I think not," she answered. "I love not to see myself in an unpleasant light," and she turned from him to reach a great cluster of grapes that hung over a rock almost to the edge of the water. It was November, and a rich purple tint was upon the overripe fruit.

He sprang down the bank to gather it for her.

That afternoon Gustavus Pors sought Axel Bonde.

"My friend," he said abruptly, "you are not in ignorance of the object that brought me to New

Sweden. I would talk with you upon the subject that is as near my heart as yours."

"Nay, that is a statement that is open to challenge," said Axel quietly. "I doubt whether your love for the bairn be as deep as that of the old man who looks less at the love than at its object. There is naught I would not do for her, even to giving her to another. Can you say as much?"

"Surely not," said Gustavus, "for I see not the necessity."

" 'Tis the eye of selfishness that is blind," said Axel. "Nevertheless, say on. I am ready to listen."

Gustavus Pors had perhaps never found it harder to 'say on' than upon the present occasion. He could not complain of want of courtesy on the part of his listener. The old man gave his words the most careful attention. Possibly the attention was too careful.

"I would gladly start for Sweden before the worst storms of winter," said Gustavus, when he had pleaded his love, and explained his intentions about the castle and lands that he had held in trust for Agneta. "I am well aware that you have legal control over her for three months longer, yet would I ask you to waive that claim and give her to me now."

"It is not a question of whether it would be best for me to give her to you at an earlier or later date, but whether I can give her to you at all," said the old man gently.

Monsieur Pors drew himself up proudly.

"Nay, but there you step beyond your privilege," he said. "She is already mine. One who had a better right to control her actions than have you—honestly as you love her—gave me the joy of calling her my own. To my dear old friend, her father, I owe a happiness the full extent of which I knew not when he placed the baby fingers in mine."

"Understood her father the character of him to whom he confided his greatest treasure?" asked Axel plainly.

The eyes that looked into his flashed.

"You are an old man," said Monsieur Pors. "Therefore will I bear with you. My friend deemed himself as good a judge of character as does Axel Bonde, and he knew more of the man in whose hand he placed that of the little Agneta."

"Would he give her to you now, think you?" asked the old man, fixing upon the face of the younger eyes that were keen to read every expression thereon. "Would you, were you in his place? Were her life yours to make or mar, and I Gustavus Pors, would you give her to me?" he added. "Would you deem heart and life fit to-day to mate with the purity of yonder bairn?"

The deep red blood rose and spread till the face and brow of the listener were darkened.

"Your question is an impertinence," he said, in a low, deep voice.

"In view of the fact that the happiness of the girl you say you love depends upon it?" said Axel. "Verily I have my answer."

For a minute they stood looking into each other's faces. Then the eyes of Gustavus Pors dropped.

"I may not be worthy of her," he said, "but I can become so."

"How do you know, friend? Have you tried?"

Again the listener was speechless. It was an unusual position for Monsieur Pors.

"You have power to set aside my happiness to-day," he said at last. "In three months the tables will be turned."

"By what means?" asked Axel, still in the same gentle tone. "Will you take an unwilling bride, my friend?"

"Nay, but she would not be unwilling if you used not your cursed influence against me."

"Has it been accursed in her life, think you?" said the old man gently. "Friend," he added, "are you thinking of the bairn, or of yourself?"

"Of myself," said Gustavus savagely. "And so are you."

The old man was silent for a minute.

"If her heart speak on your side, I may perchance learn to doubt the wisdom of my decision," he said. "Yet will I not have her disturbed until her eighteenth birthday."

Gustavus turned away with a frown on his brow, and ran heavily against one who was already within the door.

The Indian had not stopped to knock. It was not his habit.

"Surely the Swede must be running a race with the sun," he said calmly.

"I meant not to run over a friend," returned Monsieur Pors.

"It might be wiser to hear his news first," replied the old Indian, in whose features Axel Bonde recognized Amattehoorn, the husband of the squaw, who, since Agneta's first acquaintance with her, had kept up a desultory friendship with Axel Bonde's family. Amattehoorn had formed his own opinion of the "little white squaw," as he had at the commencement of the acquaintance designated Agneta.

"Come in, friend," said Axel, "for you are welcome."

"More welcome than the news I bring," responded Amattehoorn, "for the Swedes love not the war song."

The words arrested the steps of Gustavus Pors. He stopped in the doorway, and a minute after reëntered the room.

"Who would bring war to the Swedes?" he asked.

"Their brothers, the Hollanders," replied Amattehoorn.

"Nay, it is true the Hollanders have seized one of our ships that entered their port of New Amsterdam," replied Axel. " 'Twas not an act of courtesy, yet possibly might it be justified by our own behavior towards them. The hand that seizes because it is strong must be prepared to give up to a stronger."

"The Hollander is not satisfied with a ship. He would fight as my people fight. He would gather together his great canoes, and swoop down upon his enemy, and take, and destroy, and possess."

The eye of the Indian flashed. He went through the movements of sweeping down upon the foe, of conquest, and slaughter, and capture.

The faces of his hearers grew grave as they watched him. Was this thing of which he spoke real?

"Nonsense! The Hollanders do not want to fight. We white men settle such matters through our governments," said Gustavus. "We shall know if war be contemplated."

"The Swede who knows has nothing to learn," said the Indian, calmly.

"Friend," rejoined Axel, "how know you this?"

"My people have large ears. They hear up in New Netherland as well as here in New Sweden," said Amattehoorn, proudly.

"And think you that their ears are to be trusted?" asked Axel.

"I have traveled far to-day to warn my brothers," was the Indian's answer.

"It is enough, and a sure proof of your sincerity," replied Axel. "What said the good friends who told you?"

"That the Dutch Sachem has but now received from his white brothers across the great water the command to steal upon the Swedes, and drive them from their land of New Sweden," answered the Indian. "The men of the Manhattans talk of it, but they talk below their breath. They want not the winds to hear, lest they blow across New Sweden also, and carry the message with them."

"Yet our brothers, the red men, heard," said Axel.

"The ears of my people are open. They hear very far," replied Amattehoorn.

"Have any warned the Governor?" inquired Gustavus.

"We are friends of the white Sachem," replied the Indian. "We have sworn to tell him if any plot against him. Our people lie not."

"It is well," said Axel. "My brother must stay and refresh himself," he added.

"No, I go to my own people. I turned from my way to warn you," said Amattehoorn, and walked proudly from the room.

Gustavus and Axel looked at each other.

"It is but the natural consequence of a system of self-seeking," said the old man. "We cannot well complain if our aggression return upon our own heads."

"Axel," said Gustavus, "there is trouble in the air. If the words of yonder Indian be true, New Sweden has evil days before her. You told me but now, my friend, that you could bear to part with Agneta if it were for her good. What say you? Is it for her welfare to keep her in a land that the demons of war have chosen for their next play ground?"

The face of Axel Bonde was troubled. For a minute he was silent.

"I spoke truly," he said at last. "The interests of the bairn shall ever stand first. Yet have I at present no certainty that it would be for her gain to alter my decision. There is more than one form of evil. I would that I could shield her from all."

"You will expose her to all, if you have not a care," said Gustavus hotly. "Know you not that this place will be in the very track of the Dutch? Are you unaware of what that means for a maiden such as yon? The soldiery have little respect for womanhood."

Axel Bonde's face was grave and sad.

"Respect for womanhood, irrespective of its rank and its grace, is not among the commonest of manly virtues," he said. "I'll do what looketh to be best for my bairn, and you must pardon me, my friend, if at present I do not see that it is to bid you take her from New Sweden."

CHAPTER XXX

"I am afraid the Indians are nearer right than we of New Sweden want to believe."

Eric Helm sat in Axel Bonde's living room, talking to Axel himself. He had come on purpose to talk with Axel—or he told himself he had. That the conversation was not occupying all his thoughts he would perhaps have been willing to admit.

And yet the subject was, to the people of New Sweden, an engrossing one, being no other than the rumored hostile attitude of their neighbors, the Hollanders. Many in New Sweden were inclined to regard this attitude as an idle boast. Pieter Stuyvesant had enough to do to manage his own colony, they said, and to establish trade relations with the West Indies. He was about to start from New Amsterdam on a mission to Barbadoes and the other West Indian islands. He would have time to get over his anger before he returned, and the war would be one of words.

Eric Helm was not so sure. He had come over to-day to communicate to Axel a little fresh information on the subject—that is to say, this was the ostensible motive for his visit.

"There is much probability in the story the red men tell," said Axel, "though we have since heard nothing to confirm it."

"It is perhaps not conclusive confirmation," replied Eric, "yet a certain message from the home land received by Rachel Boyer yesternight surely points the same way as the words of the Indian."

"A message from the Dutch Fatherland?" rejoined Axel. "How came she by such, seeing that no vessel has arrived from foreign parts?"

"Jan Classen has been out in his sloop, fishing beyond the bay," replied Eric. "Yesterday he returned, and at night sought Rachel. On the high seas he had had an adventure, none other than the falling in with a vessel bound for Virginia. When he was hailed from that vessel by a Dutch tongue, nothing would do but he must tread her timbers. He found aboard her a countryman of his own, and had a long talk about the Fatherland. Among other things he received a message for Rachel and her husband. 'If Rachel Boyer be in New Sweden,' said the Dutchman, 'tell her to look out for herself, and not get too thick with the Swedes, for we shall have our revenge on them yet.' 'What mean you by that?' asked Jans. 'What mean I, good friend?' replied the other. 'All that I say, and much more. Why, man, every day in the week the drum is beat in the streets of Amsterdam. What for, think you? For nothing else but to enlist men to serve against the enemies of our country, even the treacherous Swedes, who took advantage of our friendship to rob us of our fort.' 'Tis a strange story," continued Eric. "I know not what to make of it, or whether to take it as an idle boast, but it pointeth, of a certainty, the same way as the tale of the Indian."

"Of that there can be no doubt," replied Axel thoughtfully. "I would gladly believe both stories without foundation, yet to me it seemeth not likely that such threats would be made for naught."

"The Hollanders are very bitter against us, else would they not have seized one of our vessels," said Eric. "It would not be surprising if they should seek yet further to retaliate."

He was addressing Axel Bonde, but his eyes were following Agneta. The big spinning wheel and the slim, graceful figure made a pleasant picture in the living room. It was December, and the inside of the house was more attractive than the outside. It needed not the December cold to make that warm living room attractive to Eric, for Agneta was there. His eyes fixed themselves upon her as she walked back and forth at the wheel, and his tongue halted a little sometimes. Suddenly she stopped, and turned her face towards him.

"I think even the capture of a fort is not sufficient ground for making the Dutch so determinately our enemies," she said. "We are kindred peoples in a land of savages. It were strange if we should fall one upon the other."

"I know a Dutchwoman who would be glad to claim the kinship of having been born upon the same continent, if she might persuade a certain Swedish lady to come beneath the shelter of her roof," said Eric. "Rachel Boyer has more than once begged me to bring Jupe's mistress to see her. To-day she was especially insistent."

"Why, I will go with you when you like," said Agneta, with a little flush of pleasure. "I have always wanted to know Rachel because——"

She stopped, and he waited with curious anxiety for the finish of the sentence. It did not come, and he did not ask for it—then. He was not as reticent the next day, when he had guided his canoe out of the South River and into a creek that ran near by the lands occupied by Rachel Boyer and honest Marten, her husband.

"Will you tell me why you were so kindly willing to give Rachel the pleasure she has long coveted?" he asked, looking down at the girl who sat in the boat, her face alight with interest.

Such an excursion was a big one to Agneta. She was enjoying every turn of the way, and looking forward to the meeting with the good Dutchwoman at the end.

"Why shouldn't I be willing?" she asked lightly. "We have not so many neighbors here that we can afford to be unneighborly, even to the remotest of them."

She thought he looked disappointed. Then he smiled.

"Would it be presumption to ask you to finish a sentence you left unfinished yesterday?" he asked. "You said you wanted to know Rachel because—I confess that that 'because' has been a subject of curiosity ever since."

For a moment the eyes he was looking into dropped. Then they were lifted again.

"I believe I was going to say, because she was so motherly to you," said Agneta, half shyly.

His face lighted then.

"I did not dare to hope that that was the finish," he said, "though I sadly wanted it to be."

Rachel Boyer took the girl's hand in hers, and looked into her face. Then she bent forward and kissed it.

"Forgive me, my dear," she said. "I could not help it. You are all he said, and I verily believe, all he thinks, and that is not saying a little."

Then, as the bright color dyed the girl's cheeks, she laughed, and helped her guest to take off the heavy wraps that had been altogether necessary accessories to a journey by water at so late a season as the latter part of December.

"I like your Dutch vrouw," said Agneta later in the day to Eric. "I think if I had known, you should not have had her all to yourself so long."

As for Rachel, she did not know how to make enough of her guest. She brought out olekoeks and head-cheese, and made waffles, and roasted game, and chattered all the time in happy contentment that was surely contagious, for the faces of her guests seemed to borrow some of her gladness, or else to have a goodly share of their own.

"I call him my boy," explained the good vrouw, when she went with Agneta into the guest chamber, and insisted on passing the warming-pan over the cold linen sheets. "Mother was never more proud of lad of her own than I am of him. I shall not easily forget the look in his eyes when he came to me directly after he learned he was not to blame for the burning of his uncle's barn. I never saw face so bright, unless, perchance, it was the same face the next morning, when he started off to tell you, and I dare not say that then it was not brighter."

Another thing that Rachel Boyer would not have dared to say was that the face of the girl before her had not acquired a tremulous gladness as she talked. Her eyes sought it for a moment, and then were withdrawn. She abstained from telling this maiden how completely the buoyancy had gone from Eric's step when he returned from the farm-house. She had looked for good news, but in answer to her questioning "Well, lad?" his eyes looked squarely into hers as he said, quietly:

"I have got a chance to begin life afresh, and to make something out of it if I can, and if I do not succeed, nobody will be the worse for my failure."

"Don't be too sure, my boy," she said.

He had never told her more, and she had not asked. But Rachel was a good guesser, and she came in time to know Monsieur Pors by name, and to understand something of his position in the household of Axel Bonde. She held her peace when for a season Eric went no more to the farm by the South River. She watched his face, however, and could have told almost to a day when the argument going on within had come to the point at which he decided that though Monsieur Pors might, as Maria asserted, be able to grant Agneta everything she could desire, it was not quite certain that Monsieur Pors himself was included in those desires.

There was a moment when he said again: "I will win her if I can," and his footfall grew firmer, and his voice had a ring in it that did not escape Rachel's ears. He had been often to the farm-house since then. Now he had brought the maiden back with him. Rachel drew a good omen from the fact, and rejoiced over Agneta, and studied her while she rejoiced.

She did not see exactly the girl whom Monsieur Pors knew best. This maiden was winsome, and sweet, and unsuspicious; yes, and she was very happy too. But when on the next day the boat was again half-way towards the farm, and Monsieur Pors hailed the occupants from the bank, her mouth fell into a mischievous curve, and her eyes became centres of light.

"Will you come with us, monsieur?" she asked.

"Surely, if you will give me a welcome," he said.

"We will give you a seat, and if you are tired, that may, perchance, be better," she replied.

He seated himself where he could look into her face. The brightness in it pleased him ill. Moreover the satisfaction upon the masculine one beyond suggested the duality of the pleasure. He was very sincere in his desire to see this maiden happy, but he himself must be the source of the happiness. He had not doubted that the source was sufficient—until to-day.

Perhaps the doubt had something to do with the fact that after he had walked to the house with Agneta he returned in time to waylay Eric, and begin a conversation with him.

It started on subjects connected with the homeland, and presently Eric found Monsieur Pors telling him of certain improvements he desired to make upon one of his estates. He launched out into a description of the house that stood upon the same, and descanted upon its disabilities.

Almost before he was aware of it the architectural instincts of the young man were aroused. He suggested a possible means of improvement.

"Undoubtedly you are right. I will make a note of it," said Gustavus.

Then he hesitated, stopped in his walk, and faced the other.

"I wish you were in Sweden," he said. "There are many other alterations that I should like to see made, and, following the example of Governor Printz, I am inclined to think that your head could find a way out of any reasonable dilemma. What say you? Will you journey at once to the old land, and undertake the remodeling of the house of which I speak? You will find me no niggard."

His face was conventionally non-committal. It betrayed nothing but a perfectly reasonable desire to provide for the improvement of his estates.

For a moment Eric looked at him without answering. That moment was one of suspense to Gustavus

Pors. He would not have liked to confess how much he desired to see this young man shake off the dust of New Sweden from his feet.

"There was a time when I should have been glad to accept your offer," said Eric calmly. "That time is past. New Sweden is to me to-day more atractive than anything the old land can show."

Gustavus looked at him fixedly, and as he looked, a light that burned steadily brighter was kindled in his eyes.

"Lieth the attraction in New Sweden itself, or in a certain inhabitant of the same?" he asked.

For a fraction of a second Eric hesitated. Then his head rose a little higher.

"Put it which way you will," he said. "I quarrel not with your statement."

The light in the other's eyes was growing dangerously bright.

"Let us understand each other," he said.

"Do we misunderstand?" asked Eric.

"You do, I think," said Gustavus, somewhat hotly.

Eric smiled.

"I await enlightenment," he said.

"You know my relations to—the maiden who has just left us," began Monsieur Pors, but Eric interrupted him.

"I have heard of your pretensions in that direction," he said. "You must pardon me if I think that the relation you desire has yet to be established."

"What? You deny my right to claim Agneta for my bride?"

"Most assuredly I do, till you have won that right from her own lips," said Eric.

Monsieur Pors certainly glared upon him. It was very unlike the usual procedure of that faultlessly polite gentleman, but he could not help it.

"And you mean that you, by your action, will contest that right?"

"I mean," said Eric quietly, "that I will win her if I can. You are at liberty to do the same. What more do you ask?"

"At liberty to stand on a footing of equality with you?" retorted Monsieur Pors, in a voice low and soft, but ringing with passion. "What do you think you have to offer her—*you*, who were but yesterday a convict?"

"What have I to offer her?" answered Eric, with a smile that Monsieur Pors did not quite understand. "I have a heart to offer her that has never beaten for any but her, and a life that she may see from one end to the other, and find in it, indeed, rashness for which I mourn, but naught that her pure eyes may not look upon. I have a strong arm that, till death paralyze it, shall shield her from all ill, and a determination to make her life one long season of gladness if love can accomplish as much. What more can you offer?"

Monsieur Pors moved aside impatiently.

"Do you realize what you are asking her to give up for *you*," he said, again with that stress upon the word.

The face of the other clouded.

"Aye, I realize it too well," he answered. "Yet, if she love me well enough to give it up, there will be little danger in the sacrifice."

"You are a presumptuous idiot!" snapped Gustavus, as he turned away.

"Perhaps I am," said Eric thoughtfully. "It is for her to decide."

CHAPTER XXXI

Monsieur Pors was in New Amsterdam. The time for which he had waited in New Sweden had come and gone, and June was here. The question that Agneta had at first felt herself fully ready to meet, and of late had experienced a growing reluctance to face, had been asked. And she was not Monsieur Pors' promised bride. Neither had he given up the dream he had indulged for fifteen years. He meant to carry this maiden back with him to the castle in Sweden, and to earn the everlasting gratitude of old Brita. But he had made up his mind to wait a little longer before he realized his dreams.

The child Agneta had been ever a pleasant picture in his mind. The maiden Agneta was something more. It was no longer the fancy of Monsieur Pors that was touched, but his heart. He had come to New Sweden determined to gratify his fancy and secure his rights. He left it pledged to himself to satisfy the cravings of his affection, and secure the girl who meant more to him than all his wealth.

When he declared his love it was in no conventional terms. The eyes that looked into hers sent their message straight down into the girl's heart. She had expected flattery and fervent persuasion, and she thought she knew how to meet them.

What she was not quite prepared to meet was the honest love that shone in the speaker's eyes, and spoke in his voice. For once Gustavus Pors did not pick his words. They came red-hot from his lips, and they were hard to answer.

Agneta had thought much about the reply she meant to give, but when it had to be spoken the words failed her. The decision had not been as easily reached as she expected. Again and again she went back to her mother's words: "Promise me that to the woman's heart within you, and not the girl's head, you will go for your answer." Yes, but which was the voice of the woman's heart, and which of the girl's head?

The picture of the old castle was ever before Agneta's eyes. It seemed as if those within it stretched forth their hands to her, begging her to come back. They had loved her when she was a child. Her eyes grew dim as she thought of Brita and Lars, and imagined Monsieur Pors going back to them alone. New Sweden looked desolate after such a thought journey to the old land, and the farm-house grew mean by comparison with the castle.

The owner of the castle, too, had a place in the picture. Monsieur Pors was very gentle and patient in those days. He came more often to the farm-house, and surrounded her with thoughtful attentions that were very pleasant, but a little trying in view of the words she must soon speak.

She was not quite sure that the woman's heart did

not give its verdict on the same side as the girl's head. When she thought of the castle, it was always with Monsieur Pors to take her to it, and to make much of her when there. And when she tried to imagine the life in New Sweden resumed on the base on which it moved before he came, the air seemed suddenly to gather to itself a chill.

There was much satisfaction in being surrounded by care such as had waited upon her through the last summer and winter. She scarcely knew whence the atmosphere of warmth and tenderness came. They all conspired to make the world a sunny place for her—grandfather Axel, and Gustavus Pors, and Eric.

It was when she thought of Eric, and his face and that of Gustavus Pors came side by side in the mental picture, that the woman's heart and the girl's head assumed different tones. Of the two men, one was not more gentle and chivalrous to her than the other, but the chivalry of Monsieur Pors was for the girl whom he had picked out from all the world to set his love upon, while, had she been the lowliest maiden in all New Sweden, and the most unlovely, the gentle chivalry of Eric Helm, though it would have been less personal in its nature, would not have failed. True, it was more than chivalry that spoke in his voice to her. To Eric Helm every maiden was an object for chivalry, but this maiden was a maiden set apart.

Perhaps Agneta hardly realized how much the thought of Eric Helm had to do with the fact that at last the woman's heart raised its voice above that of the girl's head. But she did know, before her eighteenth birthday, that she should never go back to the old castle, and that Monsieur Pors, and not herself, must carry her greeting to Brita and the rest. Then came the pleading of the castle's owner, and with it a tremor of heart and a faltering of tongue on the part of the maiden.

"I am very sorry, monsieur," she said, and he did not doubt the truth of her words. "You have been very good to me, and I would that I could give you what you desire."

"Little one," he said, gently, "you are to-day of age to decide for yourself. What you will give, none can withhold."

"Nay, monsieur," she said, "I have not made my meaning clear. It is because I cannot give that I mourn."

"Not monsieur," he said pleadingly, though he himself had taught the baby lips that word. "Agneta, little sweetheart, let it be Gustavus."

She started as the old name came from his lips.

"I have waited fifteen years for this day," he said. "Is it not enough?"

"I would that you had not waited," she replied, and he saw her lip quiver. "Surely it was a mistake."

"Was it?" There was passion in his tone. "Agneta, I would wait fifteen more rather than give you up."

She did not answer.

"Do you know what the thought of this day has been to me?" he asked, when the silence had grown very still. "It was the point to which all things tended. Agneta, I have cherished the shrine for the sake of the saint that should one day be enthroned there. The old castle has been unlike any other house. Everything in it, everything around it, has been preserved for you. I want not to boast, but its revenues have been administered with care greater than that bestowed upon any other of my estates. The land has grown rich. Not an old servant has left the place. Aye, and I have been as a slave in the hands of some of those old retainers. They have had their will with me, for were they not those who had ministered to you? Will you leave the shrine empty after all? Nay, little one, I could not bear such an ending to my hopes."

His voice dropped. The last words were low and pleading.

"I think, monsieur, that I wish you had been less thoughtful of my wishes," she said, and she tried to smile. "It would not then have been as hard for me to tell you that that for which you planned can never be."

"Nay," he said passionately, "you will not refuse me what your father has already given. It is to the influence of one whom you naturally esteem, but whose peasant outlook is too narrow to be a good guide for you, that this decision is to be attributed. Think again, Agneta. It is a question that may not be decided by another."

"You mistake," she said gently. "From my own heart, and not from grandfather Axel's judgment—which I pardon you for under-rating, since you know him not—comes the answer which I would willingly withhold."

"And your heart speaks against me?"

"Nay, not against you," she said. "It were ungrateful if it did. But it refuseth that which you ask."

He bent forward, and took her hand in his.

"Agneta, give me this, and let me win the heart," he said. "I will do it, little sweetheart, if love have any power."

The hand was gently drawn from his grasp.

"One must not go without the other," she said. "Monsieur, you would not really desire it."

"But this is already mine," he persisted. "Agneta, have your eyes never looked on a silver plate, where your name and mine are joined? I know not whether it be in your possession, or whether Axel Bonde, in his assumption of authority, may have deemed it necessary to keep it from you."

"Surely not," she said, with quiet dignity. "Grandfather Axel assumes no authority. My mother left me in his care. It is a care that has never failed. The plate of which you speak is in my own possession. It records that which should never have been—ought never to have been. Monsieur, I was a baby then. I am a woman now."

"The one woman in the world to me," he said.

At that moment her eyes met his. What he read in them may have prompted his next words.

"Agneta," he said, "I have been rash. I was in too much of a hurry to claim the desired good. I will wait. But, little sweetheart, I will not take no for an answer."

"Yet can I give you no other," she said.

"To-day I will have none," he decreed. "Come, the sun is shining. Let us go out and feel its warmth, for already it speaketh of spring."

And so it was left. To Agneta it was a question answered. Monsieur Pors judged otherwise.

Agneta could almost have imagined that the conversation had never been held, so completely did Monsieur Pors step back into the old position. He made himself more and more a part of her life, and let no opportunity to give her pleasure slip past him unimproved.

Rumors of warlike intent on the part of their neighbors, the Hollanders, reached the Swedes, but nobody knew quite how much to believe. Possibly only one dweller in the land of the South River at that time wished to believe in a coming hostile invasion. One assuredly did. Monsieur Pors saw in the turmoil and fear attending such a crisis a powerful adjunct to his own success. Axel Bonde's love for Agneta was too great, he argued, to allow him to see the girl placed in circumstances of danger. Gustavus Pors, and Gustavus Pors alone, could remove her from those circumstances. Therefore there must come a time when the influence of

Axel Bonde would be on the side he desired, always provided the threatened invasion turned not out to be a myth.

As spring advanced there was an ominous dearth of news. Whatever might be going on at New Amsterdam, no word of it was breathed in the land of the South River. It was not safe for Swedish ships to approach the Manhattans, for already one had been seized and detained by the Director-General of New Netherland. He held it, as he affirmed, until Fort Casimir should be restored to its rightful owners, the Dutch. As that day was, in the opinion of the Swedes, a remote one, there was little chance of the vessel ever again becoming Swedish property.

In the absence of vessels plying between the two colonies, the Indians were the only sources of information, and their testimony was on the side of war. Monsieur Pors, for one, believed them.

When spring came he resolved on a definite move.

"You ought to be very good to me," he said, as he walked by Agneta's side one day, "for I am tasting a joy that will soon belong to the past."

Her eyes looked startled as she raised them to his face.

"I will try not to be especially bad," she said. "What is the joy to which you are going to say farewell?"

"You!" he replied, smiling, and looking into her eyes.

She was too much surprised to drop them.

"You are going away?" she asked.

"Yes, to New Amsterdam. I cannot longer endure this suspense. I must know for myself what foundation there is for the rumors that are around."

"But—will there not be risk?"

He read fear for his safety in her eyes, and the reading pleased him.

"And if there be?" he asked, bending towards her. "Would there be any to care?"

"Surely, monsieur," she said, "else were our hearts strangely hard."

"I would that one were soft—to me," he said. Then after a minute's silence he added: "A little risk there may perchance be, but I cannot rest till I know whether or not danger threatens this land. It contains that which to me is of too much value to be risked."

To Axel Bonde he said: "I am going to New Amsterdam. I know enough about war to make me willing to adventure a little rather than be surprised by a horde of pillaging Dutchmen, while yet Agneta remains right in the track of their devastations. War is bad enough for men, but for maidens——"

He shrugged his shoulders and was silent, and Axel Bonde found no answer ready.

So Monsieur Pors went to New Amsterdam, or rather to the coast of New Jersey, for no vessel could be found, the owner of which would carry him further. The Dutchman, Jan Classen, adventured his sloop to a point on the Jersey coast, landed his passenger, and returned in haste. The rest of the journey was taken on foot, with an Indian for guide.

Monsieur Pors had started for New Netherland for the purpose of awakening the fears of Axel Bonde and his family. He had not been in New Amsterdam twenty-four hours before his own fears were aroused. He no longer asked whether the war rumors were a fiction, or an idle boast. All Manhattan was astir. Two war vessels from Amsterdam lay in the harbor, and another was expected. The return of the Director-General from the West Indies was eagerly looked for.

Gustavus Pors found it necessary to exercise caution. He did not fail to note the inquisitive stare of the landlord of the little city tavern to which his guide brought him.

"Nieuw Nederland, nor Old Nederland, never gave you birth," commented that worthy, standing before his guest with one hand on his hip and the other rubbing his broad chin.

"No," replied Monsieur Pors, in perfect French, only a word or two of which was intelligible to his host. "It requires less astuteness than has fallen to your share, my good friend, to make such a discovery. Yet, though I may not claim kindred with yourself, I would see something of your city, for I already perceive that you have in New Amsterdam men of all races."

Then, as the landlord still stared at him, Gustavus Pors changed his tone, and addressed him in very intelligible Dutch.

"I can speak other languages beside my own," he said, "yet in the French tongue I could perhaps make my meaning clearer. I want a bed in your inn, and a good Dutch meal, and while the latter is preparing, I will look at your city. Your Governor, they tell me, is not here. It is a pity. I shall thus miss a sight of his face."

"Pity! You are a stranger here, else would you know how great the pity," replied the landlord. "Man, I took you for a Swede, though, now I come to look at you, surely you are too dark for one of that race. Know you what the rascally Swedes have done in the southern part of our province of New Netherland?"

"Nay, I knew not that your people dwelt far below Manhattan," said Gustavus.

"Our New Netherland stretcheth down to the South River, yea, and that country was ours before the Swedes so much as knew there was a South River," replied the Dutchman, raising his voice and assuming a belligerent attitude. "But now have they stolen our fort, and usurped our privileges. Look you from yon door. What see you?"

"I see a goodly ship. She looks like a war ship," said Gustavus.

"That is she. A war ship! Nay, man, it is not one, but many such that should sail from our harbor before the month was over, if the Director were but back from the West Indies. There is more than one of them here, waiting to strike terror to the hearts of those thieves and scoundrels, the Swedes, who, under pretext of friendship, sailed up to our fort and took our unsuspecting garrison by guile. I tell you, man, before this summer is past we will have a revenge worthy of the great West India Company."

Monsieur Pors went out into the little city. Everywhere he saw preparations for war, everywhere he heard the name of the South River. Yet, when men spake, they looked over their shoulders, in fear lest their conversation should be overheard.

He did not need to ask whether the war would be prosecuted with vigor. A glance at the faces of these Dutchmen as they descanted on the "infamous treachery of the Swedes," sent his thoughts back to the South River, and a gentle maiden walking upon its bank to-day. Before many weeks, perchance, these same Dutchmen would be overrunning that goodly land. The brow of Gustavus Pors grew dark at the thought.

"I will stay long enough to learn something of their plans," he said, "and then the first ship that sails southward shall carry me along with it."

Already he was eager to be back in New Sweden. He found himself dreaming of a pair of blue eyes, and listening for the sound of a girl's voice.

The danger, too, looked so real that he was in haste to be at Agneta's side. There would be little time to lose if he would take her from New Sweden before the storm burst. For two or three weeks he mingled with the Dutchmen of the recently created municipality, not always without exciting suspicion. These Dutchmen were very much in earnest about keeping their designs a secret. Their city was not exactly a safe place for a Swede at that particular time. Monsieur Pors, as a rule, found it fairly easy to claim France as his native land, and a liberal use of the French language was generally sufficient to allay suspicion.

New Netherland was in a state of activity, but it was also in a state of suspense. It was waiting for the Director. When he should return, the preparations for war would be succeeded by the conflict itself.

"Not a Swede will we leave in the land of the South River," said the landlord loudly, looking round to assure himself that all beneath his roof were friends to the Dutch cause. "We're all one here, and I'm not afraid to say that our Governor has directions to turn them out of New Sweden, root and crop. They never had right there. Now shall they learn what it means to take advantage of our friendship, and defy our anger."

"It is full time for my return," said Monsieur Pors, when July was nearing its end. "I have seen enough to answer my purpose. I must even bend my energies to the procuring of a bark to take me southward. That last may not be the work of a day. Yet must there soon be a vessel going to Virginia. Once as far south as New Sweden, I will take the risk of getting myself put ashore somewhere on her coast."

That southward bound vessel proved to be a visionary good. Every sloop and yacht that left the harbor sailed towards the north, and while Gustavus was seriously considering the advisability of chartering a vessel for himself, the Director-General of New Netherland returned.

Then was there rejoicing in New Amsterdam.

"Our day has come," averred the landlord, his capacious figure swelling itself out until it occupied more than its usual share of the tavern porch, where the worthy innkeeper was smoking his pipe, and half a score of burghers were smoking their pipes, to the pleasing diversion of watching a game of bowls played on the green near by. "Now will the Swedes learn to their cost what a New Netherland army can do. Thirty-six guns carries the good ship *Balance*, from Amsterdam. I would give much to see how their forts will look after we have opened a broadside on them."

From that day Gustavus Pors haunted the harbor. He was uncharitably glad to hear that sickness had overtaken Director Stuyvesant, for this pointed to delay in the completion of the war preparations. The inability of the Governor to assume personal oversight did not, however, lessen the energy of his deputies. Monsieur Pors was on board the merchant ship, the *Spotted Cow*, when Fiscal Cornelis van Tienhoven and Frederick de Koninck, the captain of the man-of-war, the *Balance*, came alongside.

"Well, skipper," cried Van Tienhoven heartily, "we have come to pay you and the rest of the merchantmen a visit, and I doubt not we are welcome."

"Welcome enough," replied the skipper, "if so be you want not too much."

"Too much, say you?" shouted Van Tienhoven. "And what would you think too much for the purpose of upholding the honor of your country, and teaching those plundering Swedes where their place is? 'Tis not the skipper of the *Spotted Cow* that would draw back on such an occasion."

"Right you are," was the reply. "We'll refuse not our share. What want you?"

"A good vessel, and brave men," replied the Fiscal promptly. "What say you? Will you go with us to fight against the Swedes?"

"Not so," replied the skipper, with a laugh. "We have other work cut out for us. Yet will we give that which is declared to be our share. What asks the Governor? Two men, and a share of ammunition from each vessel that cannot go to the war, said he not?"

"Aye, and all the provisions you can spare," replied Van Tienhoven. "Our men must not go to the South River hungry."

"Hungry!" laughed the skipper. "Come away into the hold, and we'll see what we can do to keep hunger far from them."

As he passed Monsieur Pors, the Fiscal looked at him searchingly. Gustavus would have left the vessel had he not desired further conversation with the skipper. He had not yet learned the destination of the *Spotted Cow*. It might be Virginia.

"Now, then, skipper, here's your receipt for the

goods, and well pleased we are with what you've spared us," said the Fiscal, as he came up. "Two hundred pounds of stockfish, three firkins of barley, a ton of beef, a ton of pork, three hundred pounds of bread, and the powder to be left an open question, you agreeing to send as much as you can spare. Is that correct?"

"Aye, aye," said the skipper.

"You'll see that the two men are aboard the *Balance* when they are needed?"

"That will I," was the reply. "We'll do our share to teach the Swedes better manners. How are you off for pilots? I tell you, it wants men who know every shoal, to take such a fleet as ours into the South River safely."

"We have them," replied Van Tienhoven, in a tone of satisfaction. "Everything is arranged, and recruits coming in fast. Unless the Swedes have got warning of our intentions, you may reckon to a day when our flag shall wave again on Fort Casimir, aye, and make for itself a place on their Fort Christina also."

The Fiscal rowed to another ship, and the skipper turned to Monsieur Pors.

"Virginia! Why, man, know you not better than that?" he asked. "Think you the Governor will allow vessels to go southward now? He wants not news of his coming to be carried to the Swedes."

"But Virginia is not New Sweden," said Gustavus.

"And lieth not New Sweden on the way to Virginia?" laughed the skipper. "The Director-General is no fool. If 'tis to Virginia you want to go, truly you will have long to wait."

That night Gustavus Pors made efforts to charter a sloop. The skipper laughed in his face.

"What! With every vessel wanted for the service of the Governor?" he said. "There are few enough vessels that will be allowed to leave the port, even to carry on necessary trade. Think you one can be spared for a stranger's fancies? You have come to see New Amsterdam. You can look at it a little longer."

Monsieur Pors dared not show haste. Since the return of the Governor he had thought that men looked at him with less friendly glances. To awaken suspicion by his eagerness would be to defeat his own ends.

As quietly as might be, he visited every vessel in the harbor, and even went up the North River to find the owners of boats plying between Fort Orange and New Amsterdam. From every owner he received the comforting assurance that for the next two months his chances of chartering a vessel were of the smallest.

It was then that Monsieur Pors changed his mind about the desirability of war between New Netherland and New Sweden. He had hailed it as a friend. He was learning to see in it a dangerous enemy. Visions of the arrival of the Dutch fleet while yet the Swedes were unprepared and Agneta was without protection, came uncomfortably often. He thought of these Hollanders suddenly let loose upon the shores of the South River, and he himself unable to reach it, and he set his teeth together.

"I must get back somehow," he said, savagely. "Who'd have thought these fools of Dutchmen would have refused money for their sloops?"

In his desperation a new idea came to him.

"I will purchase a yacht," he said. "Then shall I have the means of going where I will, for once outside the harbor, none will be the wiser for the direction in which I steer. 'Tis useless to try to get permission to sail southward."

This last remark was made after he had learned that a vessel was actually bound for Virginia, but that to take passage upon her was an impossibility. Her owner had had too much trouble to secure permission to go southward himself, to risk the taking of an unknown and somewhat suspected passenger.

"Nay, I want not further risk," he said, eyeing the stranger curiously. "Know you not that the Governor and his Council have only given me leave to sail with a consignment of slaves upon my entering into bonds to the sum of five thousand pounds sterling that I will not touch at the South Bay or anywhere on the coast of New Sweden, or, even if driven thither by stress of weather, go further up than necessity demands? I have sworn that I will allow no person to come on board from there, nor give to any one on sloop or boat, or to any man whatsoever, information of the preparations going on in New Netherland. I am responsible for the doings of all whom I carry. Think you I shall desire to take a stranger with me, one of whose antecedents I know nothing? I have pledged my person and my property. I want not to come to grief with either."

It was then that Monsieur Pors told himself he would purchase a yacht.

Two days later a white man who was not a Hollander stood in front of an Indian warrior, and barred his way.

"I want to speak with you, my friend," he said.

The Indian stood in grave silence.

"I have heard that you know well the land south of here," continued the white man. "I would journey to the coast many miles below. Will you show me the way?"

Gustavus Pors almost expected to find that the Indians were like the boats, all pledged to the service of the government, or wanted for other purposes. He was relieved when the native was engaged to make the start on the next day, the destination proposed being that part of the Jersey coast where Jan Classen had put Monsieur Pors ashore. He did not dare to speak of a more southerly route. That could wait until New Amsterdam was left behind. Once beyond Dutch influence he would bribe his guide to lead him on to the land of the South River, or at worst, to hand him over to some friendly tribe who would complete the business for him.

He was in wild haste to be off. He would have started that night, but the Indian demurred.

"Daylight better than night for journeying," he

said. "The traveler stumbles who walks in the dark."

There was excuse for impatience. Already the eve of the departure of the really formidable little fleet had come. The day of fasting and prayer appointed by the Governor for the purpose of special intercession for the success of the enterprise had been observed. On that day the people of New Netherland were forbidden to plough, or sow, or reap; to fish, or to hunt; to take their amusement, or to frequent the taverns. It was a day of solemn humiliation and prayer, and as men walked through the silent streets they looked out at the ships gathered in the bay, and rejoiced to remember that in a very few days they would carry dismay and retribution to the enemies of New Netherland. Prayer and supplication, and a foretaste of revenge, mingled in the exercises of that day, and perhaps the revenge was the strongest element.

Yachts and war vessels were almost in readiness to be gone. The French privateer, *L'Esperance*, was coming in. She was to be chartered to go with the fleet.

The thought of all these preparations, and of the possibility of arriving too late, was accountable for the restlessness of the Swedish guest at the city tavern that night.

The public room of the tavern, that by the day echoed to the voices of the burghers and the travelers that even then came to the little city from the New England settlements, was at present given over to the gentle snore of a Dutchman from Long Island, who filled the niche adjoining that occupied by Gustavus Pors. The innocent looking wooden doors, at which by day Dutchmen and strangers stared stolidly, while they smoked their pipes and discoursed of the war, were now open, and in each a slaap-banck, or sleeping bench, was disclosed to view. From the recessed sleeping place appropriated to his use, Monsieur Pors peered out into the darkened room, and listened to the monotone of the nearest sleeper.

It was not long before he was aware of another sound, that reached him through an open window. He recognized the voice of the landlord in conversation with some one outside. For once that voice was lowered. Before many minutes Gustavus Pors could have wished it had been less cautious.

"I had my doubts when I first set eyes on him."

It was the first complete sentence he made out. Separate words had already aroused his suspicions. He hardly knew why he associated those words with himself. He raised his head and listened. The snore at his side went on with undisturbed monotony.

" 'Twould be strange if they made not an attempt to learn of our resources. I have watched him carefully. Surely he seemeth to me to be——"

The rest was borne away by a puff of wind, that blew the sound in the opposite direction. Gustavus knew not the voice of the speaker. He waited for the answer of the landlord. It was wisely cautious. Only one word was audible, and that was "spy."

He raised himself higher, and put his head beyond the niche that was supposed to contain him.

"A word with the Indian—easy to mistake the road.—Tell him—Van Tienhoven—not go unrewarded."

Monsieur Pors could have shaken that sleeping Dutchman in the next slaap-banck, for the increasing energy of the snore that chose this particular juncture to rise and swell till it filled the room with sound. Gustavus would not have hesitated to swear that it had become a regular roar.

"Mischief take the whole brood of them!" he muttered. "I have got myself in a trap. Yet have I something for which to thank the strength of mine host's voice. He has at least let me into the secret."

He listened intently for many minutes, but no word made itself heard above the snore that still held possession of the room. Presently the voices ceased. The landlord had retired to rest.

CHAPTER XXXII

"What next?" asked Gustavus of himself. "Shall I refuse the escort of the Indian? That were to betray my fears, and to lose an opportunity to get away. I will even go as I have planned. He who is open to a bribe is not proof against a greater bribe."

There was no doubt about the curiosity with which mine host stared at him in the morning. The face of the Indian expressed nothing but readiness to begin his journey.

They started before the city was fairly astir. Gustavus turned to look back at the harbor. Yachts and war vessels were nearly ready to be gone. Seven hundred men, well armed and eager for the fray, awaited the moment of departure. A fleet of seven vessels would almost immediately set sail to invade the South land, the most formidable hostile invasion that had yet been seen on the new continent.

Monsieur Pors no longer looked on the war as a fortunate occurrence. He thought of its possible consequences, and was feverishly impatient to be gone. His impatience was well veiled. That night he slept in an Indian lodge, and wondered whether he had already been led out of his way.

At the second resting place he perceived a comely

Indian maiden looking at him with curious eyes. Instantly a trinket was detached from his person and held out towards her. She took it with a smile of pleasure.

"How many times must the sun go down before a traveler could reach the great sea?" he asked, naming the point to which he had desired the Indian to guide him.

He spoke in Dutch, and the girl answered him in the same tongue.

"He whose face is to the big woods must walk backwards if he would reach the sea," she said.

Then he knew that he had already gone out of his way, and that in all probability he was further from his destination than on the day he started.

When all around him were asleep, Gustavus Pors lay awake, cursing his own folly in leaving New Sweden. What protection could an old man of eighty-two afford the girl about whom his thoughts centred, and for whom he felt all the dangers of the coming struggle? Would Eric Helm be near to succor her?

At one moment he persuaded himself that he would, and felt relieved that one strong man, at least, would be by her side, and the next he almost started up from the bear skin on which he lay, in impatient protest against any other hand than his own ministering to her need.

"Something must be done," he said aloud, and turned his head to see the eyes of the Indian maiden fixed upon him.

Again he motioned to her, and she responded.

"Come," he invited, and went softly out of the lodge.

"Your eyes speak good words," he said. "They are eyes for which the young braves would risk much. Tell me, which way would a brave go straightest to those eyes if they were down in the land of the South River?"

She looked at him curiously.

"It is to the sea the white man wanted to go," she said.

He took out a handful of trinkets and another of gold.

"In the land of the South River is a maiden whose eyes draw my feet towards her," he said. "I will give much wampum to any who will take me to her fast—fast as the sun travels across the sky."

She shook her head.

"I will pay all I bargained to the Indian who guided me," he said. "And beside I will give this, and more."

"When the sun shows his face, I will answer," said the girl.

CHAPTER XXXIII

"Anna, woman, stop singing to that bairn! It is weeping, and not singing, that most befits this day. For all you or I know, the little one may be fatherless this moment."

The speaker burst open the door of her neighbor's house, which, though it was the nearest to her own, was nearly a mile away. The white, terrified face she turned upon the young mother stopped the song upon her lips.

"What is it?" she asked, starting to her feet, and clasping the baby more closely to her.

"What is it? Have you not been round the bend yonder, and looked down the river to-day? Know you not that at the old fort of Elfsborg lie ships, great ships of war, the like of which our land has never before seen? War ships have sailed up the South River before, but this is a whole fleet of them. Anna, the Dutch have come!"

"The Dutch? What, Director Stuyvesant?"

"I know not whether it be the Director himself, but Elfsborg swarms with soldiers. Aye, and that is not the worst. Woman, your Olof and my Per are prisoners in their hands."

"Prisoners?"

A great cry went up from the lips of the young wife. It was echoed by the child in her arms.

"Aye, prisoners," said the other. "They went down together to see what the ships might mean, thinking of no danger, even though the Dutch flag was on every vessel. I left my house and followed at a distance, for I was afraid, though I said no word."

"Alas, I knew not but that Olof was yet on his own land," sighed the young mother.

"If he be in the land of the living you may be thankful," replied the other wildly. "I saw soldiers strike my Per to the earth. They came running up as my husband and yours were in the field, far from the fort. Their guns were leveled at the heads of unarmed men. I tell you, my heart stopped beating. The air was so still that I heard their shouts. 'Surrender or you are dead men!' cried their leader, and I screamed as they laid violent hands on my Per. He heard me, and wrenched himself loose. 'Run! run!' he called, and tried to escape towards me, but before he had gone two steps he was struck to the ground by a blow from the soldier. 'Run, Catylene! Run!' he cried as he fell, and I ran. Woe is me that I did, for now I know not what has become of my husband, my brave Per!"

The two women stared into each other's faces. The terror of the situation had struck home to their hearts. Their husbands were prisoners in the hands of the enemy, and they were at the mercy of a band of ruthless soldiers.

"Listen! Was not that a shout?" exclaimed the

young mother. "Surely they are coming upon us."

"Quick! We must hide in the woods," said the woman, Catylene, and for her baby's sake the mother ran.

Peering out from their hiding place, the women saw soldiers approach the house. It was well they had left it, for the Dutchmen rudely kicked open the door and entered the dwelling. Anna watched the little building with a terrified look in her eyes. House and contents represented all the wealth of the young couple. Would the soldiers wreck that home as well as take away its master? Fortunately they had not much time to spare. They hastily searched the house, and then left it, with the marks of their violence on more than one cherished possession.

"What do they want with Olof and Per," moaned the wife. "*We* have done them no injury. If they must have their Fort Casimir back, why do they not go and take it?"

The only reason they did not go was that the state of the tide and the absence of wind kept them here, at the little ruined fort of Elfsborg. For Elfsborg no longer menaced the South River with her guns. Her day of power was past. Her voice had not of late been heard. Deserted and ruined, she lay desolate, dreaming of the time when the Dutch flag came down in salute to her colors.

That was a past honor. Her foes had proved too many for her. They had come in swarms—the deadly marauding mosquitoes. They filled her inclosures, and routed her garrison. They even took possession of her guns, till her defenders abandoned her to her fate, and left her to brood mournfully over the past.

To-day she was more full of life and bustle than in her palmiest times. Never did her walls echo to such martial tread as now. Soldiers swarmed in her ruined courts, and looked out from her gates. And in front of her lay the goodly fleet of seven vessels that had come to possess the land of the South River for the Dutch, or in default thereof, to bring ruin and desolation to every inhabitant of the same.

Director Stuyvesant was very busy. His straight, soldierly form was seen now upon the flagship, the *Balance*, and again within the old fort. His keen eye took note of all things. The face of the Director-General was stern and determined. Pieter Stuyvesant, the man of whom one of the English officials in the West Indies had the winter before remarked that he was in more fear of him for the discovering of the raw and defective forces of those islands than of all the world beside, had come to the land of the South River to obey the command of his superiors, and that command was to subdue the country. In time of peace the Governor of New Netherland would often shew himself a man of kind heart and friendly countenance, but Pieter Stuyvesant was first of all a soldier, and when he was in the performance of a soldier's duty he looked at his urroundings through a soldier's eyes. His present duty was the subjugation of New Sweden. Therefore the fate of New Sweden was not at that moment an enviable one.

The Director was preparing for the advance. He divided his men into five companies, and gave all necessary orders. Then he waited for the tide. He was in haste to ascend the river before his presence was discovered, that the surprise of the Swedes might be complete.

The next day wind and tide proved favorable, and the expedition which the Dutchmen of New Amsterdam had all winter been preparing, and into the arming and victualing of which they had thrown themselves with a zest that had its origin in the bitterness of their hearts, came in sight of Fort Trinity, their own old Fort Casimir, now enlarged and improved.

"Improved for *us?*" said Stuyvesant significantly, as his eye fell upon it. It was the first time he had seen it since he left it, a newly built fortress, in the time of Governor Printz.

Proudly the fleet swept past the fort, the guns of which were silent, for Swen Schute, the commander, at once saw himself no match for the invading force, and deemed it the part of wisdom not to become the aggressor.

"Mother! mother! There are Dutch soldiers—thousands of them—and they are all between us and Fort Trinity."

Ian pushed open the low outer door, sending it

back with a bang as he rushed into the house, followed by Kolina. The two were wildly excited.

"Yes, and there are ships and ships on the river, and the soldiers are marching along the road to Fort Christina," added Kolina.

The child had grown since the day, four years before, when she first spied Governor Stuyvesant coming ashore, but it had been more in breadth than height. She was still little Kolina, and her voice was almost as shrill as on that occasion.

The housewife stopped on her way to the fireplace, and stared at the children.

"The Dutch!" she gasped.

"Yes. Mother, there never were so many soldiers. Will they take our Fort Trinity away?"

"Will they leave us anything? That is more to the point," replied Katarina. "Where do you say they are?"

"Everywhere," replied Ian. "A detachment but now marched up the road to Christina. Think you, mother, they are going to that fort also?"

"They would cut off communication with it," said the mother. "Truly, this looks like war. Ian," she added, "and you, Kolina, stay within the house. Go not out again."

"I know one who is out," said Maria, and in her voice there was a scarcely concealed tone of satisfaction.

"Who?" asked Katarina sharply.

"Agneta. She is on the road to Fort Christina, too, if I blunder not outrageously."

"Heaven help the girl then!" said her mother. "What are you laughing at? This is no time for folly."

"I was wondering whether the Dutch soldiers would greet her with soft words, as do all other men," said Maria.

"Shame on you!" retorted Katarina, though her voice was not harsh. "Know you not the character of an armed foe? Look to yourself, girl, and leave not room in your heart for uncharitable thought. I doubt not the grandfather will be distressed," she added. "Tell him not that Agneta is yonder, else will he be seeking her. Do you hear, Kolina and Ian?"

She turned to look from the window. All was peaceful around the farm-house, though just beyond the trees the Dutch fleet had come to anchor.

"They're not here yet," said Katarina. "Maria, stir yourself and gather together every article of silver. We must find for such a better resting place than chest that invites rifling."

They were busy gathering together their treasures when Axel entered.

"The Dutch have come," announced Maria.

"Aye, I know. Where is Agneta?"

The voice of Axel Bonde was not raised, but it thrilled through the room, and compelled attention. Katarina stopped in the middle of the floor, and turned towards him.

"Oh, the girl is somewhere about," she said. "Father, I wish you would help me find a hiding place for this silver. 'Tis too big a temptation to put in the way of Dutch rogues."

"Never mind the silver," said the old man. "Where are the bairns?"

"In the house. I have bidden them stay there."

"It is well," he said. "See that none of you go abroad. And Agneta, is she also within?"

"What think you of the cattle house for a hiding place?" resumed Katarina, ignoring his last words. "Beneath some of the provender these things might perchance be safe."

"I care not," he said, "if so be that harm come not to any of you. Are you sure that Agneta is within?"

"If she be not, it is her own fault."

"Katarina, where is the bairn?"

There was that in his voice that was not to be disregarded. Katarina turned towards him.

"She *should* be in the house," she said. "If not, she has but herself to blame."

The face of Axel Bonde grew pale. He looked at his daughter-in-law for a moment in silence.

"I thought not that my daughter would deceive me," he said quietly. "Truly, this is an evil day."

He turned to go out, but she took a couple of quick steps and was in front of him.

"Father, it is folly," she said. "Think you the soldiers will let any pass by them on the road to Christina? It is surely to prevent any communication with the fort that they have been sent thither."

"Went the bairn toward the fort, then?" he asked, a grayer pallor overspreading his face.

"I know not," said Katarina impatiently. "Maria saith that she did. She is as likely to have changed her mind and gone elsewhere as not. Where are you going?" she asked, as he laid a gentle hand on her shoulder, and moved her to one side.

"To look for my bairn," he said.

"It is folly," she asserted.

" 'Twere worse folly to delay," he answered. "Daughter, the bairn's life is more to me than my own."

"You will lose yours and not save hers," she said, but he was already out of the room.

"He thinks of none but that girl," said the mother impatiently. "If he fall into the hands of the soldiers out there upon the road, there is no telling what treatment he will receive."

Axel Bonde had but one thought—the possibility of reaching his "bairn." He remembered the words of Gustavus Pors: "War is bad enough for men, but for maidens——"

And Agneta was upon the road alone.

Axel was too wise to start boldly along the highway to Fort Christina. To do so would be to court disaster. He took to the woods. But as he could not go far without leaving the road behind him, he halted often, and listened and watched, his heart growing cold with fear. He heard the jests and laughter of the soldiers, and the minutes seemed hours as he imagined Agneta in their power. More than once his foot was lifted to step out boldly and confront them. But what would it avail? They would but take him prisoner, for they were very evidently holding the road against all comers.

He could no nothing but wait, moving from one part of the wood to the other, and listening always for some intimation that Agneta was near.

CHAPTER XXXIV

Agneta's feet were treading the road that led to Fort Christina, but her thoughts were in New Amsterdam. She was wondering why Monsieur Pors did not return. He had been long gone. It must be that there was no danger of war, or he would have come back to warn them. She breathed more freely at the thought. War in these peaceful forests would be a dreadful thing. And why should the Dutch and Swedes kill each other? There was room for both.

More than four miles of road stretched between the farm-house and the fortress on the Minquas' Kil. It was a road often traveled, for the fort had from the very first settlement of the land been the storehouse from which the colonists drew their supplies. Hither they repaired on week days for all they needed, and hither, until a clergyman was established at Fort Trinity, they went on Sunday to the church in the fort.

Possibly the remembrance that Eric Helm, who had been called northward a week before, was expected to return about this time, made the road to Fort Christina a little more attractive than usual to Agneta. The young engineer had not neglected his opportunities since Monsieur Pors left New Sweden. There was a softer light in the girl's eyes, when, by some sudden transition, her thoughts leapt from New Amsterdam to the wild lands north of the Minquas' Kil, and in imagination she saw a tall, muscular figure making its way with swinging step through the forest.

She had turned her face towards home. Above the forest trees a September sun was busy heating the air that a sea breeze tried to cool. The shadow of the wood looked inviting. Agneta stepped from the open road with a feeling of relief. She had no fear of losing her way. Every step of the distance between Fort Christina and the farm-house was known to her.

She had hardly passed into the softened light of the forest when she stopped abruptly, and stood with head uplifted. The girl was almost as much at home in the woods as a native. Every sound pertaining thereto was familiar to her. Now her quick ear caught a movement that was fresh.

"Those are not the footsteps of Indians," she mused, "and they are too many to belong to our own people."

Some instinct, which was certainly not of fear, for she knew of no possible danger, prompted her to step behind a tree. The footsteps came nearer. She heard a voice giving an order.

"Dutchmen—and soldiers," she said.

A moment later she added:

"The Hollanders have come!"

She did not stop to argue the question whether they could or could not be here. That sharp, short order, and the many feet, could mean only the presence of soldiers.

Very quietly, she told herself the unpleasant truth. She quite understood its significance. The coming of the Hollanders had been a thing to be dreaded ever since the Indians first gave warning of a possible invasion. And now they were here, and nobody was prepared for them, although the Governor had sent reinforcements to Fort Trinity as a precautionary measure.

Agneta's first thought took the form of a strong desire to be at home. Soldiers were not, as a rule, chivalrous in those days, and unprotected maidens of the enemy's race not likely to meet with generous treatment at their hands.

It was with a thrill of fear that she saw a dozen Dutchmen pass the opening by which she had entered the wood. They were near enough for her to see them plainly, and to catch in their speech the one word that was most familiar.

"Christina!"

As the lips of the Dutchmen uttered it she understood its significance.

They had surprised the fort below, and were bound for the one above. These soldiers were holding the road, that no word of their coming might reach Governor Rysingh, who was himself at Fort Christina.

"They will let none go past to tell him," she mused, "and our Fort Christina will fall into their hands."

There was nobody to see the light that a minute later came into her eyes, or to watch the nimble figure that crept round tree trunks, making swift, noiseless dashes from one sheltered spot to the next, all the time cautiously but surely advancing. In the direction of home? Nay, but away from it, towards the Christina Creek, where stood the fort of the Swedes.

"Governor Rysingh must be warned," said Agneta, "and there is nobody to warn him but me."

She made a considerable circuit to avail herself of the cover of the forest. Once she approached its edge, at a place where a view of the road could be obtained. Squads of soldiers occupied it, posted, as she partly saw, and partly guessed, at intervals along its route.

She went back into the forest and hurried on. The danger seemed more real for that glance at the enemy. It made the more exposed part of her journey doubly formidable. Before her was a stretch of low, unprotected land, across which she must pass to reach cover again. For some minutes she had heard nothing of the soldiers. This particular spot offered no facilities for investigation. She listened intently, and then stepped beyond the trees. It is not to be denied that her heart beat wildly as she came into that open space.

"Look out! There's somebody moving yonder!"

There was a rush of feet, an answering shout, and

the turning of a body of men posted further up the road.

Agneta dashed across the stretch of low land, and into the forest beyond. The wood reached, she turned aside, and penetrated deeper into its shadow. She heard orders given to watch the road, and then the trampling of feet as the pursuers came into the wood. Unfortunately the trees were not thick enough to effectually hide her movements. She crouched behind some bushes, and waited, hoping the soldiers would grow tired of the search.

" 'Tis a woman! I saw the wag of her petticoats."

"Woman or man, we've got to find her," responded a second Dutch voice. "A woman's tongue can tell a secret as well as any."

The answer was a laugh, coarse and loud, followed by the sound of crashing through the underbrush.

"This way! I'll swear I saw her pass through the gap by yonder pine," cried the first speaker.

"Spread out and let's beat the bush," suggested another. "She'll not escape further along. They're on the watch beyond, now."

They tramped round and round, coming nearer to her hiding place every minute.

Agneta kept very still. It took all the strength of her will to hold herself thus as they gradually hemmed her in. There came a moment when she saw that discovery was inevitable. Two soldiers were bearing down upon her.

Suddenly, before the foremost of them, there rose, as if out of the earth itself, a girl's figure. The face that belonged to it was pale and still; only the eyes shone with a light that looked not wholly safe. The maiden was but an arm's length from the soldier. She stood and confronted him.

"Ha! Here she is!"

He stretched out his hand. By a quick movement she placed herself beyond its reach.

"Sir, what do you want with me?" she asked, in a tone as quiet as if the meeting were but an everyday encounter.

"Want?" replied the Dutchman, taken by surprise at the question. "We want to know what you are doing here."

He advanced as he spoke, and took her rudely by the arm.

"Sir," she said, proudly, "your touch is rough. Kindly take your hand off. I have no intention of running away."

Instinctively he obeyed.

"You ask me what I do here," she continued. "'Tis a question easy to answer. What I do is that which you also are doing. This is a land free to all. I was but walking in the woods."

"Whither bound?" asked the Dutchman.

She hesitated.

"For my home, until I heard your voices," she said. Then, with a smile: "We are not well used to soldiers in this peaceful land. When I saw you, I left you the road, and took to the woods."

"In what direction lies your home?" asked the soldier.

"It lieth on the bank of the South River," she said.

"And lieth the South River in yonder part?" he asked, with a sneer.

"No," replied Agneta quietly. "The South River lay in the direction occupied by soldiers of whose chivalry towards women I was not assured."

"Aha! And so you came hither to put the chivalry to the test, eh?" laughed a broad, coarse visaged soldier who had drawn near.

He laid a rude hand on the girl's shoulder.

"Come, my beauty, speak the truth," he said. "These feet were bound for Fort Christina, or I'm out in my reckoning."

She turned upon him with blazing eyes.

"Do the men of Holland treat women thus?" she asked scornfully.

"Yes, my dear, when the women don't behave themselves," said the Dutchman, with a hoarse laugh.

She made a movement towards the other soldiers who were near.

"Sirs," she said, "I claim of you protection. You wear the uniform of soldiers. It is your duty to protect the weak. I will go with you where you desire. But I demand that you behave as men, and not as ruffians."

"Let the girl alone," said the Hollander who had first put his hand upon her. "She is a prisoner, and she must go with us. But there is no need to insult her."

"*I* don't want to insult her," replied the other, bringing his face close to hers. "But I'm going to look into a pretty girl's face when I get a chance."

His arm was round her waist. The face he looked into was proud enough to make him hesitate before he brought his own any nearer. While he hesitated, the other Dutchman gave him a rough push.

"Get away, Jansen," he said. "Let the girl alone. She's my prisoner. I took her."

Agneta came a step nearer to him.

"I will go with you where you wish," she said, "so long as I may look to you for protection."

"You'll have to go, my girl," he replied, "protection or no protection," but the hand that he put upon her shoulder was neither rough nor familiar.

"What are you going to do with her?" laughed another soldier. "You may neither touch nor look at her majesty, mind that."

"I'll go back with her, and put her into an officer's charge. It's his place to decide what to do with her," replied the other, and though his face reddened at the shout of laughter set up by his comrades, he adhered to his resolution.

Agneta had to face more than one squad of soldiers as her companion led her along the road towards Fort Trinity and the South River. It took all the force of her will to keep her face calm and proud when those rough Dutch soldiers surrounded her, staring into the eyes that more than once gathered to themselves a mist of tears. Jests and threats and coarse familiarity were met in turn by the same still, steadfast glance, that sometimes shamed and sometimes angered the Dutchmen.

They were not a mile from the farm-house when an officer was encountered.

"What have you here?" he asked gruffly.

"A Swedish maiden bound for Fort Christina," was the reply.

An oath loud and strong escaped the officer's lips.

"Hark you, girl!" he said. "This land is in our possession. Any one who tries to be the undoing of our plans will wish himself or herself underneath the waters of the South River. Do you want to be sent a prisoner on board a war ship? Life there will be little to the taste of a maiden like you, or I've lost my mark."

"Nay, sir, I want nothing but to be allowed to go home in peace," she said.

"Are you ready to swear that you will make no attempt to warn those at your beggarly Fort Christina that their loving friends, the Hollanders, are about to pay them a visit?" he asked.

She looked at him for a moment.

"Aye," she said, simply. "I will promise, for I can do naught to help them."

"You would if you could, eh?" he said.

"Sir, if this were your land, and you in my place, what would you do?" she asked.

"Give in to the stronger force, as you will have to do," he said.

"I will do it, sir," she replied.

"Let her go, Marten," said the officer. "And mind you, my girl," he added, turning to Agneta, "if you are caught at any tricks again, you will learn what falling into the hands of the soldiers means. Get you home! *We'll* see that you find not your way to Fort Christina."

She wanted to run, to put space between herself and those soldiers at a quicker rate than was possible at an ordinary gait, but she held her feet in check. There were few soldiers at this end of the road. She passed but two parties before the farmhouse was in sight. As the first building came in view she saw a figure emerge from the wood.

"Grandfather Axel!" she cried, and ran to meet him.

He hurried towards her at a pace that little fitted the burden of eighty-two years.

"My bairn, I have feared for you," he said, gently patting shoulder and arm. "Know you that the Dutch soldiers are here?"

"Yes, I have met them," she answered, trying to keep her voice steady. "Grandfather Axel, let us go in. There are many Hollanders upon this road, and their mien is far from friendly."

She was anxious about his safety. Her one desire was to hurry him indoors.

"You have met them?" he asked.

"Yes. They stopped me, but they—they let me come on."

Her voice was breaking.

"God be thanked," he said.

"So you've got back," cried Maria. "How did you get past the soldiers?"

"They let me come home," said Agneta.

She spoke calmly, but her lip quivered, and she hurried away to her own room.

"Well," commented Maria emphatically, "I begin to think there's not a man on earth that can withstand a fair face."

The door that fell to after her closed with a very unnecessary bang as she hurried away to deposit certain valuables in hiding places selected for their promise of security. Any moment the soldiers might make a raid upon the farm-house. They were at present all fully employed under Stuyvesant's orders in the construction of batteries overlooking Fort Trinity. They had no time to trouble the settlers yet.

"Swen Schute will not give in. The Hollanders will have to fight their way if they would enter Fort Trinity," said the housewife, proudly. "He has had reinforcements lately from the Governor. I'll warrant that Director Stuyvesant himself will find Swen a thorn in his side."

"He can't hold out," commented the hired servant, who had returned from a secret investigation of the enemy's forces. "Why, there's a thousand

Dutchmen yonder if there's one. The place fairly swarms with soldiers."

"God grant they may be content with taking the fort," said Axel.

"Little hope of that," was the answer. "They've made prisoners of freemen lower down by Elfsborg, and the story goes that they have threatened to carry away every man of us to New Amsterdam."

The housewife stopped in the act of lifting a kettle from the fire.

"Has it come to that?" she cried.

"Aye. So they say," replied the man, stolidly. "It's war they're here for, and war's war."

CHAPTER XXXV

A group of Swedish soldiers stood by the Christina Creek not far above the fort. The early morning sun shone upon their arms and their grim, determined faces. They were ten in number, and by their side was one who was not a soldier. He was as fully armed as the rest, and his face showed no less determination. It showed more impatience. He seemed to find it hard to wait while a boat was launched, and it was his hand that pushed it from the shore with such impetuosity that it swayed dangerously.

"Have a care," said one of the soldiers. "We desire not to begin our expedition with a ducking."

"There's no time for care," replied the young man. "If we hasten not, the fort may be in the hands of the enemy before we arrive."

"Never fear. Swen Schute will hold out," was the answer. "He has had reinforcements on purpose. We shall be there before the sun is many hours higher."

It was not so much of the safety of the fort that the other was thinking as of the safety of a farmhouse near the fort. To Eric Helm the roof that sheltered Agneta was the central spot of New Sweden. He would have liked to turn those ten picked men from Fort Christina into a bodyguard for the girl from whom his thoughts had never wandered since he heard that the Dutch were in the land. The best he could do, however, was to join himself to them, and go to Agneta's aid. They were willing enough to have his company. Every gun would count in a skirmish with the foe.

If they had known that the Dutch flag was already vaunting itself above Fort Trinity, but one of the company would that morning have been crossing the creek. He would have gone though he had been assured that all the road from Fort Christina to Fort Trinity swarmed with Dutchmen. But he would have gone more warily.

More than thirty-six hours had passed since the first hostile army of white men that ever trod the banks of the Delaware disembarked above what is now the town of Newcastle. The size of that army had brought dismay to the heart of Swen Schute. He saw at once the utter hopelessness of resistance. He was the more embarrassed that Governor Rysingh had earlier sent him reinforcements, weakening his own garrison by so doing. The warning of the Indians led the Governor to prepare for possible emergencies. He surmised that Fort Trinity would be the main point of attack should the Dutchmen come. To the best of his ability he made provision for the security of that citadel. Swen Schute was bidden to stop the fleet below the fort, by friendly negotiations, if possible, if not, by the persuasion of his guns.

But Governor Rysingh knew not the strength of

the invading fleet when he gave that order. As the commandant counted the vessels ascending the river, and estimated the number of soldiers they carried, he saw the hopelessness of a conflict with the Director of New Netherland, and decided to wait and let Stuyvesant take the initiative.

That decision was his undoing. The Dutch fleet sailed above the fort, and Swen Schute discovered when too late that he was cut off from communication with Fort Christina, and that by a foe who would make no concession.

He was called upon to surrender. In vain he asked permission to send an open letter to Governor Rysingh. The only favor he could gain was permission to put off his decision till the next day. He owed that concession, not to Dutch clemency, but to the fact—as Stuyvesant naively wrote afterwards— that the Dutch could not get their batteries ready before that time.

Swen Schute saw those batteries rise on high ground commanding his fort, and he saw no hope of rescue. Thus it happened that at noon the next day the Dutch marched into Fort Trinity with colors flying.

The little band of soldiers sent to reinforce the fort knew nothing of the uselessness of the risk they were taking. They were ignorant also of the greatness of that risk. Eric Helm breathed a sigh of relief as he stepped ashore. He was at least on the same side of the creek as Agneta. If his feet did not soon carry him to her aid, it should not be his fault.

It was he who was walking ahead when the bank of the creek was passed, and it was around him that the first onslaught of the ambushed foe waxed fiercest. The Dutchmen swooped down on that small band of Swedes, surrounding them, and swarming in upon them. Five to one was not fair fighting, but as that cry, "Surrender! You are our prisoners!" rang in his ears, Eric would have fought a hundred men single-handed.

Surrender! With Agneta unprotected at the farm-house four miles away? Not while his hand could hold a sword.

There was no time to bring his gun into position, but he drew his sword and swung it round him, for a moment clearing a space for himself in the midst of those leering, shouting Dutchmen. He was cut off from his companions, who were themselves making a firm stand behind him. A few minutes of wild, desperate resistance brought the skirmish to an end, and eight out of the ten soldiers were prisoners in the hands of the Dutch. The other two had escaped to the boat, and were putting out into the stream, while a shower of bullets fell about them, and the threats of the Hollanders rang in their ears.

Eric Helm lay on the ground, trampled upon by the victorious Dutchmen. His sword had been snatched from his grasp. The breath was almost trodden out of his body. Yet he felt not the touch of those heels. He thought only of Agneta, and the sharpness of the sting of defeat lay in the knowledge that she would look in vain for succor.

"Here, get on your feet, you madman! Do you think you can fight fifty Hollanders? Stand off here, and let him get up."

A Dutch soldier pushed away two or three of his comrades, and then gave the fallen Swede a rough kick to hasten his movements.

Bleeding and bruised, the young man struggled to his feet. Even then he struck out wildly with his fists, till a sword-thrust in the arm put a stop to further hostile demonstrations on his part.

Meanwhile, the skirmish had been seen from the fort, and one of the big guns pointed at the Dutchmen. When its great throat gave forth the first real note of war, the Hollanders scattered and retreated, taking refuge in the woods, whither also they dragged their prisoners.

Their rage at being thus opposed manifested itself in brutal violence to the captured soldiers. Eric Helm received more than his share of blows. In spite of his wounded arm, he managed to return a few of them, but when the soldiers drew off, leaving the prisoners in charge of a guard, it was an exhausted and battered Swede who glowered at his captors and meditated possible and impossible methods of escape.

At the farm-house the numbness that seizes upon the faculties when men and women wait helplessly for the falling of some great calamity rested upon the household. The first night after the army of invasion had gained possession of the land was spent by Axel Bonde and his men in driving many of the cattle into the woods.

"They may perchance be safer there," he said. "Our friends, the Indians, will not molest them."

Katarina took the opportunity to hide her treasures, and drag them forth again to find for them a safer place, all the time going about in the dark, with suspicious peerings through doorways and windows, to make sure that the enemy was not lurking without.

It was on the Sunday, the day after the capitulation of Fort Trinity, while Domine Megapolensis, the Director's chaplain, preached a thanksgiving sermon in the fort in the presence of the army of occupation, that one of the three hired men came into the house. His face, usually impassive, betrayed some fixed resolve.

"Well," said Katarina, "are all things yet untouched by those thieves of Dutchmen?"

"Aye, but they'll not be so long," he replied. "Others have fared less happily. I don't know what you're thinking of doing. I've come to give you fair notice that you'll have to get along without me. I've no mind to be sent to Manhattan along with the thirty Swedes—soldiers and freemen—that yonder marauding Director is about to dispatch to New Netherland."

"What, the freemen and soldiers from the fort?"

"Aye, the very same. He will have us all there before the war is over, if we're not a match for him. The Dutch soldiers boast that he is going to people this land with Hollanders, and send us all to New Netherland."

"What are you going to do?" asked Katarina.

"Take to the woods. The Indians are our friends."

He kept his word, and Axel Bonde was left to surmise that the other men had followed his example, for from this time none appeared at the farm.

The immunity from molestation did not last long. The very next day saw the cattle house invaded, and the best cows driven off for slaughter. Dutch soldiers entered the buildings with swords drawn and attitude menacing, and came out with coarse jokes on their lips, and quivering, half-dead poultry dangling from their hands. Katarina watched the devastation with an angry light in her eyes, but she dared make no protest. The depredations became of daily occurrence, and were continued even when the body of the army had moved on to attack Fort Christina.

Personal violence the household had as yet escaped, though their neighbors had not all been as fortunate. Every day, when the soldiers appeared, Axel Bonde mounted guard at the low door that gave access to the farm-house. With a patience that nothing could disturb he saw his cattle driven off, his hogs slaughtered before his eyes, and his poultry carried away as trophies. Not once did he offer menace or expostulation.

"Let them take them all, if they leave but my best treasures unharmed," he said.

There came a day, however, when a drunken officer brought his band of men into the courtyard. The last cow had been driven from the cattle-house. A few hens scratched in mistaken security among the hay. A couple of pigs grunted from their sty. They afforded the only promise of food to the expectant Dutchmen.

"Rout out the rascally Swede, and bid him find provisions for the owners of this land," shouted the officer, and the soldiers, nothing loth, turned towards the door.

It was securely barred within, and behind the bar stood Axel Bonde, his gun held in a hand that shook with fear, not for himself, but for the women and children who had no protector but him. An old man of eighty-two looked but a sorry bodyguard for such a moment as this.

"Open the door to your masters, you dog of a Swede!" demanded the soldiers.

There was no answer. Axel Bonde kept silence, hoping the soldiers would go away. A volley of blows upon the door undeceived him.

"Open your door, or we will burn the house over your head, you obstinate fool," cried a Dutchman's voice.

"Fasten the door quickly after me," said Axel, in a low tone, to his daughter-in-law. "I am going out to speak to them."

"You are going to do nothing of the sort," replied Katarina. "They are drunk. A sober Dutchman is brute enough at this time, but a drunken Dutchman is worse than a beast. Stay where you are. I am going to fetch another gun."

But while she went, Axel Bonde quietly unbarred the door, and surprised his foes by stepping out into their midst.

For a moment they recoiled before the calm majesty of the figure that confronted them. Then they rallied, and laid rough hands upon him.

"Here you are, are you? Why didn't you come when you were called?" demanded the officer.

"What is your business with me?" asked Axel, calmly.

"Our business? You shall soon know it," replied the Dutchman, with an oath. "What mean you by keeping empty cattle sheds when your betters are in need of food?"

"If they are empty it is your hand that has made them so," said Axel. "You have taken the cattle, even to the last. The very oxen that should draw the plow have been driven off. What will you? Can you have more than all?"

"All, say you?" demanded the officer. "Will you tell me you have no store of food upon your premises? Your family goes not hungry, I dare swear."

"That which would feed my family would suffice little for a band of soldiers," said Axel. "Would you leave women and children to starve?"

"I care not what becomes of them, you canting hypocrite," roared the soldier. "As well starve as not. There will then be the less of you to transport to New Netherland. Come, lead the way. We want food, and we are going to have it."

For answer Axel walked towards the hog-pen, his step unhurried, his tall, majestic figure drawn to its full height.

"There," he said, "they are the last. Take them, and leave my house unmolested."

"Nay, but we needed not your guidance to find these," sneered the officer. "Hark you, old man! We want all your house affords, to the last mouthful, and we'll have it, too. Do you hear that?"

"And you will deliberately leave women and children to starve?"

"Haven't I told you I don't care how soon they starve? The sooner the better," shouted the officer.

"He who neglects to show mercy will some day seek for mercy in vain," said Axel. "Your own wives and little ones may yet know the violence of a relentless foe. You are stronger than we are, but there is One stronger than you."

"Hold your tongue, and lead the way into your house. Not that we need your guidance. We'll soon make your women folks bring out their dainties," roared the Dutchman. "And take that for your insolence," he added, striking with his clenched fist the face of the old man before him.

The blow was a heavy one, and Axel Bonde was old. He reeled and fell, striking the ground heavily. A shout of derisive laughter from the soldiers greeted the old man's downfall. Before it died away a girl's voice broke in on the sound.

"Are you men, or *brutes*, to ill-treat one old enough to be the father of any one of you?" she said.

They turned and stared at her. The graceful figure was drawn to its full height. The scorn in her face silenced them.

"Stand aside," she continued imperiously, and they made a way for her till she stood over Axel Bonde. His face had grown grey as the hair that surrounded it. When he saw the girl bending over him, his eyes smiled upon her.

"Go tell my daughter to bring out food," he said. "It is food that the soldiers want. And you—stay within the house. Go, my bairn—and at once."

She smiled down upon him.

'I will go," she said, "and you shall go with me."

Then she turned to the soldiers.

"Lift him carefully, and bring him into the house," she said. "He is hurt. And you, if you need food, let one of your number come for it. You can have what there is, but you must go away. You have done enough harm for one day."

"Oh, we have, have we, you vixen?" replied the officer, who had recovered from his surprise. "It is a new thing to have a conquered foe dictating to the victors. As for that old man, he can lie where he is. It is good enough for him. And you, my proud lady, shall lead the way into the house, aye, and serve us while we feast. A pretty face is no bad appetizer, even though it be the face of a fury."

"What? You will not bring him in?" she said, looking at him with eyes that blazed. "Then are you worse than a brute. If you want food you may get it. I must first care for my grandfather."

She turned from them to summon Katarina to help lift the old man, but as she would have moved away, the officer laid his hand on her shoulder.

"Not so fast, my girl," he sneered. "I have said you shall prepare our victuals, and I stick to my word. Aye, and you shall serve us as we eat. As for yonder old reprobate, he shall lie where he has fallen. If he die there, so much the better."

"How dare you speak such words?" said Agneta, her eyes filling with tears at the thought suggested by his speech. "Are you a fiend that you thus speak?"

"Yes, my dear, the arch fiend himself," said the Dutchman. "Come, give me a kiss to propitiate me, for I swear it is not safe to anger me. I'll take my fill of such sweetness later, when my appetite for more substantial dainties has been satisfied," he added.

Agneta stood amidst the leering, drunken Dutchmen, white and desperate. Her anxiety was not for herself or her own danger, but for the old man lying helpless upon the ground. How much he had been injured by the fall she could not tell. She was frantic to find out. The grey pallor of his face alarmed her.

"Let me go," she said. "I will wait of you, if you so desire, but first I must attend to my grandfather."

"Not so fast," sneered the officer, keeping his hold upon her. "You will wait of us first, and attend to him after. Get up, you old fool!" he added, brutally kicking the prostrate figure.

A sharp cry from the lips of the girl followed the act. It rang out through the buildings and the courtyard, and reached Katarina in the house. It reached another beside Katarina. A moment later a dozen Indians stood within the door, and an old warrior, with stately step, advanced towards the staring Dutchmen.

With a piteous cry Agneta held out her hands towards him.

"Amattehoorn, help us!" she cried.

He made her no answer but he advanced towards the soldiers.

"The white men are our brothers," he said. "We cannot see our brothers kill each other. The white men say the Indian must live in peace. Now the Indians also say the white men must not kill. I have spoken. My young men are more in number than yours. Go! The red men desire not to break the chain of friendship, yet will they not see their friends killed."

The officer stared at the Indian. Then his eye fell on the warriors by the door.

"Many more wait without," said Amattehoorn significantly.

The Dutchman loosed his hold of Agneta. Then his foot spurned the figure upon the ground.

"You may look out, old man," he said savagely. "We shall come back, and it will then be the worse for you as well as your friends here. We will carry you to New Netherland with us, and see how you like that, you rascally old Swede."

He turned and went out, not without more than one fearsome glance over his shoulder. He did not know how many warriors lurked behind the corners of buildings, nor at what moment an arrow might come flying from a bow to find a lodgment in some vital part of his body. He had suddenly become very desirous of leaving the neighborhood of the farm-house. His exit from the shed was so hasty that the pigs were left to grunt in peace.

He had hardly disappeared when a tall figure strode into the building.

"Agneta—little sweetheart—am I too late? I have moved heaven and earth to get here."

He was on the floor by her side, his arm thrown protectingly around her.

For a moment Agneta's eyes looked into the face of Gustavus Pors. Then her lip quivered.

"They have hurt him," she said, and bent again over the old man.

CHAPTER XXXVI

The arm that encircled Agneta trembled, and the eyes that looked into hers burned with love and tenderness. She felt both, but she had time to think of neither. The last vestige of color had left the face of Axel Bonde after the brutal kick with which the Dutchman had turned from him. His eyes were closed, and he was no longer conscious even of the presence of his "bairn." She turned to Monsieur Pors with a frightened question in her eyes.

"No," he said gently, "he is not dead. We must take him into the house. Nay," he added tenderly, as she would have helped lift him, "thy strength, little one, is insufficient. Amattehoorn will carry him more easily."

Gustavus Pors and the Indian bore the old man through the low door, within which Madam Botorpa had passed on the day when Axel Bonde welcomed his brother Eric's granddaughter to the best place in his home and his heart. The old door had traveled to New Sweden with its owner. It was a part of the house in the dear Sweedland, and he would not leave it behind.

"He will never walk through it again," said Katarina, when she saw the old man's face.

The blow dealt by the Dutchman had been a savage one, and Axel had fallen heavily. Examination showed only a broken leg, but Axel's condition pointed to internal injuries. It was long before he rallied.

"Where are the bairns?" he said, when his eyes opened again to the world.

Then he saw Monsieur Pors. The younger man came forward.

"Will you let me care for them?" he said. "I think I can promise you that violence such as this shall not be repeated. An Indian guard is already around the house. As for me, I pledge myself to protect this family with my life."

The face of Axel Bonde was troubled.

"I am helpless, and can do no more to guard them," he said. "For the sake of the bairns I thank you, but——"

Gustavus Pors came nearer, and bent his head till the words he spoke reached no ears but those for which they were intended.

"But you hesitate to trust me," he said gently. "My friend, I thought I loved Agneta well enough to do anything to gain her. In the past few days, when it looked as if I were to be denied the happiness of being by her side in this danger, I learned that I loved her enough to deem the caring for her in itself a sufficient privilege. Let me protect her and you. At present I ask no more."

The old man breathed more freely.

"You are stronger than I am," he said. "Your arm will avail where mine has failed. I give up my charge to you."

Gustavus Pors spoke truly when he said that during the past few days he had looked in the face possibilities that had shewn the strength of his love for Agneta. He had spared neither money nor risk in order to reach New Sweden in time. He found himself practically a prisoner in the hands of the Indians.

Upon the morning after his appeal to the Indian girl he waited impatiently for the day-dawn. Before the great red face of the sun rose above the trees, he was standing where its beams could fall upon him. At the moment when the first ray shot across his face he heard a footstep, and turned to confront the old Indian who the day before had acted as his guide.

"The Swede is in haste to begin his journey," he said.

"The name will serve as well as any other," replied Gustavus, quietly. "And as for haste, judge you not that he has need to hurry who has walked all day and advanced not?"

The face of the Indian did not change.

"My friend," continued Gustavus, "yesterday I offered you wampum to lead me to the coast that lieth south of the Manhattans. I offer double to-day to him who will take me yet further, even to the land of the South River."

"The South River lieth many days' journey away," said the Indian. "The feet of the Swede would grow sore before he reached it."

"If you will lead, I will follow," said Gustavus. "The feet can take care of themselves. And the sooner we reach the South River, the more wampum shall you carry back with you."

"The white man who knows the path better than the Indian, may journey alone," said the warrior, turning on his heel and leaving the traveler to do as he pleased.

A few minutes later a young squaw passed, carrying water.

"See you the three tall pines above which the sun shows his face?" she said, without turning her head towards the stranger. "Beyond them waits a brave who will take you towards the South River."

"And at the South River is a girl who will thank you for this day's work," said Gustavus, his voice low and clear, his eyes looking off beyond the young squaw. "See, I leave among the bushes that which will remind you of her," and he placed a trinket and a golden coin upon the ground, and turned in the direction she had indicated.

It was the beginning of a series of wanderings, purposely made circuitous, but leading mainly southward. The days passed, and the patience of the traveler was worn to shreds. Not until he had journeyed far from Dutch influence did the character of the Indians change. Then, as one guide passed him over to another, he gradually met more friendly faces in the wigwams.

Day after day during that slow progress he cursed his folly in leaving New Sweden. He counted the days that had passed since he turned his back on New Amsterdam, and came to the conclusion that even with adverse winds the Dutch must be already in the land of the South River. As he tramped along the narrow trails through the forest he pictured to himself the progress of the Dutch force up the river.

He knew a little of the temper of the Hollanders. He had seen enough of it in New Amsterdam to judge of its bitterness. He imagined it let loose on the heads of the settlers. That little stretch of land between Fort Trinity and Fort Christina would be the very centre of the conflict. And the centre of that district for him was the house that sheltered Agneta. Was it even now in the hands of Dutch soldiers? Were its inmates already subjected to the coarse brutality of men who had some of them come straight from Holland to avenge the insult offered to the Dutch flag in the taking of the Dutch Fort Casimir and the making of it into the Fort Trinity of the Swedes? He would have traveled night and day if it would have availed him anything. But the Indians were immovable.

When at last he came among those who were too far south to be under the domination of the Hollanders, he made better progress. Then, indeed, he gave himself little rest, for he learned that his worst fears were realized, and the Hollanders were already in possession of the South River.

"Better stay among us till the Dutch Sachem returns to his own land," suggested a warrior in whose lodge he had rested for a few hours' sleep, "else may you quickly find yourself back from whence you came, for the Hollanders are putting the Swedes in their big ships to carry them all to Manhattan."

"Say you so?" said Gustavus. "Then must we move warily. How far are we from the South River?"

"A day's journey," replied the Indian.

Before the day was over Gustavus stood in the presence of Amattehoorn, of whose friendship for Axel Bonde he was well aware.

"Amattehoorn," he said, "I remember your face, though you have, perchance, forgotten mine. I come to ask your help for Axel Bonde and his household."

"I also remember the Swede who was in a hurry," replied Amattehoorn. "What do you ask? Axel Bonde is the brother of my people."

"He is in danger. I am going to his aid," said Gustavus. "His family may even now be in the hands of the Hollanders. I ask not that you fight against the Dutch, but only that you bring the young men and warriors of your tribe, and guard the house of your friend Axel; that you give to him protection as he would give it to his brothers the red men, if their squaws and their little ones were at the mercy of an enemy. I will give much wampum for every day you camp around his house—enough to divide amongst all your braves."

"Friend," said Amattehoorn calmly, "your wampum may be useful among the young men who know not Axel Bonde. For me, I am ready to go with you when you will. When the little white squaw needs him, Amattehoorn will come."

The hand of the proud Swede went out and touched the palm of the old warrior. It was no conventional grasp, but the unpremeditated clasp of friendship. The warrior and the traveler had an interest in common. The "little white squaw" was before the eyes of both.

It was Amattehoorn who planned the expedition, gathering together a band of young men and warriors, and stealing with them through the woods. It was he also who curbed the impatience of the Swede, bidding him keep under cover.

"The Hollanders are many," he said. "If one would strike a hundred, he must strike as my people do. The trees and the rocks and the bushes fight for us."

When the farm-house was reached, however, Amattehoorn found Gustavus no obedient follower. The voices of the Dutchmen within the quadrangle put all his caution to the rout. He forgot that he had not intended to fight—that his appearance on the scene would complicate matters. He wanted to rush at once to the rescue, but Amattehoorn's hand was on his arm.

"The Swede who is in a hurry will not bring help to his friends," he said grimly. "Axel Bonde and the little squaw will not be the better for seeing one more of their people thrown into the big canoes of the Hollanders. My people are not at war with the Dutch. Let me go in and speak to them. If they will not listen, there will yet be time to kill."

"You will fight for her?" asked Gustavus, in a voice that was not altogether under his control.

"Amattehoorn will stand by his friends," said the Indian.

"Go then, quickly," said Gustavus. "Hark! That is her voice."

It was followed by a cry, a sharp cry of fear.

"She is in danger! I must go to her."

Gustavus struggled against the hand that again detained him. He pushed Amattehoorn aside, and sprang towards the back of the sheds.

"A friend without wisdom is no better than an enemy," said the Indian.

"Go then. I will wait here—if I can," said Gustavus.

It was well he had not to wait long. He barely left the Dutchmen time to get out of the building before he entered. The minutes during which he stood behind the cattle house were the longest in his life.

CHAPTER XXXVII

Monsieur Pors was not the only man who, during the earlier days of the Dutch occupation of New Sweden, chafed and raged over his own helplessness. Eric Helm was still in the woods upon the opposite side of the creek from Fort Christina, a prisoner in the hands of the Dutch. The ships had not yet left the neighborhood of Fort Casimir, or the hold of one of them would, in all probability, have been his lodging place.

He heard the Dutch soldiers joking over the weakness of the garrison at Fort Christina, and grew hot with indignation when two messengers, a lieutenant and a drummer, sent from Governor Rysingh to hold communication with the Dutch, were, after being assured that they might adventure themselves freely among the latter, coolly added to the number of the prisoners.

"Two less of the rascals to trouble us when we walk into their fort," laughed a soldier. "If we keep on at this rate we shall have the garrison in our hands without needing to strike a blow. Verily there seemeth to be but a handful of them, when they are all counted."

"What say you, you scowling fool of a Swede?" demanded another Dutchman, turning upon Eric. "How many are there of you over yonder?"

"More than you will care to meet," responded Eric savagely. "*We* are not reduced to such straits that we must needs take to treachery to make our enemies prisoners. Go up and try, my fine fellows. You will learn that Swedes deal in honest blows, and not sneaking expedients."

It was no exaggeration to designate the young man a "scowling Swede." He would have scowled less if he could have done more. To stand by and witness the savage glee with which the enemy greeted every new discovery of the weakness of the Swedes, and to know that the main body of the army was still in close proximity to Axel Bonde's house, was maddening. He tried once to bribe his captors with big offers if they would set him free and go with him to his own plantation. They laughed in his face.

"We'll have all you've got, no fear," they said. "You needn't trouble to go through the unimportant ceremony of bestowing it upon us. You canting Lutherans have had your turn on the South River. You were ever thieves. We have come to take back our own, and to help ourselves to the wealth you have defrauded us of all these years. You and your ministers and your Governor may go back to your Sweedland together, if we slice not off a few of your heads to teach the rest of you better manners for the future."

"Slice away," retorted Eric scornfully. "You'll have to answer to our Government for all the mischief you do. I'm not sure but that death is to be preferred to the company the South River affords just now."

A kick from one of the guards rewarded him for his sally. His hands were fettered, but they strained at the cords.

Was Agneta subjected to indignity at the hands of these Dutchmen? he asked, and the question drove the dark blood to his face and the fire to his eye.

"Have a care! Looks will burn, when they are hot enough," exclaimed another soldier, in mock terror drawing a companion from proximity to the prisoner.

Fort Christina soon after became the centre of attack. Director Stuyvesant left a sufficient garrison at Fort Casimir, detaining the Swedish officers within the fortress, but putting many of the soldiers, together with the freemen who had their houses within the fort, in his own ships, that he might, when occasion offered, send them to New Amsterdam. That the vanquished would "ever be dissatisfied, and a menace to the land," was the principle by which he was guided. It would be safer to have them in New Netherland, where they would be overpowered by numbers.

The Director-General's great desire was now the capture of Fort Christina, the oldest stronghold of the Swedes. It was here—in the neighborhood where, many years later, another people built a large town and called it Wilmington—that the first Swedish vessel disembarked its passengers, and the first dwelling was erected. It was still a central spot to the Swedes. Its fortress had been their refuge before ever Governor Printz came to the country and made Tenacong its capital. They decided to stand by it now, and take the consequences.

The consequences looked serious enough when Director Stuyvesant brought his ships to anchor at the mouth of the Brandywine, and proceeded to erect batteries in positions favorable for attack. The main body of the army having been landed upon the north side of the Minquas' Kil, or Christina Creek, as the Swedes had called it in honor of their Queen, they crossed a low valley which at every flood-tide was covered with water, and came to elevated land that, even when the tide was in, stood out high and dry. It went by the name of Timber Island, and upon its west side afforded a good position for a battery. Here Stuyvesant planted four cannon pointing towards the fort, and within effective distance of it.

He was in no hurry to begin the attack. He meant to make his position sure before commencing actual hostilities. A second battery was cast up on the north side of the fort, and mounted with three cannon, and two others in advantageous positions also rose.

The fort was now invested on every side except the southeast, in which direction was nothing but a low morass, five feet under water at high tide.

is not at ordinary times bad, but the bitterness of these days will take long to pass away."

"I'm not going back to Sweden," rejoined Maria stoutly. "Anna is married, and has the farm. I will follow her example. Mother can live with me, and Ian is old enough to be useful. I wonder whether Eric is in Fort Christina," she added, significantly.

If she did not notice the trembling of the fingers held tight in Axel's clasp, another did. Monsieur Pors, from the opposite side of the bed, looked down into Agneta's face. Her lips were quivering. Did he wish to know whether the tremor was for Axel or for another that he asked of Maria:

"Is your friend Eric supposed to be at Fort Christina?"

"He was expected home before this," replied the girl. "He may be in the fort, or those villainous Hollanders may have him safe in the hold of one of their vessels. It will come to the same thing in the end, I suppose. Those within the fort must surrender at length. They are no match for an army such as Director Stuyvesant has with him."

The color that came and went in Agneta's face might well have answered any question in the mind of Gustavus Pors. He came round, and rested his hand lightly upon the girl's head. The touch was a caress.

Monsieur Pors was especially tender to the maiden in those days. He watched every opportunity to do her service, while towards Axel Bonde he bore himself as a son. He strictly kept his word, and in the household filled the old man's place.

"It is a privilege of which you must not deprive me," he said to Katarina. "I believe we need have little present fear of violence. The Indians are staunch friends of this house, and may be depended upon. As for the Dutch, they will not, I think, force a conflict with the natives. It is as much to their interest to keep the peace in that direction as to break it where we are concerned."

As regarded the present moment he was right. The marauding bands of soldiers were not willing to come to blows with the natives. The very existence of the settlers by the South River—Dutch as well as Swedes—depended upon the friendship of the Indians.

Gustavus Pors did not add, though he well knew, that the real danger to the household lay in the time when the main army should return. If Director Stuyvesant ordained that all the Swedes should be removed to New Amsterdam, even an Indian guard would be unable to stand out against soldiers who were carrying into effect the commands of their leader. Such a rough removal from his own house to the vessel as the soldiers would give the old man, would inevitably result in his death, and death under circumstances that would tear the hearts of those who loved him. For Agneta's sake Gustavus Pors dreaded the surrender of Fort Christina.

In their homes the settlers both feared and longed for it. Life was getting unbearable, and it would at least bring the end, however little to be desired that end might be.

In Axel Bonde's house there was comparative safety in the meantime. It was perhaps the safest place in New Sweden. Of the future Monsieur Pors did not speak.

But while he kept silence, there was one, at least, who thoroughly realized the danger. Agneta, knelt by the old man's side, a brave smile on her lips, but a growing anxiety eating its way into her heart. She looked upon the face white with pain that was borne without a sign, except the increasing pallor when it became more violent than usual, and imagined the rough hands of the Dutch soldiers lifting the old man from his bed and throwing him upon the hard boards of the ship, in all probability with none to care for him. She had little hope that the wives and children of the Swedes would be placed in the same vessel as the men. Her heart grew cold and hot by turns as she thought of her own helplessness to prevent the cruelty.

Even Monsieur Pors and the Indians were not a sure defence. Director Stuyvesant and his army represented, in that time and in that land, an overwhelming force. There had been a rumor of a large quantity of wampum brought in the ships for use among the Indians, if necessary. Amattehoorn would be true to her and to Axel Bonde. Of that

Agneta had little doubt. But his race might not be proof against the Director-General of New Netherland, and all the wampum with which he had provided himself.

Agneta said nothing about her fears. She told Axel of the faithfulness of the Indians, and of Amattehoorn's readiness to stay by "his white brother's house for twelve moons if the Dutch Sachem grew not tired of the South River before then."

"It is well," he said. "Amattehoorn is indeed the friend of his white brother. Is there aught left to give the red men to eat?"

"Nay, their young men bring in plenty," said Agneta. "And Monsieur Pors has promised them much wampum when, the war being over, he can exchange his gold for the same."

A shadow came over the face of Axel Bonde. Agneta was not quite decided whether to regard it as a sign of increased pain, or to connect it with her own words.

She could do little to lessen his suffering. The broken limb had not been set. There was no doctor who could be brought hither now. Katarina proposed the ministrations of the Indians, but the old man shook his head.

"It is of little consequence," he said. "I shall never use the limb again. Their handling is over rough for me now. I would keep the life that is left till I know which way this war will turn. It is not much I can do, but I shall die easier for knowing what is to become of you and the bairns."

"He's got his death blow," remarked a settler's wife, when she had looked upon the white, drawn face, and had gone into the kitchen to talk to Katarina. "You'll be left without a man of your household to stand by you. Ian is a well grown boy, but it will be years before he has a man's strength and a man's wisdom."

"There's many a one will be in the same case before the war is over, if it go on much longer," replied Katarina. "How did you get here? Is the way clear of soldiers?"

"As clear as it ever is now," said the visitor. "I sneaked in and out among the trees. Katarina, woman, I want a bit of bacon. Me and mine haven't a mouthful of anything left save meal. Them wretches of soldiers took all there was. We are not as well off as you, with that rich Swede to pay the Indians to protect you. Don't he wish he'd taken the girl away sooner?" she asked curiously.

"I don't know what he wishes. I haven't asked him," said Katarina, with a sharp ring in her voice.

The woman looked at her fixedly.

"They're going to leave us without a clergyman to baptize our little ones, or to bury our dead," she said, by way of changing the subject. "They say that none will be allowed to stay with us. So far as we who have looked to Fort Trinity for teaching and succor are concerned, it is surely true, for the good man is on board one of their ships. I doubt not that when Christina is taken, and the country falls into their hands, it will fare no better with worthy Pastor Lars Lock."

" 'Tis no good bemoaning our fate. It is hard enough, and is like to be, with the Dutch in the mood they are in, and them masters of the situation," said Katarina. "I little thought when Director Stuyvesant came under my roof, before ever their Fort Casimir was built to make trouble in the country, that he would one day return to destroy and ruin the land that smiled on him that afternoon."

The woman went her way, with a goodly piece of bacon concealed beneath her clothing. It was two days later when she returned. Agneta was in the kitchen.

"I've come to give you warning, my girl," she said. "I'd have been here sooner, but the place swarmed with soldiers. They say Christina is on the point of giving in, and when it does," here her voice dropped to a whisper, "every man in the land of the South River will be carried off to New Amsterdam."

Agneta's face grew white.

"Aye, you may well pale," continued the visitor. "It's enough to make any woman's heart lose courage. What are we to do without our husbands and our sons? That Monsieur Pors will fare no better than the rest, I'll warrant. You'll miss him, my girl, when he's no longer here to hire the Indians to protect you. But it was for old Axel my heart bled when I heard them talking. For, hark you, my girl! They're joking of the fright they will give you when they come to bear him off. They have found out he is hurt. 'I'll teach that proud jade a lesson,' I heard one of them officers say. 'We'll show her beforehand what the old man has to expect when we get him on one of our ships. We won't hurt the old fool. Not a bit of it. But we shan't handle him as if he was a baby, and if so be he should die on the move, so much the better.' I tell you it made my blood run cold to hear them," she continued. "They seemed to have a real grudge against you. How have you angered them so much?"

Agneta did not answer. She had grasped the back of a wooden settle for support. She clung to it, fighting against the numbness that had come over her.

"Why, bless the girl!" ejaculated the visitor. "It won't do to give way like that. You've got to keep up, no matter what happens. I thought I was doing you a service by coming and telling you. And I wondered if mayhap Katarina could spare me another lump of that bacon. I've risked a little to let you know the danger, for there's more soldiers than ever about the road to-day."

Agneta was not listening. She was fighting that spasm of fear. It must not get the mastery of her. Somebody must help grandfather Axel. When that tight feeling passed away from her heart she would be able to think better. Oh, the cruelty, the horribleness of designing to torment the old man to be revenged on her!

"Why, what's this? What is the matter now?"

Katarina came into the room, and the visitor began again to tell her tale, and to prepare the way for the climax—which in her mind was the bacon. Agneta staggered from the room. Her eyes were dim, but not with tears.

"What is it, my bairn?"

She had been trying to cross the living room, where Axel Bonde lay. She hoped to reach her own room without being observed. But the eyes of the old man were keen even yet.

She came and knelt by his side, hiding her head in the bedclothes.

"Little one, have I made a mistake?" he asked. "Shall I tell Monsieur Pors that my treasure is his if he can protect it? My bairn, this old hand can do no more for you. A share in the farm is yours, but even our land may not be left to us when the Dutch have done their work. I thought not to leave my bairn thus. Little one, if Eric Helm were here, into which hand should I place that of my brother Eric's granddaughter?"

There were tears in her eyes now, and the numbness had passed away.

"Grandfather Axel," she said, softly, "keep the hand yourself. Your bairn sorrows only because she fears for you."

"Little one," he said, "hide not that face. I want to see it." Then, as it was lifted, he added: "Monsieur Pors has been very patient. Can I give him his reward?"

A deep flush came to the soft cheeks.

"I think not," she said, and again her head went down.

Axel Bonde knew that he had his answer. His hand sought the bowed head.

"Eric has waited long," he said gently. "Little one, he has less to give of this world's goods than has your friend, Gustavus Pors, but his heart will ever ring true to my bairn. The evil days will not last for ever. And when they are over, Eric will return, if he be alive. Yet am I sorry for Monsieur Pors. He has done us much service."

His hand rested upon the girl's head. It was there when the sleep of exhaustion came to him.

When she saw that he slept, she crept away to her own room. The numbness had gone from her heart. She had been thinking while she knelt by Axel's bed. And the result of the thinking was the intimation to Katarina that she was very tired, and was going to her own room.

"Grandfather Axel is asleep," she said. "I think I will leave him to you and Maria tonight."

"It is time you did," said Katarina, not unkindly. "There's not been a night since he was hurt that you have stayed in your bed right through. It is no wonder you are tired."

But Agneta was not thinking of rest. Through and through her brain rang the cruel jest of the soldiers. There was but one man in New Sweden who could protect Axel Bonde from Dutch violence. That man was the Dutch Director-General.

The thoughts of the girl went to the day when Pieter Stuyvesant stood in Axel Bonde's cattle house, and spoke kindly words to herself. He seemed not a bloodthirsty man, though he looked through and through a stern one. Would he permit such wanton cruelty and insult if he knew that the old man to whom it was offered was the friend of all and the foe of none?

"I will go and tell him," she said, and when she said it she fully appreciated the dangers and difficulties that lay in the way.

She would go at once. Any time the Dutch soldiers, and especially that particular officer who had not forgiven her for being a party to driving him away, might break through the Indian guards, and vent their spite on the household within. She would not be missed until morning. She hoped to be back before then.

The afternoon sunlight was falling through the trees as she stepped outside the house. The words of the Swedish woman were ringing in her ears, "I sneaked in and out among the trees." Why should she not successfully do the same, though the road swarmed with soldiers?

"The little squaw had better stay within the house. The Hollanders are not good to their Swedish brothers and sisters."

Amattehoorn laid his hand upon her arm. She turned and looked in his face.

"I *must* go," she said. "Amattehoorn, promise me that you will not tell them at home unless I do not return by the morning. I am going to the Dutch Sachem. He was good to me once. I think he will be again."

"Amattehoorn will go with you," he said.

She hesitated a moment. The perils of the way would be less formidable with Amattehoorn by her side. But suppose the farmhouse should be attacked in the meantime?

"No. I think it will be best to go alone," she said. "You may be needed here. Oh, Amattehoorn, I would rather they should kill me than touch grandfather Axel again. Stay and guard him. Your young men are good, but Amattehoorn is better."

He looked at her steadily, standing for a long time silent.

"I will see that no harm comes near him," he said at last.

She held out her hand. He took it in his own, and stepped out from the shadow of the tree that had sheltered them.

That journey through the woods and swamps took much time to accomplish. Again and again Agneta's heart beat with fear as the voices of the Dutchmen came to her ears. She made long stoppages in the thick underbrush, waiting for bands of soldiers to leave some spot from which her next step could be observed. More than once she had to go far round to avoid a dangerous morass.

Slow and hazardous as it was, however, this part of the journey was the least formidable feature of the undertaking. When the main body of the army was reached, or that portion of it that guarded the southern bank of the Christina, the real difficulty would begin.

She did not know in what direction to look for Governor Stuyvesant. He was in all probability on the other side of the Christina River. He might be at any one of the batteries, or with any portion of the army investing Fort Christina. Moreover, the streams that below the fort ran into the South River, and the swamps through which those streams passed, made it harder to elude the soldiers. It would be very easy to get shut in between the rising water and the Dutch forces.

The tide was coming in. She could hear the water lapping around the grassy hummocks from one to another of which she carefully stepped, and see it covering deeper and deeper the low spaces between. It was over her ankles now when she found herself obliged to walk through it. It would soon make her position untenable.

She had been making longer and longer stoppages as she drew nearer to the Dutch army. Not that her courage failed her, or that she despaired of carrying out her project. She was hoping to catch some unguarded word that should tell her of the whereabouts of the Director-General. She heard many a joke at the expense of the garrison that was every day being more thoroughly hemmed in.

"I wonder how the poor wretches like the Director's last word," said a rough voice so close to where she stood that the girl started in alarm.

"Twenty-four hours he gave them, didn't he?" replied a comrade. "And no quarter if they held out. I hope the fools will hold out. My sword's quivering to bury itself in a rascally Swede's heart. I haven't come all the way from Holland to play at soldiering. The business of the soldier is to kill, whatever you out here in the Province of New Netherland may think. Put them all to the sword. That's the way to treat a set of thievish Lutherans, that have no more religion than they have honesty."

"Their Governor Rysingh went back to his fort with a longer face than he brought out of it," said the other. "The Director gave him no loophole. Surrender or take the consequences. That was the tune."

"Where's the Director now?" asked his companion, and Agneta leant forward that she might the more surely catch the answer.

"Over on Timber Island. He's inspecting the guns, to make certain they are ready to begin the attack the minute the twenty-four hours is up. What's that?" added the soldier hastily.

A loud splash in the swamp behind him was the cause of the exclamation. He raised his gun, and fired a shot at random. It passed within a foot of a girl who was floundering in water up to her knees. A treacherous hummock on which she had stood had given way beneath the pressure as she leant forward to catch the soldier's words.

"Some beast or other wandering in the swamp," said the second soldier.

"We want no beasts round here. We've got enough of them in the Swedes themselves," replied the first, and he sent another shot into the swamp by way of emphasizing his words.

It went perilously near the girl, who stood breathless as the bullets whizzed past her. She had accomplished her purpose thus far. The Director-General was at Timber Island. But how was she to get to him?

The sun had already gone down. She felt the need of haste. Governor Stuyvesant might at any time return from the island.

How to cross the water that lay between her and the Director-General was the problem. She crept slowly along the swamp till she was out of hearing of the soldiers. Then she cautiously approached the encircling trees, and peered out. The waters of the Christina lay before her, with the broad stretch of tide-covered flats beyond. She could see the men camped at high points along its shores. She could see also, less than a quarter of a mile away, a canoe upon the river bank.

Her heart beat fast. Had she courage to reach that canoe and push it out in the stream in sight of the soldiers, and within reach of their guns?

"It is for grandfather Axel," she said, and crept

out from the cover of the swamp, making a dash for a piece of forest land a few yards higher up.

She did not know that within that wood a prisoner was thinking of a gentle maiden, and as he thought, tearing at the cords that held him.

CHAPTER XXXVIII

There were many prisoners on the ships. Eric's captors had deemed it best to keep this one away from his fellows. Personally Stuyvesant knew nothing about him. It is possible that the soldiers kept him among them as much for amusement as for any other reason. It sent them into fits of laughter to look on his face when they described their violent deeds. They made the most of them in his presence.

One of them had that day alluded to Axel Bonde and his household.

"The old rascal will tread the soil of the South River no more," he said.

If looks would have killed, the speaker would that moment have been counted among the dead. Eric spake no word, but teeth and hands worked all day at the fetters that bound him. His captors had adopted the not altogether ingenious device of tying him to a tree. To all appearance, after that one fierce flash of rage, their prisoner was calmer than usual. It was the calmness of a desperate resolve.

"Who goes there! Stop, or I fire!"

The slight figure did not hesitate. It sped straight on towards the boat that was nearer to the girl than to the sentinel who hailed her.

There was a minute's silence, and then the sound of a shot, followed by a sharp cry. It was the voice of a girl, and though it was an inarticulate cry, Eric needed not to be told that the maiden for whom he would willingly have given his life was near him—and in peril.

The stimulus of that moment finished the work that had been slowly advancing all day. A broken rope hung to a tree. The two soldiers who acted as guard to the prisoner had disappeared, eager, like himself, to be quickly at the scene of interest. Eric sprang to the embers of a fire that had been lighted near by, and laid the cords that bound his hands upon the glowing coals. A minute later he was free.

One of the guards was yet within the woods as the young man passed him. Eric turned, and with a blow of his clenched fist left the Dutchman sprawling upon the ground.

"So, ho! I've got you at last. And, by Jupiter, it's the same wench that once before was bent on giving the rascally John Rysingh warning that his good friends had come to visit him. Well, my dear, what do you want now? A taste of Dutch hospitality?"

It was the same bold, coarse face that on the first day of the presence of the besieging army had been thrust into hers in the woods upon the road to Fort Christina. Agneta knew the man again. His leering eyes were looking into hers. The grasp on her arm made itself felt to the bone.

"Now then, pretty one, I want a kiss. You came hither to give it to me? Is it not so? The men of the Swedes had grown wearisome. These pretty lips longed for other kisses—kisses as ardent as that, and that!"

He smacked his lips as they abandoned their contact with the soft, shrinking ones that uttered another cry when his arm went about the girl's waist.

"Take off your hands!" she said. "I seek your Director Stuyvesant. He is my friend, from the day when he first set foot in New Sweden."

"Oh, is he, my pretty dear? And so are all his men," replied the soldier. "We will entertain you, you jade, in the absence of our Director. He is not in good trim for gallantry. His hands are red with the blood of your countrymen. He——"

But the next moment there was a mighty splash, and another arm encircled the girl's waist, snatching her from the rude hand that held her, and holding her back from the fate that had overtaken the soldier. In the water a Dutchman spluttered and swore, while a white, determined face looked into Agneta's, and Eric said:

"Where shall I take you? Do you indeed seek Director Stuyvesant?"

"Yes, oh, yes! Here is a boat. Come. He is at Timber Island," said the girl. "I must go to him. They have almost killed grandfather Axel!"

He pushed the boat into the stream, and put her in it. Before the swearing, furious Dutchman could scramble up on to the bank, the two were far out in the stream.

"And you? Agneta, my darling, I have been wild with fear for you. They have kept me bound. I was trying to come to you when they took me."

"I knew you would try," she said, and yet a strange peace came to her heart with the certainty that he had really been hastening to her aid. She was no longer afraid. She hardly knew why, but she felt as if the danger were over.

A bullet passed between the two heads. It had not much room to spare.

The second guard had reached the bank.

"Stop, both of you!" he cried, though how one could stop without the other was not very apparent.

They rowed the faster.

"Crouch low, dear," said Eric, bending over her so that his body in a measure sheltered her from the fire of the soldiers.

She looked into his eyes, and then dropped her own. Those others were alight with tenderness.

He bent yet closer to her.

"For once you are all mine, and cannot do without me," he said. "It has always been the other way."

"Did you want it not to be?" she asked.

"Agneta, I think I have always wanted you, from that first night in the snow and the darkness," he said. "I have you now—for a few short minutes at least."

Another bullet fell into the water ahead of the boat.

"You are exposing yourself for me," she said. "Don't do it. I want to share the risk—with you."

"Agneta!"

Ping! ping! Two bullets had struck the boat just above the water line.

"Are you sure that Director Stuyvesant is at Timber Island?" asked Eric.

Agneta's life as well as his own depended upon reaching the Director-General quickly.

"No. Look!"

She pointed across the stream to a high bank. A figure a little above the medium height stood upon the bank, with hand uplifted, the fine, stern face a little less immovable than usual as the Director of New Netherland watched the progress of that boat down the river.

"Surely that is none other than Governor Stuyvesant," said Agneta.

"I know him not," replied Eric. "If that be he, we will direct our course thither."

There was regret in his tone. In spite of the danger, the moments had been precious.

Neither noticed that the bullets ceased after that hand was uplifted. Eric's arm urged the boat swiftly through the water, and sent it grinding on the shore almost at the Director's feet. Pieter Stuyvesant looked upon the young Swede with stern, unbending brow.

"Who are you, and why do you force your way past my sentries?" he asked, with a voice not calculated to inspire confidence.

"I am one of the Swedish prisoners, your Honor," replied Eric calmly, "and I came hither to bring this maiden to your Honor's presence, aye, and to rescue her from the ruffianly violence of your Honor's soldiers."

The brow of Director Stuyvesant darkened.

"Your Excellency," began Agneta, stepping upon the shore, and courtesying low to the Director, "I——"

But he waved her aside.

"I will listen to you later," he said. "At present my business is with this young man. Now, sir," he added, "if you were a prisoner, how come you to be free to criticise the actions of my soldiers, and offer defiance to the Director of New Netherland?"

"Your Honor, at the cry of a maiden in peril, I broke the cords that bound me. Your Honor would have done no less," said Eric quietly.

"And where were your guards?" asked the Director.

"One of them was upon the ground when I saw him last," said Eric. "Of the whereabouts of the other I knew not until his bullet whizzed past my head."

The slightest shadow of a smile crossed the lips of the Director. It was gone in a moment.

"And what fate, think you, awaits the prisoner who turns on his guards, and bids defiance to the leader of this army?" he asked.

"I know not, your Honor. 'Twere better than

the fate of a coward who could hear a maiden's cry of distress and stand speculating on his own future," replied the young man.

"Your Excellency, the soldier knew not the rights of womanhood," said Agneta. "Had not Eric come to my rescue, he——"

"The rescued should of a surety speak well of the rescuer," said Stuyvesant, interrupting her. "Yet must the Swedes learn that the authority of the Director-General of New Netherland is supreme in the land of the South River. I will hear you later."

Then he slightly raised his voice, and called to him a soldier.

"Take this Swede to the good ship *Love*," he said. "If I mistake not, 'tis the vessel to suit best his mood. And see that he be well guarded."

He did not look at the face of the girl as the soldier led the prisoner away. But he saw her step to the young man's side, and lay her hand upon his arm.

Neither spoke, for the soldier was too near. They looked into each other's eyes, and the girl stepped back. It was a silent farewell.

"I think I have seen this maiden before."

The Director-General was studying the face and figure of the girl before him. For the moment she had forgotten the urgency of her errand. Her eyes were following Eric Helm and the soldier. Now she turned towards the Governor.

"Yes, your Excellency," she said, in a low, soft voice, "and the old man who upon that occasion so gladly welcomed you under his roof lies to-day in mortal pain and extremity. I come to ask your clemency for him."

"The old peasant?" said Stuyvesant. "Aye, I remember him well. Lives he yet? He must be very old."

"Yes, your Honor. He is eighty-two, and they talk of dragging him on to one of the ships, and he lies injured to the death by the harsh treatment of the soldiers."

Her voice broke, and her eyes filled with tears.

The brow of the Director gathered blackness.

"Who injured him?" he asked.

"The Dutch soldiers," replied the girl.

"Upon what provocation?" demanded the stern voice.

"That he sought to defend me and his household from the coarse brutality of their touch," she said.

"There seems to be more than one who will risk much for that purpose," said the Director quietly. "In what way was he injured?"

"He was thrown to the ground, and brutally kicked by a drunken officer," replied the girl. "He lieth with a broken leg, and injuries the nature of which we know not, only we know that he is in constant pain, and that he waits for death to bring him relief."

The frown upon the Director's brow deepened.

"And for what do you come to me?" he said.

"For protection from your soldiers," replied Agneta. "The same officer threatens to drag grandfather Axel from his bed, and to let him feel the power of the Dutch soldiery by torturing him in the removal from the house to the vessel, 'and if he die on the way so much the better,' saith the soldier."

The ring of indignation in her voice could no longer be concealed, but at the last words the thought of the old man left at the mercy of the merciless was too much for her. Her hand went hastily to her face. She turned her head away.

For a full minute there was silence between the two. It was the Director who broke it.

"Maiden," he said gently, "it is the business of this army to reduce the Swedish people to submission. Yet want we not to torture the old and the helpless. Your grandfather shall no more be molested. I will give orders that his person and property shall be respected."

The girl turned towards him, the light of a great joy upon her face.

"I thought *you* were not cruel," she said. "Your Excellency, one maiden of New Sweden thanks you from the bottom of her heart."

The stern face relaxed. A smile came about the lips. He looked like the Director Stuyvesant before whom Agneta had stood in the cattle house.

"Fair maiden," he said, "the duty of a Governor is sometimes to be severe. But he does not desire to be cruel. I will give you a written order from myself that will ensure the safety of your person, and the person of the old man. I will also mention the circumstance to my officers. And now, my child, how are you going to get back?"

"I know not, your Honor. I think I hardly care," she said. "Grandfather Axel is safe. The rest seems easy. But——" and she looked doubtfully in the face before her.

"But what? Is it not enough?" he asked.

The quick flush came to the girl's cheeks. They had been very white before.

"Eric Helm—the young man who risked his life to save me," she said. "Would your Excellency extend your clemency to him also?"

The color came and went in her face. The Governor looked down upon her.

"Speak you from a sense of gratitude towards a rescuer or—from some other feeling?" he asked, a smile breaking once more the gravity of his face.

The pink deepened to crimson.

"From both—perchance," she said.

His face was grave again.

"Fair maiden, I can make no more promises," he said. "The young man must take his chance. Old men and maidens are one thing; young, stalwart prisoners who can strike down a guard and loose themselves from fetters are another. He is, I think, a dangerous character."

"Nay, nay, your Honor. He is a young man who will be true to his word and his friends, and will in no wise forget a kindness," said Agneta.

"He has yet to receive one at our hands," said Stuyvesant quietly. "Here, guard," he added, as a soldier approached, "I give this maiden into your care. See that she reach her home without molestation or insult. You will answer to me for your charge."

The low courtesy, and the softly spoken thanks with which Agneta turned to follow her guide, were answered by a wave of the hand and the words:

"Adieu, fair maiden. Your grandfather's old age shall surely be respected."

Perhaps he did not see the entreaty in her eyes. Certainly he did not answer it.

CHAPTER XXXIX

The fate of Fort Christina was sealed. The grim determination that comes when the worst has to be met was in the face of Governor Rysingh, and was reflected in those of his soldiers. The twenty-four hours given by Stuyvesant for the besieged to come to a final decision drew to a close. John Rysingh had tried the effect of messengers, protests, appeals for better treatment, and even a personal interview with the leader of the great army that invested the fort. The outcome of them all was this ultimatum.

Surrender the land of the South River within twenty-four hours or take the consequences, said Pieter Stuyvesant, and the Director-General of New Netherland was not a man to say one thing and mean another. He had threatened to give no quarter if he were forced to bombard the fort. He desired a bloodless victory. If it were not to be according to his desire, a little bloodshed more or less would be of small moment to him.

It was not a fort that Governor Rysingh was preparing to give up, but a colony. For seventeen years the Swedes had held sway at the South River. They had established the most friendly relations with the natives, built forts, improved lands, and settled the country with a peaceful and industrious population. Now their rule was to cease. When Governor Rysingh left Fort Christina, and walked out upon the high land that lay between the fort and the most advanced works of the Dutch, it was to make preparations to hand over the whole of New Sweden to Pieter Stuyvesant, the representative of the Dutch West India Company.

He was in full sight of the besieging army, as well as of the soldiers within the fort. He looked at the Dutchmen drawn up in advantageous positions all around Christina, and remembered the day when he sailed up the South River in his armed vessel, and forced the Dutch flag down from the Dutch Fort Casimir. He had all along hoped that Stuyvesant would in the end be content to take back his own. Upon the fall of Fort Trinity he had sent his factor to ask the Director to stop at that point in the reprisals. But Pieter Stuyvesant had not gathered together an army simply to take back that of which John Rysingh had deprived him. The full control of the South River was what he asked as the outcome of his expedition. And to-day he was to gain it.

While the Swedes of the South River awaited apprehensively the terms of that surrender, wondering whether it would mean the giving up of their lands, and their removal in a penniless condition to a strange and unfriendly city, the two Governors met.

When the conditions of the capitulation were known, some of the people of New Sweden breathed a sigh of relief. With the surrender of the colony into his hands, the worst severities of Director Stuyvesant ceased. True, the soldiers were yet abroad in the land, and soldiers of that day were not renowned for tenderness. Moreover the policy of depriving the Swedes of their influential men was to a certain extent carried out. But there was hope for the future. The lands and property of the settlers were assured to them, though they might have to pay a rent to the Dutch West India Company in lieu of the tenths that the Dutch of New Netherland paid.

The Director-General made a concession in promising the Swedes the free enjoyment of their own form of religion. In his colony of New Netherland Pieter Stuyvesant might be a zealous Calvinist, and a hard governor where the Lutherans were concerned. In New Sweden he saw the necessity of leaving the people free to follow their national form of worship. To allow the ministers to remain was another matter. There were three of them in New Sweden. Domine Megapolensis, the Director's chaplain, looked grave at the thought of leaving so much heresy behind him.

He need not have feared. The question was not whether three should be left, but whether any should remain. And that that question was settled in favor of the Swedes was rather the effect of a combination of circumstances than of any great leaning towards liberality on the part of Pieter Stuyvesant.

The meeting between Governor Rysingh and Director Stuyvesant was ceremonious and lengthy. It ended in a complete understanding between the two leaders. Pieter Stuyvesant was willing to allow his antagonist all the honors of war. He might march out with colors flying, drums beating, fifes playing, and soldiers fully armed. He was promised conveyance for himself and his officers, and those Swedes who desired to go with him, to his own land, and that at the expense of the Dutch. All property of the Swedish crown, in the shape of guns and provisions, was to be held in trust, and delivered when called for by the Swedes.

The terms of the capitulation looked, on paper, moderate. If they were not altogether carried out in the spirit of the writing, men at the time hoped for the best.

On the twenty-fifth day of September, sixteen hundred and fifty-five, the capitulation was to be signed, and John Rysingh to march out of Fort Christina, leaving New Sweden a Dutch possession. He might have received back his fort if he would have held it subject to Dutch rule, but he refused. He would either be Governor of New Sweden, or leave everything in the hands of Pieter Stuyvesant. The future was for the Swedish government to settle.

"Well, New Sweden's dead, and her burial about to take place," announced the Swedish woman who had brought to Agneta the news of the intended cruelty to Axel Bonde. She was once more at the farm-house, possibly with an eye to further favors in the form of bacon and cheese.

"Has the Governor capitulated?" asked Katarina.

"Aye," said the woman, "that has he, in sight of all the land, upon the level ground at the back of the fort. We are Dutch subjects now."

"Are the thieves going to leave us our lands?" asked Maria, anxiously.

"So they say. 'Tis more than I looked for. It stood to fear that they would take everything. We've got to swear allegiance to them, or get out of the country."

"I'm not going to get out," averred Maria. "I'm going to make the South River yield me a living, and a good one, be it under Dutch rule or Swedish."

Maria's tone was belligerent. There had been a certain air of defiance about her from the night when a Dutch soldier led a Swedish girl up to the door of the farm-house, followed closely by an old Indian warrior.

"What do our brothers the Dutch with the little squaw?" were the words with which Amattehoorn stepped from a shadowed spot and confronted the soldier.

"What am I doing, you old meddler?" was the answer. "I'm taking the girl to her home, where she had been wiser had she stayed."

"It is true, Amattehoorn," said Agneta gently.

"He is acting as my escort. I have no reason to complain of his treatment. I have seen the Dutch Sachem."

Amattehoorn grunted. It might be all right, but he followed the pair till the low door of the house was reached, and Agneta turned to her companion.

"I thank you for your protection," she said, but at that moment the door was swung open, and Maria stood in the opening.

"You!" she gasped. "And in *his* hands! I thought you were in your bed. Come in, quick, and leave Amattehoorn to deal with him."

She pointed to the Dutchman as she spoke, and then stepped back, holding the door in her hand, ready to swing it to in the face of the intruder.

"You mistake, Maria," said Agneta. "I have to thank this soldier for protection on my homeward journey. Sir, I need trouble you no further," she added.

"What!" ejaculated Maria. "Is he another of them that think a pretty face on a delicate lady must be seen safely home, while a common Swedish woman is fit only for kicks and insults? Truly even in an invading army there seem to be many such."

"He has come from Director Stuyvesant," said Agneta, trying to keep her voice steady, but between excitement and anger not succeeding very thoroughly. "We need keep him no longer from other duties."

"From Director Stuyvesant!" exclaimed Maria,

as Agneta stepped inside. "Have you been to Governor Stuyvesant?"

"Yes," said the girl, in a tone of weariness and excitement combined. "How is grandfather Axel?"

"He is asleep?" replied Maria. "Did you go right into the army of the Hollanders?"

"Yes."

"What for?" demanded the girl.

"To ensure grandfather Axel's safety when the army returned. Didn't you hear what they threatened?"

"Aye," retorted Maria, "but I shouldn't have thought of going to the Director. *I* don't expect to bewitch all the men. Did you go through the woods to Director Stuyvesant this day?"

"Surely I did," said Agneta.

"Little one, is it not time somebody had authority to look after you?"

Monsieur Pors stood in the opposite doorway. His face was pale. A moment more and he was at her side.

"Agneta, little sweetheart, did you know what risk you ran?"

His voice was so low that Maria heard the sound but not the words.

"I could not help it," Agneta said. "It was for grandfather Axel."

"Yes—I know. But, Agneta, you are too precious to be risked. I shall not let you out of my sight again."

She smiled, but her lips were not steady.

"He is safe now," she said. "The Director-General has given me an order, written with his own hand, that we may show it to any who shall attempt to molest him, or to interfere with his property."

"His property?" rejoined Maria briskly. "Does it also insure that?"

"Yes. It was a secondary matter, but he added it of his own accord."

"It is a goodly second to us," said Maria. "Well, you're a wonder to come out of a scrape, and you've accomplished something this time. Of a surety you've less caution and more rashness than any girl I ever saw, but you have a way of walking through a place where anybody else would come to grief. Did the Director succumb to a pretty face like the rest of them?"

"Gently, kind maiden," interposed Gustavus. "Why should not the Director of New Netherland look kindly upon a fair face? 'Twould be a hard heart that could look coldly on this one. And 'tis well to remember," he added, "that the worthy man had not the good Maria's tongue to listen to, or he might, perchance, have been diverted from the intensity of his gazing."

Maria looked doubtfully at the speaker, and then left him in possession of the field.

The hand of Monsieur Pors tightened over the fingers he had not yet relinquished.

"Agneta," he said tenderly, "do you think you treated me quite fairly? I would have gone with you anywhere, little one. Do you know what it would have meant to me had I known you were in danger—and alone?"

"Though I had known, I must have gone," she said. "It was for grandfather Axel."

"Yet you must promise me that even for him you will not again encounter danger without me," he said.

"It will not be necessary again," she replied. "He is safe."

"Agneta, does *all* your heart belong to Axel Bonde?"

There was passion and entreaty in the voice. He tried to look into her eyes, but she would not let him.

"Who has such a right to it?" she asked, with a sob in her voice. "Do you know what he did for me? He took a helpless little stranger into his heart, and made her his own. He gave me a place in his love when I had no claim on it."

"Axel Bonde's is not the only heart that long ago opened to take you in," he said, but he let her draw her hand away and escape to her own room.

Once there, she threw herself upon her knees, buried her head deep in the bedclothes, and sobbed as if she had failed in her mission. Perhaps she felt that she had. She was not at that moment thinking of Axel Bonde.

The face that bent over Axel an hour later looked very white and tired.

"My bairn," he said, "you did wrong. This old life was not worth the risking of yours."

"Hush!" she said softly. "I cannot bear to hear you say that to-night."

He looked fondly in her face.

"Your journey has brought safety to you also," he said, "and to all of them. My bairn, the old man thanks you."

"Don't," whispered the girl, and for a minute the sobs gained the mastery. There were tears in the old eyes, too.

Maria, coming in, found the two thus.

"I should think you'd want to sleep, Agneta," she said. "I should, if I'd tramped through the forest, and hidden, and watched, and dodged the soldiers, as you must have done. Monsieur Pors is going to sit with grandfather to-night."

He came in while she was speaking.

"Would it not be better for you to rest?" he asked gently.

"Yes—soon. I wanted to see grandfather Axel first."

"*I* want to hear how you got to Director Stuyvesant," said Maria. "I should have thought you'd have been frightened to death."

The grasp of the old man's hand tightened about the girl's fingers.

"Where *was* the Director?" continued Maria.

"On the other side of the creek."

"And you crossed the Christina Creek to get to him?" ejaculated the girl.

"Yes."

"Well, you take it coolly, I must say," commented Maria. "Did you get that Dutch soldier to intimidate his companions, and row you across in the face of them all?"

"No," said Agneta. "He was but sent with me when I left the Director."

"Sent, was he?" sniffed Maria. "I suppose the Director would have sent his whole army to bring you safely back, had you desired him so to do."

Agneta was silent.

"And you crossed that creek alone?" interrogated Maria.

"I did not say that," was the answer.

Did Maria see the tinge of color that came to the tired face? If she did it only stimulated her curiosity.

"Then who was with you, I should like to know?"

"Eric Helm," said the girl, lifting her head and speaking in a low, clear tone.

"Eric Helm!"

For a full minute the power of speech abandoned Maria. She stood and stared at Agneta, while the soft color deepened on the maiden's cheeks.

"Does he fare well?"

It was Axel Bonde who spoke, and the words were low and tender.

"Nay—he is a prisoner."

The voice tried to be calm, but did not altogether succeed.

"Then how, in the name of all that's reasonable, did he cross the Christina Creek with you?"

Maria's tones were sharp and penetrating

"He heard me cry out, and he broke his fetters and came to me," said Agneta. "The ruffian from whom he delivered me was left floundering in the creek. And in face of the fire of the soldiers he took me to the Director himself."

There was the ring of pride in her voice. It did not escape Maria's ears, nor those of another listener.

"And he let a Dutchman bring you home," said Maria, with a sneer. "Truly he seems quickly to have tired of your company, or of the bullets of the soldiers."

"You misunderstand," replied Agneta. "He was a prisoner. He struck down his guard, and disregarded the challenge of the sentries, and he landed me at the feet of Director Stuyvesant while in the very act of defying the Director's soldiers. He paid the penalty. He is now on board one of the Dutch vessels."

Her head went down upon the hand that pressed hers in sympathy.

"Well!" said Maria, and turned away.

From that day the attitude of Axel Bonde's granddaughter was defiant and assertive.

That night Monsieur Pors watched by Axel Bonde, and in the hours that drew towards morning the murmur of voices sounded in the room. All night the thoughts of the two men had played round the same centre, and when they spoke, it was of the girl whom both loved. The talk was long and earnest, and if the face of the younger man once or twice became proud and hard, it softened again.

The room was still at last, for exhaustion had come to Axel Bonde, but as he lay with eyes closed, the hand of the peasant rested upon that of the rich land-owner, and the face of the old man was very calm.

CHAPTER XL

The invasion of the South River had been brought to a successful issue. To-morrow the Swedish Governor would march out of Fort Christina, and New Sweden would belong to the Dutch. It was a moment of triumph for Pieter Stuyvesant, and yet his face looked not like the face of a man who was satisfied with his circumstances. It was grave and sad, and much disturbed.

The Director sat in a house upon the south bank of the Christina, one that had early been taken possession of by the Dutch forces. Before him was the Christina Creek, with the Swedish fort—*his* fort after to-morrow—in full view. His soldiers were camped upon the higher lands around. He got up and walked to the window. His eye did not brighten as it fell upon the scene without. New Sweden lay at his feet, but he turned away from the sight of it with an impatient movement, and went back to the rough wooden table, upon which lay a packet, a folded paper that was responsible for the troubled expression of the Governor's face.

Yesterday he had been triumphant, but that was before the packet reached his hand. He drew it to him now, and unfolded it. He need not have done so. He knew exactly what was inside. Yet he let his eye move once more down the written page.

He had come hither to bring war to New Sweden. That paper told him that in his absence war had come to his own domain. Bouweries burned, plantations ruined, grain destroyed, cattle killed, a hundred of his subjects numbered with the dead, and a hundred and fifty more carried captive by the Indians—this was the message that innocent looking sheet of paper had brought.

New Amsterdam was in a panic. From the outlying districts Dutchmen and their families were hurrying to the city, driven by fear of the Indians. For three days, whilst the Director-General was engaged in the subjugation of the Swedes, the Indians ran riot in and around his own capital. Two hundred thousand florins, or eighty thousand dollars, was the estimated damage done by that raid.

"We blame the Swedes," wrote the members of the Director's Council.

They might with more wisdom have blamed themselves, or the man who in a fit of unrestrained rage killed a squaw for stealing his peaches, and thus put into the hearts of the Indians a rankling grudge, that only needed the absence of the Governor and a large number of the defenders of the country to make it break out in active hostility.

"The supreme chief of the Minquases has been here, conferring with all the Indian chiefs," wrote the Governor's correspondent, "and the Dutch believe that the Swedes have bribed these savages to fall on the city in the absence of the Governor."

It was a story little calculated to bring comfort to the heart of a ruler.

Pieter Stuyvesant had gained New Sweden, and his absence had brought desolation on New Amsterdam.

"We and the citizens stand guard, and are harassed day and night with watching," wrote the Council.

The Governor sat thinking long. At last he summoned to him a member of his staff.

"Is the yacht of which I spoke in readiness to sail?" he asked.

"Preparations are being completed, your Honor," was the answer.

"It is well. Let all speed be made," said the Governor. "My dispatches will be ready in an hour. Let the captain know that haste is required of him. By rowing, sailing, and drifting, he must make all possible headway, that my communication may at the earliest moment be in the hands of my Council. And send to me the captain of the *Love*. She can be spared for the protection of Manhattan. She also, with soldiers aboard, must sail, with the yacht."

He turned away and began to write. When his letter was sealed the two ships were made ready to start.

CHAPTER XLI

The *Love* had started for New Amsterdam. When she entered the South River a few weeks before, she brought soldiers eager to reach the land of the Swedes. She carried back men who were yet more eager to reach the land of the Dutch. There were Dutchmen on board whose wives and children had been carried away captive by the Indians, and Dutchmen whose families were exposed to the danger that still threatened New Amsterdam. The men were in haste to go to the relief of the frightened little city, that, small and helpless as it was, stood as the representative of the power and authority of the Hollanders in New Netherland.

Feeling was divided between elation at the victory gained in New Sweden and dismay at the evil wrought around New Amsterdam. There was more than one perturbed face on board the *Love* that day, but none that looked quite as anxious as that of a young man whose tall, straight figure made him conspicuous among the rounder and stouter built Dutchmen.

The neighborhood of Fort Casimir was being neared, and for the time the victors forgot the troubles ahead of them, and gave themselves up to the contemplation of this proof of their prowess. The *Love* had just sailed majestically past the house of Axel Bonde.

"Wonder whether the old man's dead yet, or whether he's waiting for the returning army to pay his house a last visit," said a soldier, with a loud laugh, and a nod of his head towards the farm-house.

He did not see the angry flash in the eyes that belonged to the tall figure behind him.

Eric Helm had heard nothing of the fate of Agneta since he left her in the presence of Pieter Stuyvesant. The words of the soldier were the first reference made in his hearing to the family of Axel Bonde. He had at first been kept a close prisoner upon the *Love*, but latterly his captors had given him more freedom. That he had experienced no actual ill-treatment he owed to the orders given by the Director-General.

"Keep the young man in safe custody, and carry him with you to New Amsterdam," commanded the Governor. "In the meantime, treat him well. When I return, I will see him myself."

Eric Helm's anxiety to know whether Agneta had reached her home in safety had made the days seem long upon the *Love*. Now, as the farm-house was passed, he looked longingly at the uncommunicative walls. Was all well within?

The brutal joke of the Dutchman brought the color to his face. Would the soldiers indeed enter that dwelling upon their return? The thought of Agneta, left to face them alone, without even the protection of the old man's arm, was too much for his equanimity, and perhaps for his wisdom. The gleam of anger changed to a light that was possibly hardly more sane, though it was the light of a swift resolve. He glanced quickly round the vessel, making a mental calculation of chances that were all against him.

The sun had gone down, and the brightness was fading from the sky. The trees upon the shore looked dark and gloomy, especially in the stretch of woodland that lay between Axel Bonde's house and Fort Casimir. The *Love* was abreast of that thicket now, and every eye was turned towards Fort Casimir. For a minute elation took the place of anxiety in the breasts of the Dutchmen. Engrossed with the visible representation of their own success, they paid no heed to a figure that edged towards the side of the vessel, and then, swinging itself up by a rope, was outlined for a moment against the evening sky. Even the splash that came after it dropped over the ship's side was lost in the babble of Dutch voices, all talking at once, and all in loud praise of Dutch prowess.

There was only one pair of eyes that saw that frantic break for liberty, and they belonged to neither Dutchman nor Swede. The young Indian brave who stood by the bank towards which everybody's back was turned, not only saw, but recognized the Swede before he dived beneath the water, and came up in the wake of the vessel. It was four years since he followed that tall figure through the forest, his hand more than once upon his bow for the purpose of avenging an unintentional wrong. The brave was an older Indian now, but the animosity of that day had not been quite wiped out from his heart, or the sharp, shrill cry, half whistle, half call, with which he drew to himself the attention of the soldiers, had not been uttered.

More than a minute had elapsed between the splash and that long call. The swimmer was already some distance behind the boat, striking out for the shore.

When the soldiers turned, there stood upon the bank an Indian with arm outstretched, one finger pointing towards the water behind the boat.

"What's the matter?" shouted a Dutchman, and all eyes traveled from the Fort Casimir side of the river to the other.

"Your boat carries one man less," said the Indian, in slow, clear tones, that reached every ear.

"What do you mean?" demanded the soldier, impatiently.

The finger still pointed towards the water.

"The Swede desires not to go to Manhattan," replied the Indian.

"What? Where is he? Look out! The wretch has escaped us!"

For one moment the Dutchmen caught a glimpse of a head above the water. Then it disappeared, and for the shot that rang out there was no result but a bullet that went scudding along the surface well to the right of the diver.

Orders confusing and contrary took the place of the peaceful clamor of self-praise. The boat and the swimmer were combining to increase the distance between the two, and the mists of evening were all in favor of the prisoner. When he came up again a long stretch of water lay between Eric Helm and the *Love*. One or two bullets fell near him, striking the water harmlessly.

"Lower a boat! Stop the vessel! We're responsible to the Governor for him! Fire on the wretch, and done with him!" were some of the cries that reached Eric's ears.

He was nearing the bank, and the stretch of uncut forest afforded almost immediate shelter. He had no intention of going straight to the farm-house. That would be to draw upon it the very visit he dreaded. He would take to the woods. The *Love* could not long delay her departure. Unless the soldiers found him quickly, they must give up the search.

As he came to the shallow water the bullets dropped splashing round him.

"A little more luck, and one strong right arm will be between her and any villain who dares to molest her," he thought, as he drew together his forces for the dash up the bank.

The arm in question had already healed of its wound, and was doing good service in helping its owner through the water.

When his feet touched the bank, Eric turned, and saw a boat with soldiers in it preparing to leave the ship's side. He had still two or three minutes' lead. He did not despair of success.

At the very moment that he turned his head, an officer on deck was seen to take aim at the figure that now offered a better target. A bullet whistled through the air, and this time did not fall short of its mark.

"Hit, by all that's lucky!"

The officer lowered his weapon, and coolly surveyed the prostrate form.

"Pick him up, and bring him aboard," he shouted, addressing the men in the boat.

"Wait a bit, my fine fellow," whispered lips that had grown white.

The force of the missile as it entered his shoulder, and cut its way through to bury itself somewhere in his breast, had laid Eric low. He did not try to rise. That would be but to tempt another bullet. Not ten yards away the trees stretched out sheltering arms to him. Scarcely raising his head, he crawled towards them, the movement being at first unperceived from the vessel.

"Hullo! He's not done for yet!"

The speaker leaned over the ship's side, and strained his eyes to watch the progress of the wounded man. Twilight favored his escape.

"Put a little more lead into him!"

The words were addressed to the officer.

"Oh, let him alone," replied that worthy. "He's about done for. Our men will pick him up and bring him aboard."

But before the boat touched the shore, Eric had reached the trees. Then he stumbled to his feet and ran. It was but a short spurt. Drops of blood marked the way.

"No good. I can't do it. I should be no help to her now if I could."

He sank down in the shelter of the trees, and looked up at the darkening sky. He was near to Agneta—very near—but he might as well be miles away. She would have none to help her if the soldiers came. Axel was perchance dead, and he——"

Rallying all his strength, he drew himself up by the trunk of a tree.

No use. He could not stand. He reeled, tried to hold on to the support that seemed in some mysterious way as unstable as himself, and fell into the arms of a man upon the other side of that apparently swaying trunk.

"Quick, Amattehoorn! I hear the boat grinding on the shore. Throw them off the scent. I'll get him into the house."

Monsieur Pors lifted the limp figure and bore it away, and the Indian bent his head for a moment, and listened. Then he crept on all fours in the direction of the sound, ostentatiously causing the leaves to rustle and the twigs to crack.

When the soldiers rushed up the bank they caught sight of a figure crawling in the shadow thrown by the trees.

"Here he is! Come on! He's past running, and has taken to the animal's method of locomotion."

But when the pursuers came into the shadow themselves, the figure had disappeared. They heard its movements further on, going in the direction of Fort Casimir.

"How, in the name of thunder, has the villain escaped us?" cried the leader. "Push ahead. He's wounded, and cannot long hold out."

And while they pushed ahead, Gustavus Pors carried his burden by a circuitous route to the house, never once coming out into the open.

As he entered the courtyard, Eric opened his eyes.

"Don't take me there," he said. "I swam ashore to help her, not to put her in danger."

"I'll take care of the danger," replied Gustavus, and passed beneath the low doorway.

"Hush!" he said peremptorily, as Maria came forward, uttering a shrill exclamation of dismay. "Be cautious. This is no time for outcry."

"Where did you find him?" demanded Maria, her voice rising again. "The wretches have shot him!"

"Silence, girl!" commanded Monsieur Pors, sternly. "Go, call your mother, and say no word to either your grandfather or Agneta."

But the warning came too late. There was the sound of an opening door, and the vision of a white, frightened face. Then Agneta crossed to the side of the wounded man.

"He is hurt," she said softly, but her tongue was stiff, as if a cold hand clutched her heart and stilled all movement of the body.

"Not of necessity seriously," said Gustavus.

"Go, little one, and keep the grandfather from knowing."

She looked in his face.

"I cannot," she said. "I must do what I can for him."

He carried the young man to the room that had been assigned to himself.

"Agneta," he said, as he laid him upon the bed, "I will do all that can be done for him. Can you not trust me?"

She looked again into his eyes.

"My place is here," she said.

For a moment he hesitated. Then he stooped suddenly, and put his lips to the fair forehead.

"So be it, little one," he said. "You shall return. Now I must see the extent of the danger. Go. Find bandages, and send the good house mother with them to me. I will call you when I have done."

She went without further demur.

Half an hour later, when he opened the door to call her, he found her standing before it.

"You have waited there?" he asked. "Poor little girl!"

His hand caressed the soft hair, and for a moment he stood barring the way. Then he led her in. Eric's eyes were open now. They turned eagerly towards the door.

"Agneta!" he said.

She came swiftly forward, and put her hand upon his. The fingers clasped it hungrily.

"I wanted to come to your aid. I did not know——"

His eyes went from her face to that of Gustavus Pors.

"He swam ashore from the Dutch vessel," said Monsieur Pors, and his voice was very low and gentle. "He wanted, I think, to bring a strong arm to the aid of a certain fair maiden."

"And I have brought only added danger."

The thrill of sorrow and despair in the tone brought the tears into the girl's eyes. She lowered her head till it was very close to his.

"You brought me—yourself," she whispered.

A new light was born in his eyes. As he saw it deepen, Gustavus Pors stood aside. For a minute no word was spoken.

"Well, we have worried at the bullet till it is out, and our patient stands a fair chance of doing well," he said cheerily, after that minute of silence.

Agneta looked at him gratefully.

"Monsieur, how can we thank you?" she said.

At that "we" his face contracted. It was but for a moment.

"By looking less as if the skies had fallen," he said. "A youthful knight does not die of one such wound as that. You have need to take a cheerful view of life, little one, for you have two patients to care for now. Your hands will be full."

She smiled at him, but it was through tears.

At that moment the door opened, and the face of Amattehoorn was thrust in. Then a beckoning movement called Gustavus. He went outside, and those within heard the sound of voices.

When Monsieur Pors returned, he went straight to Agneta.

"Little one," he said, taking her hand in his, "there is a certain silver plate that has long been to me a sweet memory of the past and a precious promise for the future. When I am gone, drop it into the flames. Just this once I will take that to which it entitles me."

He folded his arms about her, and pressed a kiss on the quivering lips.

"Little sweetheart, farewell," he said. "The soldiers are here. They seek a prisoner, and are in haste. I am going with them. It is dark. Eric is of the same height as myself. They will not find out their mistake until the ship has sailed."

He released her, stepped to the foot of the bed, and lifted from it a torn and bloody coat. Then, divesting himself of his upper clothing, he put on Eric's in its place.

"Farewell, young man," he said. "If you do not value as you should the gift I make you, you are worse than a brute."

He turned and was gone. At the door he put into the hand of an Indian warrior a heavy packet.

"It is gold," he said. "When the war is over, exchange it for wampum, and divide it among your young men. And until the war is over Amattehoorn will guard the 'little squaw.' "

Aboard the Dutch ship *Love* the captain watched in a fever of impatience.

"The Director's orders were peremptory," he fumed. "We were to sail with all haste. Why have not the soldiers returned? Do they not know that the wretched Swede is not worth the waste of time? We will even sail without them if they come not in a few minutes."

"Yonder is the boat, sir," replied a soldier.

"What do you mean by thus delaying the vessel?" shouted the captain. "Think you any rascally Swede is worth this delay? Get you aboard. What is a prisoner by the side of our orders?"

"The prisoner is in our custody, sir," replied the officer in charge of the boat.

The captain turned away with an oath.

"Pitch him into the hold," he said, and a tall Swede was rudely thrust into the lower recesses of the vessel, and left to his fate.

It was the roughest handling that had ever fallen to the share of Gustavus Pors, but the proud, fastidious Swede thought not that night of his surroundings, nor of the indignities to which he had been subjected. His thought was of a maiden with swimming eyes and quivering lips.

"Little one, I love you enough to give you to another," he said, but upon the hand that he could not see in the dense darkness of the ship's hold, there fell a hot, round drop.

CHAPTER XLII

New Sweden had ceased to exist, and New Netherland had grown larger. Director Stuyvesant would have liked to stay longer in the land of the South River to personally direct the affairs of the same, but his presence was urgently needed in New Amsterdam. Thus it was that the fleet which had struck terror to the hearts of the Swedes sailed at an early date from the South River, leaving the forts garrisoned by Dutchmen, and the land itself breathless and terror-stricken.

True, the haste with which the Director had departed worked in favor of the conquered people. Pieter Stuyvesant had not time to stand out upon every point that might have been demanded by the Dutch. He was willing to convert such of the Swedes as desired to remain in the land into loyal citizens of New Netherland. He called upon them to take the oath of allegiance, or in default thereof to leave the country in a year and six days. To those who remained he allowed one clergyman of their own faith to minister. Domine Megapolensis looked grave at the concession, but haste, and the inability to supply a Dutch pastor who could preach in the Swedish tongue, settled the question. Pastor Lars Lock remained among the vanquished Swedes, to help them begin a new life under Dutch rule.

As the vessels sailed past the stretch of forest that lay just above Fort Casimir, the eye of the Director-General fell upon a great square block of buildings, and his thoughts passed to a gentle maiden and an old peasant. But a moment later he turned away again. The fortunes of individuals were of little account where the welfare of a province was at stake. Pieter Stuyvesant was Director-General of New Netherland, and in the interest of New Netherland he had brought war to New Sweden. Sorrow must ever follow in the wake of war.

THE END

www.ingramcontent.com/pod-product-compliance
Lightning Source LLC
Chambersburg PA
CBHW022100300426
44117CB00007B/529